spirals of contention

spirals of contention

why India was partitioned in 1947

satish saberwal

LONDON NEW YORK NEW DELHI

First published 2008 in India
by Routledge
912 Tolstoy House, 15–17 Tolstoy Marg, Connaught Place,
New Delhi 110 001

Simultaneously published in the UK
by Routledge
2 Park Square, Milton Park, Abingdon, OX14 4RN

Routledge is an imprint of the Taylor & Francis Group, an informa business

© 2008 Satish Saberwal

Paperback edition published 2013

Typeset by
Star Compugraphics Private Limited
5-CSC, First Floor, Near City Apartments
Vasundhara Enclave, Delhi 110 096

All rights reserved. No part of this book may be reproduced or utilized in any form or by any electronic, mechanical or other means, now known or hereafter invented, including photocopying and recording, or in any information storage and retrieval system without permission in writing from the publishers.

British Library Cataloguing-in-Publication Data
A catalogue record of this book is available from the British Library

ISBN 978-0-415-84196-2

... most significant historical developments result from the concurrence of many circumstances, each of which might have had quite different effects in another context.

Hodgson 1974: vol. II, 67n
[citing Myrdal, *An American dilemma*]

Most of the key questions of sociology concern processes occurring through time; social structure is inherited from particular pasts; and a large proportion of our "sample" of complex societies is only available in history. But the study of history is also impoverished without sociology. If historians eschew theory of how societies operate, they imprison themselves in the commonsense notions of their own society.

Mann 1986: vii

... an adroit marshalling of seleted facts so as to create the maximum of goodwill and self-confidence may easily become an evasion of the truth, and deprive the Indians as a people of the courage to face reality.

Mujeeb 1967: 556

for mubarak ali and bilal ahmed

contents

Preface ix

Acknowledgements xi

Introduction xiii

1. Medieval Legacy 1
2. Facing the Future 1 32
3. Facing the Future 2 55
4. Nineteenth Century Anxieties 81
5. Parallel Processes 110
6. Drifting Apart 131

Concluding Review 156

Bibliography 179

About the Author 195

Index 196

Preface

In the course of a week-long visit to Lahore in March 2000, I happened to meet Dr Mohammad Jawwal of the Department of Philosophy, Punjab University. When I called on him at the University, he generously took me to students in his class and told them that they could ask me any questions they wished. One student asked: "We find that there is a good deal common between people in India and Pakistan. Why then did we have the Partition?" I had not thought about the issue in any depth, and therefore my response was necessarily brief and tentative. This volume is part of my effort, over the past seven years, to figure out an answer to that question.

During the twentieth century, the Partition of 1947 was surely a defining moment for South Asia. It affected millions immediately, and would affect hundreds of millions for generations to come. The question that the student in Lahore asked troubles many in both Pakistan and India, people whose own knowledge of the past may not be enough for placing that social and historical event in an adequate perspective.

The experience of Partition has received much scholarly attention in recent years: there is fiction (as in the collections edited by Bhalla 1994 and Hasan 1995), there is interpretative recounting (as by Butalia 1998), there are studies of the late stages of the steps to Partition (as by Jalal 1985 and Bhargava 2000), and there are reviews of long-term, principally political, processes (as in Prasad 1999, 2000). Yet "foundational events such as those of August 1947 in India", Partha Chatterjee writes (1999: 117), have "many different roots ... running along different levels of determination and with very different temporalities." Such is the quality of these "foundational events ... that they supply each of these narratives with a closure that identifies it as a history of [P]artition".

The analysis that follows is one among the many that are possible. It concerns principally the *social* processes which – drawing from the medieval period memories of symbols and happenings, and of forms of collective action – gained scale as well as ideological and institutional triggers during the nineteenth century. Through all this society in India was reconfigured in ways that accented the differences, and eroded the commonalities, between the various religious groups markedly. This reconfiguring became more contentious with passing decades, the religious identities became increasingly adversarial – and the growing stock of antagonisms facilitated the passage towards Partition. To recognize this, as the study before you does, is not to deny the political circumstances of the 1940s, nor the role of the immediate protagonists through whom the Partition became a fact.

This study recognizes the British culpability in sharpening the cleavage between Hindus and Muslims; but, in the themes on which I concentrate, they appear only as bit actors. The major actors were Indians, who claimed to speak and act on behalf of Muslims and Hindus. I explore the issue from both sides, but I do not try to balance the scales at every step. Here and there, it is the Muslim experience, and institutional developments, that engage me rather more; the reason for this is simply that my own ignorance of the Muslim scene had been considerably greater. This does not mean that the Hindu culpability in the rise of hostilities was any less.

The study offered here is *sociological*. It explores the working of some aspects of a society and some of its social processes over the long term. As a glance at the bibliography will show, I rely overwhelmingly on the large body of socially and culturally sensitive work by historians over the past generation. In effect the historians are my "informants", and the information that their work provides goes into answering the questions, concerning long-term social processes, that I formulate as a sociologist.[1]

The following pages employ a small number of terms from Persian, Urdu, Arabic, and Hindi. I have tried to make their meanings clear in context at their first use; that location can be reached through the index. The use of diacriticals in this study, even if I could provide them, would make it pointlessly pedantic. Sometimes a single term has been transcribed in the literature in different ways: e.g., *hadis* and *hadith*. I have consulted Dr Razi Aquil for some of these terms but have finally taken decisions on the basis of what is most likely to be familiar to readers in India.

[1] Earlier I have written at some length about the varied personal experiences, and academic activity, over the decades which have gone into shaping my sense of the problem as it appears in this volume. See Saberwal 2005b.

acknowledgements

While doing this piece of work I have been free from any substantial institutional affiliation though, for several years, I had a visiting arrangement at the Academy of Third World Studies, instigated by its Director, Mushirul Hasan, who has subsequently been an active Vice-Chancellor at Jamia Millia Islamia. My first thanks go to Mushir, then, for his hospitality, his many ideas, and his countless courtesies.

I have continued to incur debts to my old friend and colleague, T. N. Madan, who has also been a generous neighbour while I worked on this book. He has often backed up bibliographic advice by loaning me his personal books, and he helped me gain access to the library at the Institute of Economic Growth. To cap it all, he commented on an earlier version of the text, and suggested that I offer the manuscript to Routledge!

Then I must mention Razi Aquil, a wide-angled medievalist, at the Centre for Studies in Social Sciences, Calcutta. For about four years now we have been in regular contact, and I have found many of his writings beneficial. I have always thought it safe to sound my most outlandish notions off him, and he has scrutinized in detail every chapter in this book.

Other colleagues who have commented on earlier versions of parts, or whole, of the following work, or have discussed the underlying ideas with me at length, include: Muzaffar Alam, Mubarak Ali, B. D. Chattopadhyaya, Pradip Datta, Sasheej Hegde, Sudipta Kaviraj, M. Rajiv Lochan, Vasant Palshikar, Gyan Pandey, Alok Rai, and Akbar Zaidi. Many of them have gifted books or papers to me, or provided vital references, and all these have helped strengthen the arguments that follow. Bibliographic aid came also from Ramesh Bairy, Kunal Chakrabarti, Roma Chatterji, Sunil Kumar, Vandana Madan, Anindita Mukhopadhyaya, Veena Naregal, Aditya Nigam, Asiya Siddiqi, Bajrang Tiwari, and Susan Viswanathan. Historians, sociologists, and others at more than a dozen universities and other institutions all over India have heard, and reacted to, my presentations concerning the Partition, raising questions that have helped shape my arguments over the years. Seven years is a long time, and there is no way I can list all the friends and colleagues who have helped in various ways; my debts to them all remain. The thoughtful assessment by the publisher's anonymous reviewer helped me sharpen the argument at several points. I have had access to the collections at the Centre for the Study of Developing Societies, India International Centre, Indian Institute of Public Administration, Jawaharlal Nehru University, and Nehru Memorial Museum and Library. My salutations to the institutions and the staff that maintain their libraries.

I have four more sets of debts to record and then I am done. My impulse to view the past sociologically took shape during my long years at the Centre for Historical Studies, Jawaharlal Nehru University, New Delhi. Romila Thapar had suggested initially that I move there – and she has been a source of firm support over the decades.

Second, my visit to Lahore in 2000 became possible through invitations from Bilal Ahmed and Mubarak Ali. Bilal hosted me at his home graciously, and for six days he drove me around all over Lahore, usually in the company of Nadeem Omar Tarar. Without their generous hospitality, the theme of this book would never have occurred to me.

Third, the reader will find in these pages repeated references to events in Europe and China long centuries ago. These references come in course of arguments that bear on my theme. These have been possible because of my immersion in medieval European history during the 1980s and in pre-modern Chinese history during the 1990s. On Europe I have published a little; on China much less. I wish to place on record here, nevertheless, my numerous debts to the Indian Council of Social Science Research, to the University Grants Commission, to the Indian Institute of Advanced Study, Shimla, to the Maison des Sciences de l'Homme, Paris, to the Nordic Institute of Asian Studies, Copenhagen, and to the British Academy. All these institutions aided my readings on Europe and China. The British Academy's support was for a month of work in the Leeds University Library. I commuted to Leeds from York, where T. V. Sathyamurthy hosted me for the month most generously – just a few days before he passed away.

Finally, my immediate family. My wife, Edith, and our daughter, Gayatri, both read earlier drafts critically; and from them and from Vasant, our son, and his wife Farah, I have had all the moral support that helps to keep the bonds of family alive.

introduction

> ... we need to work hard at doing away with our selective amnesia about the past, to come face to face with our memories, and to begin from there the process of learning how to deal with the future.
>
> Butalia 2001: 95

Soon after an offer of a faculty position from the University of Alberta, at Edmonton in Western Canada, reached me in early 1965, a letter came from a gentleman in that city with the surname Sabharwal, a variation on my own. He offered me welcome to his city – and any help I might need. In fact, when we reached Edmonton, the family invited us to lunch and was very friendly. Our shared surname gave us a tie of clanship though, for many like me, it remains a tie in name alone, literally, devoid of substance. Here was a case of putative social ties getting stretched across continents, common enough in our time, at least for some. Many of us, though, remain confined to the groups of our origin in telling ways, in our minds and social universes, even after moving vast distances physically. One would have grown into an identity acquired at one's mother's knees, which therefore seems to be one's "natural" identity. That is the common sense view. In the social sciences, however, there is now an axiomatic proposition: that *all* identities, and the associated mutual expectations, are human constructs, part of how persons grow up in a society and, in turn, how they bring their children up. Our identities, that is to say, do not come from nature; these come from our experiences, and from the choices we make – or do not make – as we grow up.

For my new friend in Edmonton our clanship nestled within other shared identities: our being Punjabis, Hindus, Indians, and so forth. This was expressed first in a phone call I received from him late in September, when the India–Pakistan border hotted up: Indians in Edmonton were issuing a press statement for India, he said, and they wanted my name on it too. My nationalist convictions are fairly tepid, however, and I said no. In fact, the University had interesting colleagues from Pakistan, and I saw no need to let jingoism disfigure my academic relationships.

Some months later I had to disappoint my namesake again. He asked me if I would help him get a Ph. D. in the department where I taught. The best I could do was to indicate to him the departmental procedure and say that he would have to try his luck. By then I had also decided to shift to McGill University in Montreal at the end of the academic year. Unfortunately I had had to let down someone who had been so friendly and hospitable – and also let down, at the same time, numerous identities ranging all the way from our clan to that of being Indians.

I had gone to Edmonton from Cornell University in the United States where I had been doing my Ph. D. Among foreign students there then, Indians were the largest group, and a Cornell India Association was active. At its annual elections, I think in late 1960, some of us persuaded Ali Ashraf, the political scientist,[1] to stand for Presidentship. His candidature aroused opposition – because he was a Muslim! Sensing the straws in the wind, Ali withdrew. In place of an assumption of mutual trust, until someone proves to be unworthy of that trust, here was a case of *a priori* rejection. It reflected a "bar of separation" between Muslims and Hindus in India which, I have argued, has been hardening since the late nineteenth century (Saberwal 2005a).

That separativeness has braided a variety of strands together. One strand was brought home to me by my friend and colleague, Mushirul Haq, during a conversation at Shimla in the early 1970s.[2] There is a point upto which, he said, Muslims in India share their sense of the

---

[1] The late Professor Ali Ashraf taught at the Indian Institute of Technology, Kanpur, and later at Jamia Millia in New Delhi – where he became Vice-Chancellor too, and where he retired.

[2] I met Mushirul Haq first in 1966 or 1967 at McGill University where he was doing his Ph. D. Later we were both Fellows at the Indian Institute of Advanced Study, Shimla. Professor Haq taught at Aligarh and Jamia Millia in Delhi before going to Srinagar as Vice-Chancellor, University of Kashmir. There he fell victim to militancy.

past with Hindus; beyond that, the Muslim sense of the past diverges into west Asia.

I asked him why it had to be so. Why should our sense of the past be fixed, given to us by that past? We can choose which parts of the shared human past we wish to make our own. My own sense of my past includes a good deal from outside India – it is vastly different from what my parents would have regarded as their past. (Today I would put it somewhat differently. We have to be discriminating over what aspects of the past to accept and what to reject. I reject various parts of Indian tradition, say the caste order and much else of the beliefs and practices associated with Hinduism. I would apply the same critical judgement to elements in the Islamic and other traditions available to me.) Mushir was the gentlest and kindest of men I have known. He heard me out politely, and appeared to agree, but I doubt that he saw my kind of stance as viable for himself. His mind had been formed in a *madrasa* – and he was comfortable in a particular identity: comfortable enough that he felt no need to try other ways of being.

Narrating these three episodes says something about the mutual perceptions among Muslims and Hindus in my shifting milieu about four decades ago. It also reports on what I said or did then. It should be clear from my behaviour then that hard, exclusive, religious identities had no place in my personal life; but also that I recognized the significance of such identities for those who live by them. I have not changed this overall stance much during the decades since, and it informs the argument in the pages that follow.

ଔଛଓ

The history of the Indo-Pakistani subcontinent has been remarkable for its contradictory tendencies. For long centuries it seemed that Muslims and Hindus could live and work together, amicably enough, in countless localities, in their commercial relations, in the conduct of numerous governments, in forging a lingua franca, Hindustani, and in cultural creativity – in music, dance, literature, architecture. By the late eighteenth century the scene began to shift; the assumptions of existence, at least in north India, began to change in consequential ways. Colonial rule brought profound changes in the rules of the game – such periods are always a time of uncertainty. Even the preceding centuries had carried mutual antagonisms, and occasional communal riots, and then in 1947 came the mother of all riots:

Close to three-quarters of a million Punjabis died in mutual massacres during the first days of independence. ... Between August 1947 and March 1948, about 4.5 million Hindus and [Sikhs] migrated from West Pakistan to India and about 6 million Muslims moved in the reverse direction. From 1950 to 15 October 1952, over [932,000] of Hindus came from East Pakistan to India, while nearly 384,000 Muslims went from India to East Pakistan (Hasan 1997: 167; see also Rao 1967).

Beyond numbers, and beyond one cataclysmic moment, there are now ingrained attitudes, imbibed during childhood and early youth – and matters of everyday experience.

Reflecting over her visit to Bidar, northern Karnataka, for fieldwork in August 1970, Ratna Naidu wrote:

> I recall the uncanny fear which I experienced when the bus speeding me to field-work ... suddenly took a turn to reveal a skyline studded with the beautiful domes of Islamic culture which was my destination. Later introspection made me realize that the absurd fear was that of a Hindu (even educated and cosmopolitan), on the eve of close interaction with an isolated *Muslim* dominated small town. I have tried to analyze the fear and am certain that it was an instinctive reaction to the architectural character of the city skyline (1980: 149).

The "instincts" are formed early in life. A former (Muslim) university professor told me once that his family had easy visiting relationships with various Hindu families in their town in eastern UP. When he was a young boy, however, there was just one thing his mother asked him to practice: he was to take care never to allow his sight to fall on an image or a statue of one of the "gods", for that is forbidden. My friend took the injunction seriously then. He is reminded of it even now, say, when he boards a bus and sees a little statue that the driver often has on the dashboard. A profound sense of difference, of cultural distance, had been imprinted on the young mind.

At another level, a judicious appraisal of the social scene may persuade one to take precautions. Professor Shahid Amin, the distinguished historian at the University of Delhi, related at a seminar in 1995 how, at times, he considers it advisable to travel in India under an assumed (Hindu) name.[3]

---

[3] I refrain from reciting the recent expressions of similar processes, considered at some length in Saberwal and Hasan 2006.

introduction xvii

⊘⧲⊘

The social equation between the categories Muslim and Hindu in the subcontinent has clearly been ambiguous. Anyone who looks can find a great deal of evidence both of mutual relatedness and caring across religious lines and of mutual distrust, animosity, and worse. Depending on how the evidence is selected and organized, these precolonial relations may be presented as overwhelmingly cordial, as thoroughly conflictual, or something in between. The fact of that ambiguity has been obscured by the writing, both lay and scholarly, from several sides. There is the partisan writing, from one or the other viewpoint, taking the wickedness of the other as given. Then there is the secularist writing, which would not grant the separation and the antagonism as ever having had much social and cultural depth. Gyanendra Pandey has argued that this writing was not very sensitive to questions of "specific historical consciousness in [its] specific time and place", and therefore to the prevailing forms of "rationality"; it was insensitive, that is, to "the units of solidarity, the requirements of status, the understanding of honour and shame ..." (1990: 20). Some writing by secularist historians has alleged even that the whole phenomenon of communalism has been the product merely of contemporary history-writing with communal overtones.[4] Occasionally, a scholar has only had to use the categories "Hindu" and "Muslim" to invite the allegation that it betrayed the author's own communal outlook. In such a view it would be illegitimate to hold that such categories, identified in religious terms, have had any significance in South Asia's social history![5]

This will not do. Troubled pasts do not fade away by themselves. Especially in large societies, time does *not* heal by itself. "To try to get away from one's past by turning one's back to it is simply to misunderstand the nature of the historical reality of the present" (Kaviraj 1995: 90). In order to comprehend the past, it is imperative that we try

---

[4] I reviewed the then literature on, and the phenomenon of, communalism at some length in 1981, reprinted, for instance, in Saberwal 1996a: Chap. 6.

[5] Professor Bimal Prasad has produced a comprehensive, if not exhaustive, long-term narrative in which the categories Muslim and Hindu loom large (1999, 2000; a third volume is forthcoming). The underlying social processes, our focus in these pages, occasionally do seep into his predominantly political analysis, as in his reference to "the anti-cow-killing agitation and the widespread Hindu–Muslim riots of 1893" (2000: 89).

to understand it in all its complexity and ambiguity.[6] We *should not* try to forget the past merely because some people distort it for partisan ends, for that past is a priceless record of human experience, waiting to be deciphered, interpreted, and understood: a matchless resource for learning to form judgments and to make informed choices for the future. We *cannot* forget the past: if we do not make the effort to scrutinize such a past actively in our consciousness, but try simply to forget it – as is sometimes urged – we remain prisoners to that past, ever prey to its obsessions. We might try to repress our memories but, as Freud taught us, memories stay on, dormant in the preconscious, personal and collective[7] – to haunt us in wholly unexpected ways, playing emotionally with what we see and experience, and distorting our understandings thereof.

A more creative approach to troubled pasts, personal or collective, is to meditate on them, to reflect on them, by asking, as honestly as we can manage, what exactly happened and why. We have to work out for ourselves a different sense of selfhood – one purged of the burdens of conquest, of past humiliations, of the Partition, and of all the manifold wrongs of centuries past. We have to bring it all into the open candidly, and to recognize that these were acts of another era: an era when the scales of existence, the priorities, the worldviews, the resources for understanding, and the gamut of possibilities and available alternatives were far narrower than what lies now within our reach. As we externalize our troubling memories, as we make them public, as we examine the origins of our troubling emotions, and consider the conduct of actors past, placing *their* reasons in relation to *their* own time and situation and experiences, appraising their conduct in relation to that of others down the millennia – in the light of such *understanding* of another era, some of our troubling emotion may begin to ebb away. Once the emotional charges from the past have been examined and understood and overcome, we may, in full knowledge of that past, make reasonable choices for the future. While some may wish to, and indeed be able to, "forget the past", that would give them no defence against those who, for whatever reasons, insist on continuing to rake up that past.

---

[6] For examples of fair-minded appraisals, see Mujeeb 1967, Sayeed 1967, and Prasad (1999, 2000). For prejudice, see Stephens 1964.

[7] The collective preconscious – that which is shared by many – is carried from one generation to the next in people's shared habits, attitudes, proverbs, myths, folklore, and the like.

This book is a move in confronting our collective troubled past in the South Asian subcontinent – as a step towards transcending it.

Perspectives

It was in course of reflecting on ongoing social reconfigurations in nineteenth century Europe, as industrialization and its social consequences spread, that the discipline of sociology was born there. Europe's early sociologists had emerged from relatively undifferentiated intellectual backgrounds; and they had a sense of history.

Early twentieth century sociologists in India, men in the generation of Benoy Kumar Sarkar and G. S. Ghurye, perceived Indian society as a carrier of ancient (Indic) traditions, linking their discipline with Indology. The discipline of sociology was being reshaped in India in the 1950s, its defining research method being fieldwork; and the period saw dozens of studies centred on particular villages. Robert Redfield at Chicago, M. N. Srinivas in India, and Louis Dumont in Paris stressed the significance of the Indian village being located within a civilization; all had the Indic civilization in mind.

In the sociological understanding of India, Muslims have been notably inconspicuous.[8] Of the several factors in this neglect, I shall mention only three here. *Ideologically*, "nationalism" sought to ignore *all* marks of difference within Indian society. In the words of a student of feminism, an "emptying of India's history of all conflicts characterizes the dominant nationalist grid for imagining both the nation and its past" (Chaudhuri 2004: xxi). The search for solidarity against the colonial power induced an underplaying of conflicts, and of the social differences – gender, caste, class, region, or religion – which led to the conflicts. To deny that religious differences had, or could have, any legitimate political significance became central to the nationalist consciousness promoted by the Indian National Congress. This ideology has percolated into the practice of social sciences in India extensively.

Conceptually, insofar as the dominant grid for apprehending society in India has been in terms of the caste order, it was relatively easy to

---

[8] The sparsity of basic enquiry – and, even more, of conceptualizing – concerning the Muslims was clear in the early major reviews: Srinivas 1966, Bose 1967, Mandelbaum 1970. Subsequently, as researcher and as editor, T. N. Madan has advanced our understanding of this social category significantly.

show the importance of castes, or caste analogues, in Muslim social arrangements: this was mistaken as its central feature. What seemed then like a comprehensive consideration of Muslim society in India appeared in a fieldwork-based quartet edited by Imtiaz Ahmed (1973–83). The overall assessment of these volumes was that the Muslims' social organization is of a piece with that of their neighbours – the differences being "within normal limits" of the caste order, as an ECG report might say. The question – Why did we have the Partition? – did not arise. In the early 1940s, the sociologist D. P. Mukerji at Lucknow had written about the then stark cleavage between Muslims and Hindus, but the issue did not figure in the "field-centred" vision which came to overwhelm the field in the 1950s. And *methodologically*, Indian sociologists have been largely unconcerned with long-term historical developments: how exactly did South Asia's enormous Muslim population become "Muslim"? how exactly have their ideological currents over the generations changed their conceptions of themselves – and of their "others"?[9] To anyone considering the twentieth century scene in India coolly, a separation between Muslims and Hindus – for most people, a matter of fact, for some, one of principle – was clear enough; how and when did it arise?

The impulses for this cleavage go back, but how far back? Various time horizons are possible – and valid. Bhargava (2000), for example, rests his explanation of the Partition on the attitudes of the principal actors – Jinnah, Gandhi, Nehru – during the decade leading up to 1947. In my view, a phenomenon as complex as the Partition needs consideration in multiple time frames. Sandra B. Freitag has demonstrated the growing local contestations in the mid-1800s; and the work of C. A. Bayly and Haider, which we shall consider later, takes us to the "prehistory" of communal conflict in the 1700s and earlier; all this will engage us in later chapters.

It will be conceded, however, that sectarian differences – not only between "Hindus" and "Muslims" but also within Hindu and Muslim groups, by themselves – have long been the loci of conflict. Given a general sectarian tendency, then, have the relations between Muslims and Hindus had a special edge? Some answers to that question are

---

[9] Francis Robinson's critique of the Ahmad quartet (1983) was a rare moment of dialogue between historians and sociologists writing on Islam in India; it yielded an exchange with Veena Das and Gail Minault in the same journal in 1984 and 1986.

inherently flawed. One flaw arises in some "secularists'" disdain for the categories "Hindu" and "Muslim" altogether. Another arises in certain "essentialist" views, which give these categories, their opposition, and the consequent conflicts, an eternal, timeless quality: these views have existed on both sides of the fence.[10] This study considers the issue over the long term, going back to the medieval period. It holds that the tenor of relationships has varied greatly: the levels of mutual trust have ranged from very high to very low, depending on the forces at work at different times. This judgment arises from attending, in equal measure, both to "the long-term formation of mentalities" and to "their modern transformation" (Ray 2003: 33). While the overall legacy has been ambiguous, the scene began to shift during the nineteenth century. Numerous sociologically sensitive historians' monographs since the late 1970s have shown that, from the late nineteenth century onwards, institutions such as Deoband and Arya Samaj generated ideologies and messages which provided strong triggers for separativeness. Several regions and localities felt the separative pulls, and reconfigured their social spaces around the Hindu: Muslim cleavage substantially, in areas which had been managing their social diversity within the caste order.

To consider such long time horizons is sometimes taken as an expression of, or as an aid to, a "communal" approach to the issue. Those who pursue communal or other intimidatory agendas, however, do not wait for scholarship to do its work. Scholarship in my view has nothing to gain, and much to lose, if it allows its agendas to be set by such anxieties. A study marked by an exemplary balance between engagement with the field and a fine sense of scholarly judgment, *Modern myths, locked minds* by T. N. Madan, covers the terrain that will concern us too. Madan's central concern there is with the strands of "fundamentalism", and of "secularism", arising in the Sikh, Islamic, and Hindu traditions. In contrast, the present study explores the historical roots of animosity between some of those who saw themselves as Hindu and Muslim, and the growth of this animosity, leading up to the Partition in 1947. Our concerns differ but the following chapters rely on his judgments at several key points.

While the importance of sociology and history for our enquiry is clear enough, we have to remember also that we are concerned with

---

[10] For a secularist view, see Chandra 1984; for essentialist views, Qureshi 1962, and the writings of Dayananda, Vivekananda, Aurobindo Ghose, and Savarkar examined in Sharma 2003.

the connections between the changing perceptions, individual and collective, and the shaping of mutual attitudes between large social categories. These are matters of social psychology, a bridge field which we in India have not found the energy to nurture much (Saberwal 2003).

ርአ80

In any case, it is necessary to attend to multiple, long-term, reconfigurative processes which have been active in south Asia. Concluding her study of shifting identities in Jharkhand, in eastern India, up to the 1990s, Susana Devalle says, "*Ethnicity should be viewed as a process whose meanings can only be understood in context*, evolving within the flow of history and according to the particular circumstances of a given people at different points of time" (1992: 229, emphasis Devalle's). The processes at issue, concerning "Muslims" and "Hindus" and their mutual relationships, have included older ones like the spread of an Islamic space, variously mixed in with the older segmented order. Then there were the nineteenth century transformations: growing numbers moved, physically or mentally or both, from a locality-centred existence to greater involvements in wider physical and social spaces. This reconfiguration happened as Indians in their enormously complex society coped with their disempowerment – and with all the new technologies and worldviews, which became available through the contact with the West. Indian responses drew on their internal resources and drives; and these included the diverse nodes around which groups and categories came to cohere – *jatis*, or caste groups, and symbols and religious traditions. The outcomes of these shifts were many, among them that of communally-centred confrontations, sharpening over a period of roughly two generations. All this can be seen clearly in a substantial corpus of sociologically sensitive work by historians which will engage us presently. This has included, on one side, studies on regions (UP, Bengal, Punjab) and, on the other, those on institutions (Arya Samaj, Deoband, Barelwis, and others) whose agendas – religious, social, cultural – have catalyzed that reconfiguration.

Among the most influential of the emerging processes was the growing salience, the growing significance, of the ideological visions that projected Muslims and Hindus as distinctive, contrastive identities. This made a difference to the patterns of social relations, and of social distance, between Muslims and Hindus. Numerous actors began to invoke certain memories of recent centuries: collective memories of (one's co-religionists) having been the rulers on one side, memories of having been subjects on the other. In later decades, these contrastive identities would gain in salience and spread, in an ambience of recurring confrontation, involving aggressive behaviour, including violence, along communal lines. These identities would increasingly be the lens through which fresh experience would be interpreted. These emerging matrices of identity, difference, and opposition were to configure the politics of the Partition. All this we shall have to consider.

CRSO

How do we make sense of this extraordinary situation? We have here a phenomenon of great diversity and many dimensions, a variation that can be mapped against the flow of time on one side and the territorial spread on the other. The variation in *time* can be seen in the contrasts down the generations. One need think only of the contrasts between the eleventh century conquest in north India; the end of the sixteenth century, as Akbar worked on building his empire; and the mid-twentieth century, as the post-colonial arrangements worked out. The operative logics have varied a good deal over the different periods. Over that flow of time, there are further variables at play, shaping the attitudes which changed over time. One is the shifting *locus of power*, as with the decline of Mughal regime, and later the Indians' disempowerment under colonial rule. The other is the rise of comprehensive *ideological visions* from mid-1800s onwards, as in Arya Samaj (estd Bombay 1875, Lahore 1877) and the Islamic seminary at Deoband. These visions were to inspire powerful efforts at consolidating religious identities in exclusive modes.

Cutting across the variation in time has been that in space, and here the differences between regions have been compounded by those between different social strata in the same region. Communications in this vast subcontinent were slow until the twentieth century; and the historical experiences of different regions, with their distinctive social structures, have been far from uniform; and the tenor of social relationships in each region has reflected its particular historical trajectory. A later chapter will review two specific instances: the region now Bangladesh, and Mewat, the home of the Meos, near Delhi. Within a region, there have been considerable differences between different strata. Ruling strata, traders, custodians of the several religious traditions, and local communities: between these several levels, the plays of interests, ideologies, and strategies have diverged markedly. Reflecting the regional diversity, the peninsular south has had a notably different social dynamic; but it will not engage us much, since the region was marginal to the processes that led to the Partition. That landmark was a product largely of northern India.

Given this enormous diversity, our question, why the Partition happened, takes us to a complex issue, with the promise of infinite detail. One obvious simplificatory move is to narrow the focus territorially, and I shall say very little about regions other than Bengal, UP, and Punjab: either because I have not had access to pertinent studies on them (like Sind and Assam) or because these have been peripheral to the Partition story (as with western and eastern India). Even then it is easy to surrender to detail, risking thereby the loss of perspective necessary for addressing our central question. Take the categories "Muslim" and "Hindu". Brajadulal Chattopadhyaya (1998) has examined the epigraphic and literary texts in Sanskrit between the eighth and fourteenth centuries. In that long stretch, the authors of the Sanskrit sources used a variety of terms for identifying the newcomers, using for them "generic terms which were in use in earlier times to denote outsiders or others to the society": Musalamana, Tajika, Turuska, Gauri, Mudgala, Turuti (Turbati), Pathana (*ibid.*: 29f; Appendix 1, pp. 92–97, lists many more terms, specified by date and source). Chattopadhyaya reads this diversity of labels to suggest that such categories as "Muslim", and implicitly "Hindu", were not significant for the experience at the time.

T. N. Madan (1997) has reviewed the question of the diverse practices and self-identifications within a social space in the subcontinent which, "in both political and scholarly discourses", was designated "Hindu" by the early twentieth century. These numerous entities had been "dynamically interrelated over the millennia", says Madan, invoking the model of the Great Tradition – the textual, more reflective, tradition carried by specialists spread far and wide – in continual communication with the numerous Little Traditions – the numerous local, oral, less reflective traditions lacking in full-time specialists.

> Depending upon what the purpose of a particular inquiry is, one may focus on the congeries that is Hinduism, or on its constituent religions, individually or collectively, which share a 'family resemblance' ... (*ibid.*: 177–79).

What does it look like from the side of the Persian literature? Reviewing the history of "Hindu" and "Muslim" and related terms, Rajat K. Ray notes that, in al Beruni, "'us' is unambiguously designated as 'Muslim', while 'they' are 'Hindu', the pagans of another land."

The implicit equation here of Hindu with native and Muslim with newcomer moved gradually: "the meaning of the formula [shifted] from the distinction between native and alien to a recognition of two separate religious communities living in India" (2003: 85f).[11] Razi Aquil writes of several groups in the Saltanat centuries – the ruling dynasties, the Muslim officialdom, the *ulama*, religious scholars, the Sufis, mystic adepts – held together by their shared anxiety, their sense of vulnerability, surrounded as they were by vast numbers of Hindus, despite some indigenes taking to Islam in certain regions (Aquil 2006).[12] That anxiety has been recurrent, it has spurred movements through the centuries, and many feel that anxiety down to our day.

The variation in terms (Tajika, Turuska, etc.) and in attitudes, is a fact, then, and recognizing that variation, my argument rests on the assumption that some of these social categories tended to come together more easily than others, thanks to their historical interrelationships, and what Madan calls their "family resemblance". These linkages had been carried in webs of texts and symbols and symbolically important "structures", say the ubiquitous temple or the pilgrimage complex at Benaras, or the Quran, the *ulama*, and the Sufi orders, *silsila*s. All social experiences, and social identifications, are subject to reinterpretation over time; and clusters of groups which had such affinity, or which were persuaded that they had it, were brought, through reinterpretations, to accept that they were "Muslim" or "Hindu". We shall see that this long-term process accelerated during the colonial period.

൩൸

In dealing with a complex phenomenon in an orderly manner, there is no escape from having to think at a level of some abstraction, locating various contrary tendencies in relation to each other. One has to abstract

---

[11] From a reading of Sanskrit and Telugu inscriptions in Andhra, between 1323 and 1650, Cynthia Talbot comes to a similar conclusion, except that the native identity emerging – framed by language, territory, and remembered local history – is Telugu, not Hindu (1995: 700f, 714).

[12] In Sunil Kumar's reading of the mid-thirteenth century chroniclers, they were anxious as they contemplated the future of "Muslims" in India, that is, the ruling groups, that lived in a string of cantonments. This was an anxiety in relation to indigenous non-Muslims, an anxiety that merged with that from another non-Muslim category, the Mongols, who were then menacing from the north (forthcoming).

from the phenomenon, to "model" it – some say, to "conceptualize" it – looking for the most significant, the weightiest, the most consequential elements: to "weigh" the significance of each, and to pick, out of the welter, elements which have had long runs – and long run consequences. In the long run course of events, there is nevertheless the play of social chance, partly in the form of unintended, and unforeseeable, consequences of actions; we shall elaborate on this issue shortly.

There is, first, the relationship between the actor and the "structure" of society in which one acts: we may think of "structure" as the totality of conditions within which one acts.[13] A later chapter will explore the diverse links between actors and their contexts (pp. 100–11). These links are comprehensive and would cover a great deal; but we need just a few points of reference. In the making of a large group, elements at two different levels are vital. At one level, its members' material *interests*, the basis on which they make a living, an element central to the Marxist tradition, and the location of interests in the structure of *power*; at the other level, the bonds of *kinship* and, beyond these, bonds arising in shared *ideas* and *symbols* which may include the group's shared *name*(s). I should add that shared *animosities* towards others, who are believed to be common adversaries, can be bases for bonding as effective as any other.

These two levels – one, interests and power, and two, kinship, ideas, symbols, names, animosities – are not tied to each other firmly. That is to say, common interests (say of agricultural workers) do not necessarily produce shared symbols and other marks of shared identification; and, conversely, shared names and symbols do not necessarily mean common interests.[14] A region may, for instance, have both Muslims and Hindus as agricultural workers; and also as landlords; so that there could be diverse patterns of active relationships, those between, say: *all agricultural labourers* (Hindu as well as Muslim); or *all Hindus* (landowners as well as agricultural labourers); or *a landlord with all his tenants*, Muslim as well as Hindu. In this polycentric conception of society, in principle a member may have multiple options regarding whom to ally with, whom not, and whom to oppose. Within the available

---

[13] This simplifies further the already rather simple conception of "structure" in Sibeon (2004: 124). For my task, any further complication would be a waste.

[14] This elementary insight has long been familiar to sociologists (Cohen 1974) and continues to be restated, as in Schryer 2001.

options, one may tilt one way or another, depending on personal disposition, pressures of economic need, diverse currents of ideology, and the like.

At certain junctures, this diversity may yield to exclusive mobilization: all agricultural labourers – Muslim and Hindu – may stand together against the landlords, thanks, say, to mobilization by a Communist Party; or all Muslims may stand together, against Hindus, inspired by Islamic activists. Which kind of combination jells into conscious groupness, then, depends on the effective influence of the most active mobilizing agencies and their ideology in the region at a particular moment. In other words, our mental maps of our social milieu – our "social cognition" – use various sets of social categories. And our patterns of social cognition can change: a change, that is, in the way we would see who "we" are – and who "they" are.

In our discussion of the social background to the Partition in the following pages, we shall notice certain recurrent patterns. It will become clear that the patterns of social cognition began to change during the nineteenth century. For example, a widespread pattern in nineteenth century eastern Bengal: Muslim peasants began to hold back on customary payments for their Hindu landlords' ceremonies as being un-Islamic. This seemed an act of defiance to Hindu landlords, who responded by asserting that cow sacrifice at Id was offensive to their religious feelings and therefore would not be permitted on their lands. The contention could call for police intervention (see p. 148 below). A pattern of established mutual accommodation had given way to one of charged opposition.

In the process, the prevailing common sense changed, the meanings people saw in their social milieu changed – or, as sociologists say, the prevailing "definitions of the situation" changed. A conception of society that I have called "polycentric" declined – but it did not disappear. Ashis Nandy (2005) provides us instances of persons involved, simultaneously, *both* in hostile communal activities *and* in remarkably positive cross-communal personal bonds. The world that human beings inhabit is often ambiguous, admitting of multiple stances and interpretations. We read into our situations particular meanings out of our repertoire of familiar ideas; and we may read different, sometimes mutually contradictory, meanings as we move from one context to another. All this has consequences for what we try to do, and what we can manage to do. "If men define situations as real, they are real in their consequences", so goes the "Thomas theorem".[15] How we act in the situation depends on what meanings we see in it, on how we define the situation.[16]

The issue bears some elaborating. How we understand a situation, how we define it, what meanings we see in it, is something we share with others: others who may be within my *jati* or organization or profession, with whom I have more or less close relationships. This kind of sharing, as of norms, is part of social existence; but the extent of this sharing is variable. In close-knit relationships one can expect to find shared values, attitudes, skills, and familiarity with certain social forms. All together these may be called a shared culture, or sub-culture, and a shared mindset. Given a shared mindset, members of a group are likely to interpret their social milieu in terms of these shared social categories. We shall return to this matter of definition of situations in the next chapter in a somewhat different context.

I wish now to make this framework a little more complex. Central to modern social theory is the concept of "unintended consequences". Social existence is riddled with unintended, and unanticipated, consequences of given actions (Merton 1936; Giddens 1979: 59 and elsewhere). This happens because we work always with imperfect information; or with imperfect understanding of what others intend to do, or how others would interpret, respond to, our actions.

How I define a situation, then, influences how I act in it. To my action, in turn, my neighbour responds by her own lights: what she does in response to my action may not be wholly a consequence of my action; she may have misread my intentions, and therefore her response

---

[15] In elaborating upon the Thomas theorem, Robert Merton (1968: 475) compared it with a Newtonian theorem, possessing "the same gift of relevance, being instructively applicable to many, if indeed not most, social processes."

[16] The enormous effort in "science" in recent centuries, both natural and social sciences, is part of our cumulative judgment that this mode of approaching our world facilitates understandings which are more "objective". Historically, this effort at anchoring to objective understandings has helped improve our grasp of "reality" – and therefore our capacity to cope with the world around us.

It is part of this objective understanding of the social world that we recognize also that, in any situation, human beings act in terms of their own understanding, their own "definition", of their situation: in ways which are inescapably *subjective*. Sociologists recognize this subjectivity to be an objective fact.

may be a wholly unintended consequence of what I did. Put otherwise, we have to recognize the importance both of intended actions and of their unintended consequences: the latter arise because no one can wholly anticipate the consequences of one's actions, partly because others interpret these actions in ways that violate the actor's intentions, but more generally because the world is much too complex for anyone to anticipate its working fully. On the wider screen of history, D. P. Mukerji wrote of the colonial regime's encouragement for learning English to meet its need for clerks. Those who learned the language however went on to read much else – and picked up ideas on freedom, self-government, and all the rest, wholly unintended by the colonial government (see p. 98). The following account will argue that countless acts of contention during the nineteenth and early twentieth centuries contributed to a reconfiguring of the social space in ways which made something like the Partition more likely; however, such an outcome was not intended by any major actor before, say, 1940 – or, some would say, before the summer of 1947, just on the eve of the event.

The foregoing has introduced a series of concepts which the subsequent chapters will use to identify certain recurrent patterns. An act of analytic judgment lies at the heart of this effort at modelling. My judgment may well be mistaken. Taking as central some elements that I consider marginal, others have produced, and will continue to produce, other interpretations – which some will find more satisfactory than mine. Still others may conceive of my theme in entirely different terms. Open, plural perspectives of this kind mark the republic of scholarship – as against bigotry and propaganda.

The Argument

My argument here may be put briefly. It will be noticed that successive chapters address a range of *divergent* considerations. I begin with a quick look at the "Medieval Legacy". The period saw the spread of Islam in the subcontinent, a *modus vivendi* in numerous shared spaces, and conflicts and myriad insecurities – which were not very different from those in other comparable regions of Asia and Europe. Most religious specialists among both Muslims and Hindus continued to live with a sense of difference, indeed of animosity, towards the other tradition. It gave many of them a "we–they" framework within which to interpret the many ups and downs in successive generations; and something of these habits of thought carried into the colonial period. The legacy from the medieval period, then, was ambiguous; and it included, alongside numerous shared spaces, something of a culture of contention: centred on the temple and the mosque, the pig and the cow, and similar elements. As we shall see, elements of that culture continued to be renewed, modified, and invoked through the nineteenth century and later, in ways that the actors of the day would see fit.

Then follow two chapters on "facing the future". The nineteenth century was a time of manifold turbulence for people in India; and for coping with the uncertainties, many had to draw on whatever resources, material and social, that they could muster. The central argument of these two chapters concerns the contrasting ways in which this effort worked out among Hindus and Muslims respectively.

Chapter 2, on the Hindus, considers the variety of uses to which the bonds within the *jati*, the caste group, could be directed; but the reach of these bonds was inherently limited. The tradition had, however, long carried another kind of social entity, the *sect*, whose membership could sometimes stretch well beyond the reach of any particular *jati*. Given the wider reach of some sects, some nineteenth century men found ways to work through their networks for ambitious secular purposes. Indeed some of the most influential sects were new, having arisen during that century. The Arya Samaj, for example, became a base from which numerous educational, and other, institutions were built in Punjab. Then there were the numerous Bengali settlements outside Bengal which had followers of the Brahmo Samaj. Surendranath Banerjea travelled to these groups repeatedly, during the decade preceding the establishment of the Indian National Congress in 1885, establishing links for wider political activity. Such *institutions*, then, and the experiences of fostering them – and of working, or studying, in them – became another resource with which to meet the uncertainties of the times. In matters of coping, the formal institutions, and all that could be learned in them, augmented the initial resources in the *jati* and the sect.

The story among Muslims, in Chapter 3, was different. In the mid-nineteenth century, most Muslims would have had more or less clear identities in terms of castes or caste analogues. Yet those who spoke for Islam in India have taken a dim view of caste society. Consequently, Muslims could rarely act on caste bases publicly, say to mobilize politically or to draw resources to build an institution of the modern kind. Furthermore, although dozens of sects have flourished among Indian Muslims, this proliferation too ran, as it were, against the spirit of Islam, so that sectarian energies have also not been available for addressing wider public purposes – with one major exception.

The exception found energy in Sunni Muslim religious leaders' anxiety concerning the future of Islam in the subcontinent, bereft of ruling power, amidst much larger numbers that did not abide by the faith. There was the further difficulty that vast numbers whose ancestors had accepted Islam at some point had remained closely integrated with their non-Muslim neighbours, in the main, participating in the caste order and in the locality's ceremonies and festivals, oblivious of Islam's stern stance on idolatry. The most influential consequence of these anxieties was a large new *madrasa*, Islamic seminary, founded in Deoband in western UP in 1867. In a multi-faceted drive, it sought to bring all believers to the true path of Islam shown in the Quran, the *hadis*, that is the collections of the Prophet's words and deeds, and in the *shariat*, Islamic law, which had been developed out of the Quran and the *hadis*. For reasons we shall see, the Deoband line became, and continues to be, influential throughout South Asia.

The ideological influence of Aligarh, where Syed Ahmad Khan founded his College a little later, had rather different thrusts. Overall, however, Muslim initiatives in the field of modern education were few. This was due, in part, to a scarcity of resources, owing to the Muslims' virtual absence from substantial commerce, at least in north India, so that they were missing out on the circuits of wealth slowly growing in commerce and industry. In looking to the future during the nineteenth century, then, between the internal social resources that Hindus and Muslims tried to harness, there were substantial differences. This differential was displayed in their experience of building modern institutions, for instance, those for education, commerce, and other public activities.

Chapters 4 to 6 deal principally with developments in the nineteenth century. What had earlier been shared spaces began to cleave as religious identities hardened, amidst widespread anxieties of disparate origins. First, in the changing economic and occupational milieu of the early colonial regime, established patterns of dominance came under pressure, from neo-rich merchants or bearers of new occupations, at least in some urban areas. In the absence of political arenas for Indians, however, their claims were often pressed under cover of "religious" activities, defying the older elite's disapproval. Contestatory moves were couched in symbolic terms, say in routes for processions, or in abrogating customary obligations, as of tenants of one faith to their landlords of another, or *vice versa*.

Second, nineteenth century India had tens of millions who lived a folk, some a tribal, way of life, amidst whatever traditions had evolved or become available. They had managed without the apparatus of high religious traditions: scriptures, pompous religious functionaries, elaborate rituals and pilgrimages, and the like. As the new institutions like Arya Samaj and Deoband (as well as the Christian missionaries) pushed their respective agendas, however, many who had lived by tribal and other folk traditions were persuaded to make clearer commitments to exclusive religious identities. Millions that had lived outside the influence of the scriptures and the specialists of the "great" religious traditions began to receive clear signals about what they should believe, and do, and what they should not, where they belonged and where they did not. This was especially useful for men who moved, say from a village to a distant metropolis where they often found advantage in taking over lifestyles and identities associated with one of the major religious traditions. From older settings, with shared local traditions, they were moving to new ones, accepting religious traditions and identities which were more sharply defined and, in some areas, beginning to be poised more separately.

Orientalist and other research from the late eighteenth century on uncovered much about ancient India: ancient texts, diverse religious traditions, genetic linguistic relations with languages of Europe, archeological sites and so on; and Hindu ideologues tended to appropriate these findings avidly as testimony to their exalted past. Muslim ideologues' search for an exalted past led them, apart from dynasties in India whose rulers were Muslim, to the political, commercial, legal, literary, and other achievements of Muslims over a large arc reaching from southern Spain to Indonesia.

Our consideration of diverse settings, then, will point to the consolidation of a sense of distinctive identities, tending to become exclusive, among many leading Hindus and Muslims through the nineteenth century. This consolidation of exclusive religious identities received powerful impulses from other directions. I shall argue that the strongest impulses took the form of persistent contestation between men on the two sides. Its early forms we have met already; and the protagonists learned also to deploy symbols that resonated widely: like the cow, on one side a sacred being, on the other an animal for the customary Id sacrifice; or a procession that honoured a god on one side, became an irritant to the other when it passed a mosque. Given the new technologies of communication, over the decades, the underlying contestation gained in scale – and then threatened often to spill into violence, known in India as communal riots, as local episodes would be reported in the print media extensively, often in biased ways. Experiences of violence, or of threats of violence, it is now clear, have contributed much to a hardening of religious identities in adversarial terms. We shall see that "communal violence" and "adversarial religious identities" have a reciprocally aggravative relationship. By the late nineteenth century, the worldviews and symbols were becoming organized around the categories Muslim and Hindu, tightly enough to renew themselves more or less routinely.

This growing cleavage received the stamp of authority in 1909 when the colonial government accepted the principle of separate electorates. Muslim and Hindu candidates at elections would henceforth have to look only to their co-religionists for support.

> [Separate electorates] symbolized, as nothing else did, the position of Muslims in the then Indian society – 'a nation within a nation' as the Aga Khan put it. That position, of course, was already a fact of life and did not suddenly emerge in 1909. But the constitutional recognition of that position under the act of 1909 solidified it and made it difficult for the Muslims to be absorbed by the growing current of Indian nationalism (Prasad 2000: 118).

The social and the political, then, were separate levels, but interconnected, though loosely. The looseness of the link can be seen in the following: shortly after the Indian National Congress and the Muslim League signed a pact, in 1916, agreeing on a framework for separate electorates, communal riots in northern India reached a high point in 1917–18 (*ibid.*: 153). When Gandhi came on the stage the political space had already been bifurcated. His attempt to run together, in 1920–22, the twin movements of – *Khilafat*, one that mobilized Muslims in defence of the Khalifa, head of the then collapsing Ottoman state, and *Non-cooperation*, a wider mobilization challenging colonial rule – generated a relatively brief, euphoric phase that seemed to reverse the prevailing trend towards separativeness.

With the suspension of the movement in 1922, communal riots and bitterness rose to new highs. A campaign headed by an Arya Samaj leader persuaded more than a lakh and a half Malkana Rajput Muslims in the Agra–Mathura region, during 1923–24, to switch from Islam to Hinduism. The shock of this event made Muslim leadership even more anxious about the allegiance to Islam of the many millions whose commitment to the faith had not been deep. This crisis saw the emergence of the Tablighi Jamaat, a formidable movement for Islamization, which has since attained global reach.

The collapse of the Khilafat had another consequence: after the extraordinary camaraderie of the movement, the mutual trust between the political leaderships on the two sides began to slide. Back in 1916, leaders of the Muslim League and the Indian National Congress had joined in endorsing the principle of separate electorates that had been introduced by the government seven years earlier. After the Khilafat, such agreements became scarce. The social cleavage tended to harden – and to continue to gather adversarial emotions. The contentiousness, by itself, we shall see, became a "deep-seated generative mechanism" (Morgan 1983: 16). It shaped the conditions which enables some of the leading political actors in the 1940s to force constitutive choices which made the Partition inescapable.

This experience of long-term contention contributed to a consolidation of both the "Muslim" and the "Hindu" identities: it *pushed* people into these distinctive spaces in some measure. This combined with other processes that were internal to the two sets of spaces which, we noted, will be considered in Chapters 2 and 3. Together the two sets of processes yielded contrary outcomes. We shall return to this theme towards the end (pp. 159–61).

1

medieval legacy

> He whose vision cannot cover
> History's three thousand years,
> Must in outer darkness hover,
> Live within the day's frontiers.
>
> Goethe[1]

Civilizations are complex human creations, evolving historically in course of encounters with diverse realities – ecological, social, political, and so forth. Distinctive ways of thinking and of doing things develop in a civilization, ways that gather weight, and exercise moulding influence, in its historical experience; I shall call these ways its "cultural styles". Illustratively, I think of China's great bureaucratic tradition, of the varied institution-building in western Europe since the thirteenth century (Saberwal 1995: Chap. 4), and of the idea and practice of *umma* in Islam, which will concern us later. Given the array of concerns that bear on a civilization's evolution, any that survive and flourish can do so only by learning to nourish multiple, *contrary* purposes – and concomitant cultural styles and orientations. China, say in the twelfth century, is a rich example. The repertoire of its Confucian literati, the mainstay of its formidable bureaucracy, included: a gentle, Taoist contemplation of nature; exceptionally resourceful technological capabilities; bureaucratic traditions which could underwrite some of the largest empires in human experience, able also to organize resistance to potential horse-borne conquerors from the vast northern steppe – all this and much more was part of the Chinese tradition (Gernet 1982).

---

[1] Epigraph in Waltham 1972.

Diverse cultural styles for coping with the world have found nourishment in the Islamic tradition too.[2] An expansive, open, outgoing style has been central to Islam's repertoire: large numbers of bearers of the Judaic, Christian, Pahlavi, and other traditions swelled its ranks in its early decades, bringing their older ideas, expectations, and practices with them, making these part of Islam. Arab and Persian merchants had long travelled to the edges of the Indian Ocean, and after the seventh century, they carried the Prophet's message too – to the east African coast on one side, and India's west coast and southeast Asia on the other – relating to local communities everywhere. Following the early Arab conquest of Sind in 712CE, "The Arabs, who took wives from amongst the women of Sind, were absorbed by the population in a few generations. Sind reverted to the rule of the various Hindu clans. ... The Arab conquest of Sind was a passing episode: yet another instance of the cellular structure of Indian society successfully absorbing strangers with a different religion (Ray 2003: 129)."

Sufi mystics reached out to peoples and to the indigenous religious traditions wherever they went; and numerous Muslim rulers – the Abbasids in the Fertile Crescent, the Umayyad dynasties in southern Spain, the Ottoman Turkish empire, the Mughals in India – drew strength from the social, cultural, and religious diversity of their peoples, and promoted extensive commerce in ideas as well as goods.

Hidden here was a key moment in the intellectual history of mankind. The Roman imperial ruling class had made Greek its *lingua franca* but, as the long twilight of empire ended in the mid-fifth century, the motivation to master the Greek language faded and, by the mid-sixth century, Romans could rarely read texts in Greek. Their familiarity with the riches of the Greek tradition, and that of Europeans at large for five centuries after, would henceforth be limited to whatever little had been rendered into Latin by the sixth century. Continuing older connections, between the eighth and the ninth centuries, Arab thinkers had absorbed large parts of that Greek tradition, then available in the Byzantium, translated these into Arabic, and carried these with them to the emerging Arab kingdoms in Spain (Hodgson 1974: Vol. 1, Chap. 5). From the eleventh century onwards, European scholars discovered, in the Arabs' libraries in Spain, something of the vast, unsuspected parts of the Greek corpus, which fitted in with the texts they already had.

---

[2] This section builds on Saberwal 2006.

Challenged by this sudden infusion of ancient Greek and recent Arab thought, scholarship in western Europe took a quantal leap.

Alongside this open, outgoing style, Islam has carried a stern, scripturalist style too. Shaped by religious scholars, the *ulama*, between the eighth and the tenth centuries under the Abbasids in the Islamic heartlands around the Fertile Crescent, this style turned on the *shariat*, the Islamic Law, codified by the scholars on the basis of the Koran, and the *hadis*, the Prophet's sayings and deeds, all of which they believed had been divinely inspired. The *shariat* was a social code for living a worthy life, a life of individual responsibility to God's will, as revealed in the Prophet's words and deeds, and addressing the mores that prevailed at the time of its codification. The interpreters of the *shariat* – the *ulama* – wished to stay aloof from royal courts, which embodied organized power, for they believed that those who lived by Islam, following its law, the *shariat*, needed no external power to govern them. In practice, though, the *ulama* have been appreciative of the advantages that accrue from royal patronage for Islamic religious establishments – and, indeed, for advancing the frontiers of Islam.[3]

One open and outgoing, the other scripturalist and conservative: these two styles, in mutual opposition or in convergence, in more or less stable arrangements, have always been present among Muslims. During its long and eventful history, several other styles also came to be associated with Islam; of these I shall mention only one, which followed from its spread into central Asia. As the medieval horsemen in the central Asian and Mongolian steppes, with their mobility and flexible social organization, gained skills at combat as mounted archers, they were able to generate, recurrently, remarkable war leaders (Unger 1987: 72–74). Among their best known leaders was the thirteenth century Mongol, Changhez Khan, whose religious inclination was, if anything, to Buddhism. Other central Asian war leaders, several clusters of Turks, who were more or less recent converts to Islam, were at their devastating worst when they conquered Islam's own heartlands, like Iran; these recent converts expressed "a particularly assertive identity" during their initial incursions into northern India (Pollock 1993: 286). In later centuries different Turkish groups founded several empires, among them the Safavid in Iran, the Ottoman in Turkey, and the Mughal in India.

---

[3] Here and elsewhere I owe my understanding of the Islamic tradition largely to Marshall G. S. Hodgson's magisterial *The Venture of Islam: Conscience and History in a World Civilization*, 3 vols., 2004.

When a small, mobile body of conquerors, astride their swift war horses, targeted a territory with a large sedentary population, dramatic violence offered a quick route to decisive victory.[4] This style of conquest was not limited to the Saltanat; it marked medieval warfare involving horse-borne central Asians of the medieval centuries everywhere. In the late nineteenth century Hindu- and Hindi-nationalist imagination, however, as Shahid Amin notes, "the foreigner-Turk conquerors of north India [were conflated] with the entire population of Muslims in India" (2002: 26).[5] The Central Asian prowess for raising warhorses rested, in any case, on their vast pasturages, something that the more densely populated agricultural civilizations did not have. Within the technological limits of the early second millennium, a large contingent of warhorses brought decisive advantage in warfare. (This advantage vanished ultimately before artillery.) The Indian experience in this regard was comparable with that of peoples in West Asia and in China, when these were conquered by Central Asian Turks or by Mongols between the eleventh and the fourteenth centuries (Unger 1987: 70–77, 154–70). Nineteenth century Hindu ideologues misread the event, not realizing the importance of the central Asian horses; and they built up the stereotypes of the weak, effeminate Hindu facing "the Muslim" as the oppressive Other (Datta 2006 has a critique).

There were differences between the regions, however, in the aftermath of conquests. The Mongols could hold the bulk of China for less than a century – and withdrew rather abruptly amidst the Ming uprising in the 1360s. Before the Turks conquered West Asia in the eleventh century, they had already accepted Islam (Hodgson 1974: Vol. II, 40ff); and the leaders of the Mongols, who followed them in the thirteenth, did likewise by the end of the century. Events in South Asia took a notably different course. The conquerors faced *polities* which could not match their horse-borne power; but the local *society* was unusually resilient. Relying on the caste order, it could hold its internal ordering despite repeated conquests. That society had, in centuries past, offered earlier conquering groups from the north, including Arabs

---

[4] Down the centuries, would-be conquerors have repeatedly turned to this formula: think, for instance, of the savagery of the armies of the United States, in Vietnam in the 1960s and in Iraq four decades later.

[5] What Shahid Amin says is true, but the coin had another side. At about the same time began, too, and independently, the drive to foster the *umma*, a sense of the community of Islam that sought to erase all differences of ancestry, caste, sect, and language. The next chapter will return to this theme.

and Turks, the possibility of settling in the host society as a ruling *jati* (Pollock 1993: 285). For this possibility the new conquerors had no use. On the other side, large parts of the host society did not take to the new faith wholesale.

The patterns of relationships between Muslims and Hindus in nineteenth century colonial India were remarkably varied. This variety has had varied sources. There was the unparalleled diversity within indigenous society, in its ecological settings, and in the prevailing ways of making a living. There were the diverse origins of immigrant Muslims – descendants of Arab merchants in Gujarat and Kerala, of the eighth century Arab conquerors in Sind, of Afghan and Turki conquerors of north India in the twelfth and sixteenth centuries, of those coming away from the turmoil in central and west Asia following Turki and Mongol conquests, and others in search of opportunity and adventure. And there was the variety of ways in which indigenes took to Islam in India. In the several regions, the diverse patterns of relationships had evolved over a thousand years and more. I wish to explore something of the range of these patterns, what went into shaping them, and the consequences that flowed from them. The events we shall consider have principally been small in scale, localized, spasmodic. With processes so complex, analysis cannot aspire to certainties; it can hope at best to suggest the more probable of connexions, and the more consequential of the prevailing patterns.

The Context in India

In the subcontinental theatre of power, the establishment of the Saltanat in north India introduced a new, expansive force, but its rulers faced a dilemma. The early thirteenth century Mongol conquerors had "torn apart the fabric of Muslim power in Central Asia" (Alam 1989: 44), closing off the only possible line of retreat for the Saltanat rulers, so they had no option but to come to terms with their situation in India as best they could. Within India, they had to contend with opposing pressures: from the *ulama*, Islamic clerics, to advance the cause of Islam; and from the indigenous society, where a variety of political contendors continued to be more or less active, sometimes organized as caste brotherhoods. The Saltanat rulers lacked the wherewithal for imposing Islam upon their subjects; yet their religious bonds were crucial in holding together the variety of immigrant groups on whom their power ultimately rested (Mujeeb 1967: 264; Aquil 2006: 76): for the tiny ruling class, shared faith was the vital cement. "The rulers needed [the Muslim religious leaders] to legitimate their actions and were therefore constantly extending concessions to them" (Alam 1989: 54).

Divergent interests and visions continued to be at play through the centuries: Akbar had an empire to build; Shaykh Ahmad Sirhindi had a creed to spread. The rulers' prime concerns were to ensure their revenues, and internal peace for further expansion: if the clerics had their way beyond a point, the indigenous reactions could be violent, threatening the conditions needed for steady revenues. The rulers tended by and large to be pragmatic, trying to maintain a certain distance from the men of religion, and seeking to promote co-existence between the several religious categories. In Muzaffar Alam's reading, they did this in two principal ways:

A. Tolerance for indigenous customary law and religious practices regardless of Islamic religious law. Conciliatory towards Hindus, "... [Saltanat rulers] emphasised that their conflict was only with those who challenged their paramount political power and control over revenue. With the rest of the local population they had no quarrel" (Alam 1989: 44).

> [The fourteenth century courtier] Barani lamented that even at Delhi, the capital of the sultanate, Hindus went in procession, beating gongs and cymbals, and passed beneath the walls of the palace to immerse the idols in the river and the sultan, as the historian presented, was powerless to interfere with them (Alam 1989: 52, citing Barani, *Tarikh-i Firuz Shahi*).

The general policy was not to interfere in Hindu beliefs and rituals, not even in such practices as *sati*. Akbar gave this policy of "tolerance and non-sectarianism" formal ideological cover, *sulh-i kul* (peace with all) (*ibid.*: 52f). We shall return to matters of practice later.

B. Indigenous intermediaries. Even during the Saltanat, the later rulers, especially Sikandar Lodi, encouraged Hindus to learn Persian and enter state service, particularly in the revenue departments. Mohammad Habib has suggested that the Kayastha *jati* may have originated among "those Hindus who, regardless of caste, began learning Persian in the thirteenth century, gradually acquired the culture of both the communities and ultimately made themselves indispensable in revenue and accounts" (1958: 231). Indigenous participation in government expanded under Akbar, and the tradition established by him of absorbing Hindus "in the higher ranks of the nobility and of ruling through Hindu hereditary landed elites continued until the very end of the Mughal empire" (Alam 1989: 52; similarly I. A. Khan 1978: 458). This openness of the ruling class suited the indigenes' willingness to partake of the framework of power.

Muzaffar Alam has documented the importance that Mughal rulers, and even their predecessors, attached to working with a political ideology, *akhlaq*, that called for the welfare of all subjects, of all faiths (2004: Chap. 2). This ideology had built on Greek and pre-Islamic Iranian thought; and it stressed the necessity for rulers to abide by ethical norms, distantiated from religious injunctions, and urged them to provide justice to all their subjects, Muslims and others. Manuals outlining the *akhlaq* ideology circulated extensively in the Mughal ruling class. In medieval Islamic circles by the twelfth century, the rival schools of thought, like the Mutazilite philosophers, had been marginalized. Consequently, the authors of these Greek-inspired *akhlaq* texts thought it prudent to stay "within the circle of what was considered to be acceptable Islamic practice". These texts:

> inevitably begin with a proper sequence of references to the Creator and the Prophet, and seek initial legitimacy by inserting their authors into a system of erudite references that makes their texts immediately recognizable to fellow Muslims. ... The formal similarities between these treatises of political ethics and other treatises of a purely religious nature (which were, paradoxically, intended, among other things, to be refutations of the Hellenic tradition) may also have lent them some weight of legitimacy. (Alam 2004: 191.)

Granting the significance of this literature, how well it shaped the Mughal administrative practice on the ground remains rather uncertain; to this issue we shall return later in the chapter.

The men of religion among the immigrants, coming during the Saltanat and later, were not bound in a unitary religious organization. There were the specialists who led in prayers in mosques; there were the scholars in Islamic law, the *shariat*, who would administer law for, and be general advisers to, the ruler; there were the Sufis, engaging rather more in personal quests for fresh, transcendental, experience. Sufis had their orders, *silsilas*, yet the great Sufi masters were strong individuals who kept their own counsel. These various groups were predominantly Sunni; but there were significant Shia elements too, owing, first, to several waves of missionary activity, in Sind, Gujarat, and Rajasthan, by Ismaili Shias (Khan 1997), and, second, to immigration from Iran (where the Shia sect had overwhelmed the Sunnis in the sixteenth century: Hodgson 1974, Vol. 3: 23–24). Gujarat did have great merchant communities who were Shia; but bids for sovereign power in India have rarely found Shia leadership, excepting the late eighteenth century regime in Awadh – which made the city of Lucknow an important Shia centre.

In the long run, the Sufis could take on a variety of roles, responding to the changing opportunities and challenges. Richard M. Eaton (1978) has tracked the Sufis' trajectory in Bijapur, in latter day northern Karnataka, between the fourteenth and the seventeenth centuries. As warriors, they accompanied, and splintered off, the Saltanat expeditions to the south, in the late thirteenth and fourteenth centuries, prior to the founding of the Bahmani kingdom (1347–1498). On the outskirts of Bijapur town, the Chishti order of Sufis settled to establish its hospice, a centre for learning, where disciples would learn the Chishti mode of Sufi devotion. Over time these men took to the regional language and produced an important stream of Deccani literature. Other Sufis came in small groups, dependent on state patronage, independent of the Chishti hospice. Tombs of famous *pirs* became centres for popular veneration, founts of *baraka*, grace, drawing large followings. Under state patronage, their managers became large landholders – and pillars of the state. As the state of Bijapur tottered in the late seventeenth century, the operative Sufi form changed again: to that of the *darvesh*, the renouncer, a man of ecstasy. Of the various kinds of religious men, it is the Sufis who are remembered most for having "brought Hindus and Muslims closer together …, [explored] the common ground of spirituality between [them] and opened the way for a mutual appreciation of aesthetic values …" (Mujeeb 1967: 166–67).

There was tension at times between the *ulama* and the Sufis. The *ulama* brought the *shariat*, Islamic law, to the tasks of governance, so that their leading figures could be close to the rulers. For the Sufis, their personal, sometimes ecstatic, religious experience counted rather more than the *shariat*, and this gave them greater flexibility. Many of them believed in *wahdat al-wujud*, the doctrine that there is a divine unity underlying all the diversity of religious beliefs and practices; the doctrine authorized "the process of religious synthesis and cultural amalgam" (Alam 2004: 91). Their aura of holiness drew to them Hindu followers too who, gaining familiarity with a broadly Islamic milieu over time, might accept the new faith ultimately.

Sufis are well-known for their willingness to reach out and relate to others. Muzaffar Alam provides a remarkable instance from the early eighteenth century career of a renowned Sufi, Shah Abdur Razzaq Bansawi of Awadh region. Razzaq's adult life was lived in a milieu in which ordinary Muslim social life shared many social practices, rituals, and folk beliefs and performances with their Hindu neighbours. Razzaq himself participated in them while recognizing that many of these violated the *shariat*; there is even a report of Ram and Lakshman appearing to him in a vision (Alam 2004: 105, 109). Echoing earlier Sufis' understanding, Razzaq saw that "The closer a Muslim's contact with his non-Muslim neighbours, the greater his ability to show care and concern for them, the greater the glory to Islam" (*ibid.*: 108). Razzaq encouraged open and friendly relationships between Muslims and Hindus in his region, a stance not inappropriate for the conditions of his time – with the Mughal hold over the area declining, and one's own control over one's landholdings dependent largely on one's neighbours' goodwill.

Elsewhere, and especially during earlier centuries, when the great Sufis were remembered, the miracle stories surrounding their memories mentioned repeatedly their superior powers, directed at rival Hindu religious adepts or at unfriendly rulers. In these stories, the Sufi's power prevails unfailingly – and is acknowledged. Often the rival then submits to Islam. Sufis in the medieval period, by and large, are not to be mistaken as living in the same hut as, say, the non-sectarian Kabir. The Sufis did loom large in the expansion of Islam in South Asia, facilitated in many regions by Muslim rulers – even if the latter resisted occasional pressure from the Sunni orthodoxy to advance the cause more peremptorily (Hardy 1983 has reviewed the literature justifying such peremptoriness).

The *ulama* and, indeed, some Sufis too, were uncomfortable with the doctrine of "unity of being" and tended to dismiss it as *wahdat al-shuhud*, "unity of perception": a unity, that is, not of being, of existence, but only of certain Sufis' perceptions (or delusions?) in their states of ecstasy (Alam 2004: 163). In this alternate doctrine, the supremacy of Islamic revelation, belief, and practice was absolute, incommensurable.

Apart from the *ulama* and the Sufis, religious men of Islam, numerous *bhakti* teachers too flourished during these centuries, and the continual bickering between their various sects would sometimes turn violent. Drawing upon sources both in Hindi and in Persian, Bajrang Tiwari has explored both the long standing skirmishes between these several sects (2003) and the functioning, especially, of Vallabhacharya (1478?–1530), the powerful sixteenth century Vaishnava leader. While many Muslim and Hindu men of religion may have avoided each other's company, Tiwari documents the relationship between Vallabhacharya and his successors on one side and the Saltanat and Mughal rulers on the other (2001). Vaishnava leaders accepted large gifts from these rulers, of course, bestowing on them high praise; they were also willing to use their access to the powerful, in Akbar's reign, to force members of a rival sect, in one case Bengali Brahmin managers of a temple at Govardhan, near Mathura, out of a position of vantage (Tiwari 2003: 86f). Alongside this mutually supportive relationship with ruling dynasties, Vallabhacharya wrote texts addressed to his followers, referring bitterly to the hardships which men like him, and their sacred sites and rites, were alleged to suffer at the hands of the *mlechha* – impure – rulers. The regime may have given him wealth, and allowed him influence, but he could not partake of the kind of honour that was reserved for the religious men of Islam, even under Akbar.

Ulama, Sufis, Vaishnava sects – all these were rather clearly defined social categories. The *ulama* and certain categories of Brahmins would have maintained exclusive social spaces for themselves; but Sufis drew Hindu followers, and Vaishnavas too claimed to be open to everyone regardless of caste or religious background. Various sites came to be seen as dispensers of grace, which devotees could avail, regardless of their personal backgrounds. And there emerged, too, a series of religious figures, like Kabir, whose poetry was dismissive of religious and sectarian differences, animosities, and conflicts – and instead projected inclusive visions. Insofar as their followers did not get organized into distinctive religious bodies around a corpus of scripture and associated specialists, however, visions such as that of Kabir have had to retreat ultimately before the claims to sovereign truth asserted on behalf of resurgent high religions and their scriptures.

Countless adjustments, contextually, were inevitable; yet "The symbols were so contrary in the two religions, and the sensibilities were so opposed," notes Rajat K. Ray (2003: 95), "that a clash of fundamentals could not be avoided." His illustrations of this opposition include the direction in which to face when praying, the mode of disposing off the dead, and the attitudes towards the cow. And there was a "recurrent pattern of religious and sexual transgressions, mutually", which included the desecration of temples and mosques, especially by armies engaged in conquest (*ibid*.: 99ff). While these were surely not everyday affairs, a vocabulary for mutual provocation – in words and in deeds – did emerge. It was remembered, and its use would increase during the nineteenth century.

※

In appraising what happened in another era, it is not proper to judge the conduct of men by standards we recognize today. Yet we need to understand the experiences that contributed to the making of attitudes between communities. Here we note a few seventeenth century cases, from Jaunpur, in latter-day UP, from Gujarat, and from the border between Orissa and Bengal. First, a case of blatant arbitrariness. In his autobiographical account, Banarasi Das, the early seventeenth century Jain merchant, related his experience in his early youth in the town of Jaunpur:

> Nawab Qilij Khan, ... then the governor of the city, brought his terrible wrath to bear upon every single jeweller and dealer in precious stones who lived in the town. He put them all into prison and demanded of them something so beyond their reach that the jewellers were quite unable to meet the demand. He felt affronted, and early one morning in a frenzy of rage he stood each one of them in a row, ... and began to whip them ... till they nearly died of their agonising wounds. But he spared their lives and allowed them to go free (Banarasi Das in Lath 1981: 18).

Power and force were used arbitrarily in this instance, but Banarasi Das accepted such incidents as an elementary fact of life, beyond complaint (Lath 1981: vi–vii). While the jewellers were all Hindu and Jain, and the city governor Muslim, there is no indication that either party saw religious difference as material to the event. This low salience of religious differences is evident, too, in Ashin Das Gupta's account of commercial rivalries in Surat between the late seventeenth and mid-eighteenth centuries (1979). At about the turn of the century, his principal protagonist, Mulla Abdul Ghafur, repeatedly sought to rally the city's Muslim merchants, claiming that the Dutch merchants' activities were putting "Islam in danger". His success was limited, for his motives were suspect; and many of his adversaries – in commerce and in city administration – were Muslim too.

In the Mughal regime, such experiences of highhandedness, *pace* Muzaffar Alam, were not unique. "The Mughals gave Surat her finest years", wrote Ashin Das Gupta (1979: 134), "but even then the Gujaratis had ... seen two major bouts of civil conflict and known occasions of searing royal oppression." A footnote adds: "To take only one example of official tyranny, the merchants of Ahmedabad found the administration of prince Khurram (later the emperor Shahjahan) so intolerable that they celebrated his defeat by his father in 1623 with considerable joy." There was insecurity, then, but it has to be seen in relation to practices normal at the time: how did the seventeenth century Mughal administration compare with the practices then current, say, in China, Iran, or France? That important question lies beyond our ability to pursue here.

Elsewhere, the Mughals showed remarkable sensitivity to local, indigenous practice and sentiment. We have a report from a Portuguese Catholic friar, Fray Sebastiao Manrique, who travelled through Orissa and southwestern Bengal in August 1640. At one of his halts, his Muslim attendants seized, killed, and cooked a couple of peacocks – which infuriated the local Hindu villagers. Manrique's party fled to a town nearby. There the town's (Muslim) Mughal official, responsible for law and order, heard the case. Manrique pleaded that his attendant had done nothing contrary to Islamic precepts, but the official–judge maintained that

> when Akbar had conquered Bengal – sixty-five years previous to this time – he had given his word 'that he and his successors would let [Bengalis] live under their own laws and customs: [the official] therefore allowed no breach of them.' (Eaton 1994: 181.)

Killing a living thing in a Hindu district was not permissible; the erring attendant was found guilty. He would have suffered "whipping and the amputation of the right hand", but got away with whipping only, thanks to Manrique's private appeal to the judge's wife, laced with a substantial gift (*ibid.*: 182). In the relations between the rulers and the people, then, there was a diversity of experiences, and there would be a corresponding variety of attitudes.

The Realm of Imagination

Our discussion above has stayed close to the level of groups and institutions and what would have been observable experience. This would have included numerous forms of give and take and, in any case, overwhelming numbers of "Muslims" had long and deep roots in India. The variety of forces at play between "Muslims" and "Hindus" is evident in the realm of imagination too: in folklore, in myths and rites, in the various kinds of literature. Here we consider some of the evidence from the medieval period; a later chapter will return to the tendencies in the nineteenth and twentieth centuries.

We begin with the relatively relaxed world of medieval south India. Vasudha Narayanan examines the Tamil text, *Cirappuranam*, Life of the Prophet: "The most famous work on Islam in Tamil", written c.1700, published 1842 (2002: 77f). This is a Tamil biography of Prophet Mohammad. In this text, Umaru Pulavar (Omar the Poet) seeks to portray the prophet's life – but he was familiar with his Tamil milieu, and with conventions of Tamil literature, not with Arabia nor with Arab literature. His account of the prophet's life, consequently, echoes those in Kampan's ninth century *Ramayanam*, an instance of Tamil Muslims' immersion in Tamil literary life.

> However, even though the details are exquisitely similar in spirit and in concept, each poet has his own inimitable style. Reading both descriptions is similar to listening to the same raga played by two maestros (*ibid.*: 85).

Dominique-Sila Khan has traced the Ramdev sect in western Rajasthan, where Ramdev has two faces: he is believed to be an *avatar* of Vishnu–Krishna, and also a *pir* called Ramdev Pir or Ramshah Pir. A fifteenth century Rajput, his *bhajan*s identify him as an Ismaili (1997: 60). The Ismaili tradition had sanctioned *taqiya*, the practice of camouflaging one's true faith in adverse circumstances, say Sunni hostility. An ancestor of Ramdev, Ransi, may have become a Nizari Ismaili convert "who chose to cling to a Hindu exterior as a method of precautionary dissimulation" (*ibid.*: 78) in order to evade Sunni attention. We shall return to Khan's work when considering the influence of religious men in advancing conversions to Islam.

Aziz Ahmad has written that, at least until 1857, Muslim poetry in Persian and Urdu tended to work with images and metaphors drawn from Persia and to ignore its subcontinental ambience. Ahmad saw here the "unconscious operation of group psychology, an instinctive effort to preserve in a culturally alien and hostile milieu its own cultural roots, signs, symbols, and insular patterns of expression" (1964: 252). Recent work suggests, however, that the patterns may have been much less insular. Madhu Trivedi (2005) has tracked the course taken by the *marsiya*, an Iranian Shia musical tradition, from the Deccani states in the sixteenth century, to Delhi in mid-seventeenth century, and to Awadh, and its capital Lucknow, by the mid-eighteenth. Over these three centuries, the genre underwent many transformations. A *marsiya* narrates at Muharram an account of the martyrdom of Imam Husain, the Prophet's grandson, and his kinsmen at Karbala. Tradition had tied *marsiya* to an occasion for mourning, but it left details open, allowing the mourners, or their leaders, space to improvise. In the consequent variation, one dimension was *language*: *marsiya* composers drew on the language of their locality, on its compositional traditions, and on its physical and social features – indeed, Hindu composers were active too. Yet, there remained the pull of the Persian language and traditions, and the urge to Islamize the narration, for Muharram is a Shia religious occasion. These persistent contrary pulls, toward the local and toward the Islamic, together shaped the course of *marsiya*-writing and recitation in India.

Over the same centuries, Shantanu Phukan (2001) has explored an extraordinary body of bilingual poetry, written by Sufis and by several members of the nobility – both Muslim and Hindu. A single composition could have some passages in Persian and others in "eastern Hindi" – from the Bhojpur region. These men wrote for audiences which, at the time, were at home in both languages.[6] The Persian poetic tradition had principally been a male creation, at home in the world of men at Court, in war, and so forth. In contrast, Hindi provided, as Persian does not, for nouns, verbs, etc., to be inflected for the speaker's gender, so the poet could present a feminine voice unobtrusively; besides, Hindi poetry had customarily explored the domestic scene in a way that the Persian had not, so the poet could use Hindi passages to introduce domesticity in a familiar way. His listeners could appreciate the nuances of, and the poet's achievement in, this bilingual genre, for they too shared a facility in both languages.

At a different social level, Shahid Amin has worked on the figure of a man, said to be a nephew of Mahmud of Ghazni, "the notorious early-eleventh-century despoiler of northern India": Syed Salar Masaud Ghazi, also known as Ghazi Miyan, who died a martyr at age 19. The man's memory has for centuries been woven into the ballads of

---

[6] The seventeenth century Jain merchant–scholar Banarasi Das taught Qilij Khan, then governor of Allahabad, "Hindi versification and poetic usage" (Lath 1981: xxiii)

the region around Bahraich in northeastern UP, bordering Nepal: the warrior is remembered as a protector of cows and of their Ahir masters, his tomb seen as an auspicious site for routine marriage rituals (Amin 2002).

Then there is the legendery figure of Satya Pir, around which two kinds of texts have spread through eastern India over the past five centuries (Stewart 2002). In one set, essentially a *purana*, Visnu/Narayan appears in the *avatara* of a Muslim looking Satya Pir, who reveals his true identity when necessary. Faithful devotion to Satya Pir is held to facilitate general welfare and access to wealth; negligence can invite great misfortune. In the other set, Satya Pir is projected as aiding the spread of Islam, demonstrating his (Islamic) powers to (non-Muslim) commoners and kings alike. In Stewart's reading,

... the differing genres of stories suggest not so much identification with different groups as they suggest differing visions of hierarchies of power within a common world (*ibid*.: 24).

A sense of *difference* between the two sets of texts around Satya Pir, turns, in the next case, into one of *opposition*. In his study of the making of the Islamic tradition in Bengal, Asim Roy writes of Saiyid Sultan, a prolific early seventeenth century author, who wrote in Bengali "a comprehensive history of all prophets, culminating in Muhammad" (Roy 1983: 12). In Sultan's, and other texts, Muhammad's birth and triumph, and other initial Islamic victories, were seen to be located in a milieu where they had to contend against powerful Hindu rulers and gods (*ibid*.: Chap. 3). These authors transported their sense of Hindu resistance in Bengal to the moment of Islam's origin, making it a "genetic" opposition between the then nascent faith and its supposedly hostile Hindu environment. Yet Bengali Muslims and Hindus continued to share textual forms, myths, rites, and festivals until well into the nineteenth century.

This sense of opposition found expression on the other side too: it was coded, in Sheldon Pollock's reading, into the spurt in the Rama cult, manifested in such matters as the forms and similes used for indigeneous kings, in the appearance of Rama as the presiding deity in temples, and in the contrary metaphors used to characterize the conquerors. To this theme we return later in the chapter.

All the local converts among Muslims apart, even the immigrants' descendants, as they settled down in the localities, would share with others the experience of living as neighbours, of the changing seasons, of the local ecology, flora and fauna, and often the modes of propitiating the supernatural. All this would define a regional identity that held within it numerous differences of beliefs and practices too. We have noted the echoes that this sharing of experience found in the life of the imagination.

Among the legacies of the medieval period, then, was a very large body of people whose multiple identities would include that of being a Muslim. I proceed now to review some of the processes whereby indegenes came to preponderate historically in the category "Muslim". Muslims in India, to be sure, have not lived in a limbo, in a world apart. They have always been part of the larger society. Yet, by the nineteenth century, this category became a node for persistent drives to foster a distinctive sense of community, so there is a particular story to tell. It may be appropriate, then, to give some attention to the social logics that have been at work.

The Making of Indian Muslims, or, The Various Modes of "Conversion"

Large numbers in the subcontinent came under the influence of Islam, with concentrations in the northwest and in eastern Bengal. While eighth century Kerala and Sind already had significant numbers of Arab sailors and rulers – and their descendants – respectively, Islam spread elsewhere during the centuries after the Saltanat was established in north India, making things easier for Islamic religious workers in some other parts of the subcontinent. The process was slow; and there was not much effort at creating a distinctive Islamic community, marked off from its non-Muslim neighbours. Consequently, the Muslim presence in their localities in different regions has been variable. It was shaped as diverse actors, in particular localities, pursued a variety of agendas and responded to what others did. Some *ulama* might have wished that the new converts live by the *shariat*, the laws of Islam; but medieval rulers in India were rarely theocratic; and, until the nineteenth century, as we shall see, the bulk of the *ulama* were in no hurry to secure conformity with the *shariat*.

In conversions, as in other matters, some rulers did use both the carrot and the stick, off and on, but more gradual processes have also been at work. Each case is unique. The social complexity among

Hindus – their sects, castes, languages – is well-known. That among Muslims was even greater. For instance, what had been the immigrant ruling class, the high status *ashraf*, had forged alliances with high status indigenous groups; but, commonly the former had kept a distance from the indigenous converts of lower caste and artisanal backgrounds, the *ajlaf*. Until the nineteenth century, the *ashraf-ajlaf* line was almost as sharp as that between upper and lower castes on the Hindu side.

The following pages explore some of the ways in which people "became" Muslim – or, less self-consciously, came to be recognized as Muslims. This variety of ways may be arrayed along a continuum. At one end was the *personal influence of Muslim religious men*; and the great bulk of the Muslim population in the subcontinent has descended from those who turned to Islam under such influence. In the middle is the interesting *case of Kashmir*, where the influence of religious men combined with political pressure to advance the process. At the other end were what might be called *political conversions*: some people took to Islam in *anticipation* of economic opportunity, or of gaining political favour, or of escaping political disfavour; others found that their proximity to (Muslim) rulers, possibly sharing food and drink with them, made them unwelcome to their Hindu castemates, and then the conversion could be a *consequence* of such proximity. Occasionally the political pressure could be highly coercive (Hardy 1972: 9ff has an earlier review of the literature on medieval conversions; see also Hardy 1983).

Influence of religious men

More than 60 years ago, Nirmal Kumar Bose wrote of what he called the "Hindu method of tribal absorption" (1941/1967), citing instances of the Juang from central Orissa and the Oraon and Munda from the latter day Jharkhand. A tribal group at the edge of Brahminical society would gradually absorb Hindu elements in ritual, deities, and concepts, while maintaining large parts of its older cultural beliefs and practices; and, enjoying a virtual monopoly of a particular craft manufacture, it would enter into economic relationships with the wider society (Chaudhuri 2002 revisits the theme). Over time its members might find a place in the caste hierarchy, usually at a low level; but Surajit Sinha (1962) showed that a ruling group within a tribal society would be assimilated with the Rajputs. We may speak similarly of a Muslim method of tribal absorption – a general model of gradual change of religious identities, ranging from being nominal to being thorough. In many cases, affiliating with some elements of Islamic tradition was a simple matter, with only a minimal shift in religious practice or in the group's social locus: a seamless rearranging of indigenous and Islamic beliefs and practices.

Where the social framework of the caste order was already in place, such a group would continue to live, and function, much as it had previously. In Tamil areas, Susan Bayly finds a variety of influences at work: as in other parts of south and southeast Asia, Sufis in their orders, as well as the unattached, wandering adepts "provided a focus for the transmission of Islamic ideas and teachings", aided by the similarity of their flexible ways with those of "local non-Muslim holy men" (1989: 74f); Sufi saints' tombs were seen as bearers of supernatural power and attracted seekers of different sorts; and there were the numerous wealthy and influential Muslim communities in port towns, going back to the ninth or tenth centuries, which had provided extensive maritime links between the Arab world, the west coast, and southeast Asia (1989: Part I).

In a study of extraordinary range and depth, centred on Rajasthan but stretching over all of northern India, Dominique-Sila Khan (1997) has sought to recover the little remembered Ismaili missionaries, also known as Nizaris, who were active especially in the fourteenth and fifteenth centuries. It was a time of diverse religious tendencies, both indigenous and Islamic. The Ismailis' style was remarkably flexible, illustrated in one major figure: "The Nizari ... Hasan Kabiruddin [d. 1470?] himself acquired two additional personalities, first as a Suhrawardi Sufi Pir named 'Hasan Darya' and second as a Shaiva ascetic, clad in ochre-coloured clothes, as 'Anand-jo-dhani'" (Khan 1997: 221). Given also the Ismaili tradition of camouflaging one's faith, which we noted earlier, we get a complex, fragmented story of numerous distinctive groups, with their usually secret beliefs and ceremonies, which drew on the diverse traditions flourishing in their milieu. The Ismaili missionaries and their local disciples connected especially well with the lower castes owing to their egalitarian style.[7]

These various groups drifted apart over the centuries into three principal channels. Some erstwhile Ismailis took to 'orthodox' Sunni ways, largely abandoning their earlier complex heritage. Some others have inflected their legends and practices to approximate one or another Hindu model, while preserving Ismaili elements, partly secretly, as

---

[7] I thank Shail Mayaram for loaning me her copy of Dominique Sila Khan's work.

among two communities of folk musicians in Rajasthan, Langa and Manganiyar (Bharucha 2003: 181–88, reporting on his conversations with Komal Kothari, the folklorist of Rajasthan). And, finally, the Khojas: after the first Aga Khan moved to India in about 1840, he urged Ismailis, who observed their faith in secrecy, to come into the open since secrecy was no longer necessary.[8]

Eastern Bengal

Richard Eaton has examined the spread of Islam in Bengal meticulously (1994), especially in its eastern parts, since before 1204, the time when the Saltanat regime was first established there. For an overwhelming majority of the people who became Muslims, the process he describes was one not of "conversion" in a particular moment but of constituting a community, initially for an economic activity, that of clearing densely forested land, under the leadership of a man of religion, a maulvi and the like. Apart from contemporary observers' records, he draws on evidence of epigraphy, numismatics, architecture, and artwork to produce a thick analysis. It enables him to demonstrate that by far the largest increases in the Muslim population in rural eastern Bengal came in the wake of the Mughal conquest of the region, in the seventeenth and eighteenth centuries.[9]

The foregoing was *not* a consequence of pressure from the state; the Mughal administration took pains to ensure that its officials would not engage in proselytizing (Eaton 1994: 175–79). Rather, it was part of the process of clearing, for paddy cultivation, lands which had until then been thickly forested; this major economic shift followed from the Mughal search for revenue from these hitherto forested territories. The spread of Islam followed principally from the ability of pioneering Muslim religious men to draw forest and hill people, and others of diverse religious backgrounds, into labouring groups, which they formed for clearing the forest lands. The communities so forming took on the religious practices of the men who had drawn them together – there was no particular moment of "conversion" in the whole process.

---

[8] In Dominique-Sila Khan's reading, the Bohras were constituted in Gujarat during the twelfth century, following earlier Ismaili activity (1997: 31). Subsequently, they received much hostile attention from Sunni Muslim rulers of Gujarat, and underwent several splits (Misra 1964: Chaps 2 and 3).

[9] Asim Roy's earlier work (1983: Chap. 1) had anticipated several elements of Eaton's account.

In a vast region, where there were few previously established rights over land, the Muslim religious men's initial claims took varied routes in different regions: they might install themselves, and their followers, in virgin land, clearing it for paddy, and then seek recognition from Mughal authority as collectors of revenue for the government (Eaton 1994: 224); they might buy "permanent land tenure rights" from "non-cultivating intermediaries, or *zamindars*", high caste Hindus, who had acquired the rights from Mughal authorities, but who would not do the work themselves owing to "social taboos" (*ibid.*: 220ff); or they might get a land grant from the government for bringing land into cultivation and "to promote Islamic piety in the countryside" (*ibid.*: 246).

Men entering these relationships and communities carried with them their prior ideas concerning the supernatural. From such beginnings, the passage to a relatively sharp and self-conscious identification with Islam took more than two centuries. Eaton sees them as journeying through three distinct phases in relation to beliefs, symbols, and practices:

A. inclusion: Islamic elements were mixed into the prior stock of beliefs and practices concerning the supernatural, as often happens in folk practice (Eaton 1994: 269, 270–75);

B. identification: particular Islamic figures came to be identified with specific indigenous ones, as being the "same", or as being linked with each other in specified relationships, say one being the *avatar* of the other (*ibid.*: 275–81); and

c. displacement: a process beginning in the early nineteenth century, in a colonial milieu, once the political reasons for mutual accommodation, coming from the Mughals and their successor states, had worn off. Religious identities and practices began to move from being relatively fuzzy to being more sharply defined (*ibid.*: 281–90). As we shall see below, there have been long-term pressures, for such groups as the Meo in north India and Muslims in eastern Bengal, to remove the pre-Islamic beliefs and practices, in the cause of securing what some believed to be purer Islamic beliefs and practices.

Eaton sees the Muslim religious men in Bengal as well endowed for the role they entered:

> ... from the culture of institutional Sufism came the asymmetric categories of *pir* and *murid*, or shaikh and disciple, which rendered Sufism a suitable model for channelling authority, distributing patronage, and maintaining discipline – the very requirements appropriate to the business of organizing

and mobilizing labour in regions along the cutting edge of state power. It is little wonder that Sufis appeared along East Bengal's forested frontier (1994: 257).

The forested delta had earlier been populated only thinly. Pivotal to the spread of Islam in this setting was the ability of the Muslim religious men to relate to others in an open-ended manner; this was in sharp contrast with the attitude of long-settled Brahmins in western Bengal who considered lands further east, inhabited largely by "tribal" peoples, as being ritually polluted, not really suited for Brahmins to live in (Eaton 1994: 7). As later generations remembered it, the challenge was "the forest, a wild and dangerous domain that [the Sufis] were believed to have subdued; ... the supernatural world, ... with which they were believed to wield continuing influence" (ibid.: 218). The forest was the same. The Brahmins ignored it; the Sufis embraced it, aided no doubt by their own long-held belief in their own superior hold over supernatural forces. We have here an instance of two groups, bearers of contrasting ideologies, "defining" the same physical situation in different ways – definitions which had marked historical, if unintended, consequences (pp. xxviii–xxix). Muslim religious men entered this region vigorously.

In reclaiming forest land for paddy, the Muslim religious men drew to themselves not whole *jatis* proud of their collective identities from the past, but individuals and small groups. The land rights that these men would acquire arose from their participation in work which had been organized by the men of religion. People entering the communities being formed had no stake in the ideology underlying the caste order, which has been part of a wider Hindu ethos. In the society that emerged in eastern Bengal, consequently, Muslims enjoyed an overwhelming preponderance.

Similarly in Punjab. Here again Richard Eaton has uncovered the evidence. Between the seventh and the eleventh centuries, Jat pastoralists moved up "from Sind into the Multan area". By the thirteenth century, they were settling between the Sutlej and the Ravi; by c.1600, they had spread greatly, becoming "the dominant agrarian caste" (2000: 212f). Many, meanwhile, were accepting Islam too. Eaton tracks the process by analysing a set of 14 genealogical charts of a set of prominent families available in a mid-nineteenth century publication. Distributing the names in the charts between "Punjabi secular names" and "Muslim names", he finds that the latter begin to appear in early 1400s, become a majority by mid-1600s, and a 100 per cent by 1815, indexing a slow, barely conscious, process of entering Islam spread over four centuries (*ibid.*: 221f).

For all their irenic qualities, however, we find numerous references to Sufis for whom a little coercion in the cause of Islam would not be a bad thing. S. A. A. Rizvi, for instance, mentions the Turkistani warrior-saint Shaikh Jalal, a militant evangelist active in Sylhet, Bengal, in the fourteenth century. In the areas he conquered, he left hundreds of disciples behind to propagate Islam themselves (1977: 26f). And there is the eighteenth century Mulla Muhibb Ali Sadi:

> Shah Jahan gave orders that if any Hindu desired to become a Muslim, he should be put in charge of the Mulla, who also recommended what pension should be given or favour conferred upon the convert. He is reported to have made a large number of conversions (Mujeeb 1965: 308).

The state had taken a forward role much earlier in Kashmir.

The case of Kashmir

Kashmir's case is unusual. Conversions there have often been linked with the use, or threat, of force by the late fourteenth century ruler, Sultan Sikandar (1389–1413). Recent studies argue that these attributions have flowed from texts by Kashmiri Pandit chroniclers who, to be sure, were under pressure at the time; but their difficulties may have been of another sort (Khan 1994; Hangloo 2000; Wani 2005).[10] The new interpretation reads the Pandit chronicles more critically, and it marshals a wide range of Kashmiri and Persian sources, and several kinds of oral tradition. It goes as follows.

Since the eighth century, Muslims had come to Kashmir from elsewhere – soldiers, traders, artisans, Persian speaking Sufis, refugees. They came in groups small or large, and their numbers grew as the rule of Muslim dynasties spread closer to Kashmir. Preceding the establishment of the Saltanat in Kashmir in the mid-fourteenth century, the region was riven with pervasive political conflicts, as noted in the twelfth century Kalhana's *Rajatarangini*; and the revisionists stress the acute social tension between the dominant Brahmins and the vast numbers

---

[10] I thank T. N. Madan for telling me of these revisionist studies – and loaning them to me.

of others. The field of political contention in Kashmir was wide open: a Ladakhi Buddhist gained the throne briefly, 1320–23, during which period he took to Islam under Sufi influence; and in 1339, a Muslim from Swat in Pathan country, in service to the previous king, was able, with support from Hindu Chiefs, to mount the throne.

Sufis from west and central Asia continued coming to Kashmir, sometimes in large parties. One leading Sufi concentrated on the ruling group: persuading the Sultan and his family to Islamize their lifestyle more fully; and getting his senior Hindu officials to accept Islam (c. 1390). Both Ishaq Khan and Muhammad Ashraf Wani deny stoutly any use of force by the Sultans to speed the drift to Islam that followed. They concede the demolition of numerous idols and temples but insist that this was instigated by the newly converted officials, especially a senior minister of Sultan Sikandar – Suhabhatt, whose name changed to Saifuddin – and by non-Brahmin villagers, abandoning their lowly ranks in the Brahminical order, and demolishing its symbols. A later Sultan, Zainul Abidin, 1420–70, invited any neo-converts who wished to return to their former faith to do so; none did.

The picture becomes a little fuller, and more credible, with an older account from R. K. Parmu (1969: 116–30), which indicates a series of elements converging around the year 1398. A peremptory, very large demand was presented on behalf of the central Asian invader, Timur, to Sikandar, Kashmir's relatively young and inexperienced ruler; and he was persuaded by his advisers, including the recently converted Suhabhatt, to meet the demand by despoiling the lavishly endowed Hindu temples. This move soon swelled into a general assault on Brahminical practices. Many Brahmins left Kashmir; people of other *jati*s converted to Islam.

In the spread of Islam in Kashmir, Ishaq Khan holds to the centrality of the "Muslim Rishis". This movement was initiated by a man known as Nund Rishi or Shaikh Nuruddin (1379–1442) whose poetry castigated Brahminical beliefs and practices and referred reverentially to Prophet Mohammad and to much that followed from him: "the bulk of Nooruddin's poetry is a Kashmiri rendition of the *Quran* and *Hadis*" (Zutshi 2003: 23n, citing G. N. Gauhar's biography of Nuruddin). Nuruddin and his followers lived ascetic lives, celibate and vegetarian – a familiar lifeway, long practised by indigenous holy men. Through Nuruddin's poetry and singing, the ideas and symbols of Islam acquired general currency, commended by their local, renunciatory associations. Collective singing of the praises of Allah and Prophet Mohammad became a distinctive mark of folk Islam in Kashmir. By the end of the sixteenth century, nearly all Kashmiris, except Brahmins, had taken to the new faith. Here we have conversions in which the influence of religious men was augmented by political pressure. The next section considers situations where the play of the latter was stronger.

Political conversions

One might take to Islam in *anticipation* of economic opportunity, or of political favours, or of escaping disfavour; or it could be a *consequence* of proximity to rulers.[11] Analyzing an early nineteenth century report about a village in Kaira District, Gujarat, A. M. Shah has written about a Muslim Rathod Rajput group whose members had accepted Islam, in the fifteenth or sixteenth century, owing to "the policy of the Sultans of Gujarat of creating such social groups in the region as would provide abiding support to their political authority" (2002: 58). Apropos a late nineteenth century court case concerning property, the historian Asiya Siddiqi considers a Muslim butcher family, apparently descendants from the Dhangar *jati* in Maharashtra, cattle breeders and shepherds by traditional occupation. Siddiqi surmises that at the time of the first Saltanat conquests of the Deccan, about the thirteenth century, an opportunity for supplying meat to the substantial Muslim population would have arisen. In response, some Dhangar would have converted to Islam "in order to meet the canonical requirement for slaughter (*zabiha*)" of animals (2001: 114). In both cases, Rajput and Dhangar, the Hindu and the Muslim families had maintained close relationships with each other.

The Meo of Mewat

Numbering rather more than 300,000, the Meo of Mewat, in the districts southwest of Delhi, are a mainly rural, landowning caste, with a self-image of being Rajputs, of having been warriors in the past; they are also Muslim. When and how they took to Islam has been a matter

---

[11] In the course of an evening of Dhrupad music by the Dagar Brothers at a home in the late 1980s, the senior brother stressed the affinity between the Dhrupad style of singing and Vedic chanting. He added that his ancestors had been Brahmins; but because they performed at the Mughal court, their castemates broke off relations with them; and therefore his ancestors had taken to Islam.

of folk memory – which places the move variously between the eighth and the seventeenth centuries. In some versions of this memory, the use of force was a sporadic element in their conversion. After reviewing various reports, Partap Aggarwal concludes, "The Meos, because of their active interest in Delhi politics, were constantly under pressure to accept Islam for its value as a useful protective shield" (1971: 40). Until the mid-1940s, the Meo carried their Islam lightly, functioning as a dominant caste, quite like other large landowning castes, confident of their place within the caste order. They were firm in marrying other Meos, following their own rules, ignoring the more common ideas among Muslims about marriages with preferred kin, as well as the possibility of marrying non-Meo Muslims. They patronized Brahmins, who legitimized the high Meo place within the hierarchy, and they lived by the ideas of purity and pollution, much like the other high castes, but they did not employ Brahmins in ritual roles. Their rituals, say at marriages, had forms that they largely shared with Rajputs, except that it was the father's sister who would act as the "priest" in place of a Brahmin. In effect, they were a cluster of Rajput clans. What identified them as Muslim was the following: their names, their occasional recourse to mosques, their practice of circumcision, and their burying, not cremating, their dead; that was about all (Jamous 1996: 191f).

The Meo and their neighbours participated in a variety of festivals in a relaxed manner; Muharram was occasion for a common *mela*, and there were various shared sacred personages. Engaged almost exclusively in agriculture, the Meo had travelled very little outside Mewat and had only limited contact with the outer world. Since the mid-1940s, however, the Meo have changed course substantially (see p. 152).

Modest coercion to secure conversions, though on a small scale, was fairly widespread under dynasties abiding by Islam. Under the Husain Shahi rulers in Bengal (1494–1538), for instance, Hindus had to convert in order to be able to take government employment (Rizvi 1977: 23). For the late seventeenth century, Muzaffar Alam mentions the case of Bikramajit Singh, a Chief of the Gautam Rajputs from the Azamgarh area in UP, who "had hatched [a conspiracy] to kill his brother"; he "had to become Muslim to avoid execution at Aurangzeb's order" (Alam 1986: 159). Granted such retail coercion – and Rizvi (1977) mentions cases on somewhat larger scales – it remains true that the largest blocks in India accepted Islam through absorption, not through coercion.[12]

In sum, then, the streams of Islam spread through the subcontinent through a variety of channels. However tolerant the dynastic political norms, this was also a period during which *ulama* and the Sufis were pushing to spread their faith (e.g., Aquil 2006: 67–72 *passim*), and to this end they would have the state's at least tacit support. The emphasis by and large was on having Islam accepted, by saying the *kalima* – a statement of faith in the unity of God and the prophethood of Muhammad – often under the influence of Sufis and their grace; beyond that, the prevailing social arrangements were ordinarily disturbed only minimally. The streams spread, finding their own courses and levels locally; but there was no central authority to shape strategy or give this process direction. The *ulama* might chafe at all the un-Islamic goings on, but they had neither the resources nor the will to work on a general promulgation, say, of the *shariat*.

Yet a subtle pressure towards Islamizing had been at work in certain settings. The pressure arose in the *ulama*'s informal networks and in the Sufi orders that strung numerous Sufis together. From their viewpoint, how well a convert from a Hindu background could be accepted into Muslim society, and what status he could be accorded as a Muslim, would be a function of how well he had erased his origin as a Hindu – and how clearly he kept his distance from Hindu society (Ahmad 1969: 1141). Our study has a recurring theme: that Muslim leaders in the subcontinent have long had anxieties that their always modest body of followers might be absorbed by the capacious Hindu society.[13] During the Saltanat centuries, the number of Muslims was small; but the anxieties did not abate even when the numbers grew. The prospect of acceptance and appreciation among Muslims, then, was a lever that leading Muslims could use for those who would make an unambiguous commitment to the tenets of Islam.

---

[12] Relatively small numbers of Hindu literati, merchants, and the like also took to Islam, e.g., Imtiaz Ahmad (1973a) has written of an ex-Kayastha group, known as Sheikh Siddique, in Allahabad and Lucknow. The motivations, and the circumstances, for change of faith in these stray cases have been diverse.

[13] These anxieties were reciprocal; see p. 149 on an early twentieth century text on the Hindu side. Need one add that Muslim: Hindu was scarcely the only axis of anxiety in an era when so many political adventurers were abroad.

I wish to return now to the social processes during the Mughal period which would have left marks in the memories of generations of Muslims and Hindus subsequently.

Power and Force

All states use force, and the upper strata within a state have informal advantages, if not formal privileges, compared with others. For the Mughal period, C. A. Bayly (1985: 189–93) notes something of the advantages of the higher Mughal strata. They were able to expand the lands under their control substantially, aided by their place in the government. Their employment in, or proximity to, the government helped by way of their salaries and *jagirs*, which allowed them access to the land; it helped them also in terms of the support that the local representatives of the government, the *kazi* and the *kotwal*, could provide in making their rights more secure.[14]

The units of advance and retreat in these, ordinarily silent, struggles were the extended kin groups which loomed large in social organization. Among some Hindu groups like the Rajputs, their marriage rules served to disperse their marriages widely, creating thereby an extensive field for intimate, kin-based interaction: their sense of being under pressure would be felt throughout their *jati*. This interactional field, resting on kinship and *jati*, persisted, amidst vivid memories of their retreat in the past; and all this would abet their mobilization when the political tide turned (Fox 1971). It would then be the turn of the established ruling class to feel the pressure. We may expect that, in both rounds, such essentially political contention, turning on land and power, would be inflected in the hands of ubiquitous exclusivists, its meaning assimilated into the enduring identities, linked with religious traditions.

Bayly calls our attention to another process (1985: 194ff). The political flux between the twelfth and the nineteenth centuries saw the rise and fall of many dynasties in South Asia. Once a state was stabilized, its rulers tried generally to be equitable towards their subjects of various persuasions; to that effect, they would try to rein in their religious specialists, armed forces, and the like. In other phases, when a warrior

---

[14] The use of governmental position to advance one's personal interests has been common enough historically. Indian officials in the early colonial apparatus also could effectively use privileged information, not to mention the then scarce cash resources, for feathering their own nests (Stokes 1978: 84f, 247, and elsewhere). Practices in the early twenty-first century have long antecedents!

group – Afghan, Maratha, Sikh, or whatever – was struggling to establish its dominance, or when the state was decaying, its hold over its soldiery tended to be lax. In course of warfare in contested territories, Saltanat armies (or those of other Muslim dynasties), moving beyond the dynastic frontier, sometimes displayed a similar lack of control, or assaulted temples deliberately, appropriating their movable property (Prasad 1999: 78, quoting Mohammad Habib 1974: 20; Talbot 1995: 718–20). Such incidents of soldierly or political aggression, then, would be interpreted and remembered in terms which would reconfirm a belief in an opposition between "Hindu" and "Muslim".

Commercial rivalry, in Ahmedabad in 1714, between some leading men led to violence between "Muslims" and "Hindus", the spark coming, as so often, from offensive Holi revelry – and possibly from cow sacrifice at Id in another episode at about the same time. The events were serious enough for the adversaries to travel to the court in Delhi – where they seem to have settled their dispute voluntarily (Haider 2005). Aziz Ahmad has written of serious rioting, at about the same time, "when Muharram coincided with Hindu festivals like Ramanavami and Dashera" (1964: 157, citing Jafar Sharif, tran. in 1921). Rajat Ray's list for the eighteenth century (2003: 29) includes Delhi, Agra, and Kashmir (1720s during the festivals of Holi, Muharram, and Id) and Surat (1788, 1795, between Muslim weavers and Parsi and Bania contractors).

⊗

To sum up our sketch of the legacy from the medieval period. The Saltanat victories, from the twelfth century on, arose in the central Asian horse-borne warriors' ability to concentrate the application of force to telling effect. Alongside the matching of arms, there was also an encounter of "cosmic schemes", of worldviews. Commenting on this overall process, Rajat K. Ray notes that "This was not a conflict between the Vedic religion of antiquity which had nothing against the sacrifice of cows, and the original Islam of Arabia, which did not require it" (2003: 104). He sees it rather as "an encounter between two parties defined by the confrontation itself: an interface between Hinduism, newly denominated by Islam, and the latter, recontextualized by the former (*ibid.*)." It was an encounter with much silent give and take, and acceptance and rejection, on both sides.

While the hosts lacked the means to meet the conquerors on equal terms militarily, both sides had strong reasons for helping things to settle down. In later generations, the caste system, and the imperatives of governance and neighbourliness, provided frameworks for organizing basic social and economic cooperation, and for maintaining the agrarian cycle, commerce, and revenue flows under conditions of some stability.

We can say a little more. Medieval social arrangements were such as to allow even the *same person, even in the course of a single day, to participate in both a shared space and an exclusive one*. Illustratively, the Kayasthas and the Khatris in the Mughal establishment participated in a Persian, if not a thoroughly Islamic, milieu in their administrative functioning; but the "brahmanical notion of pollution", notes Muzaffar Alam, prevented even these limited influences from entering "the life of a Hindu beyond the threshold of the inner apartments of his house" (1989: 56). Their Persian and Turki colleagues would no doubt have participated, with equal facility, in settings which would be exclusively Persian, emphatically Islamic, or both.

In all this, Muzaffar Alam has argued for the influence of the *akhlaq* literature of ethical governance which he sees as promoting "an atmosphere of mutual trust and confidence" (1989: 53). Nevertheless, there were struggles, often violent, over political and revenue matters; and Mughal functionaries were not always shy about using the strong arm. The level of insecurity could rise; yet how it would compare with other major polities of the era remains a moot point.

Insecurity, it must be remembered, was not limited to the subject population; it affected the ruling groups too. Many of them were refugees from disturbed conditions in central and west Asia. In India, there was always the potential threat from Hindu chiefs to Muslim life and religious places. In overwhelming numbers, the local population was Hindu: not only did they fail to recognize what seemed to be the manifest superiority of Islam to its believers; the latter were also surrounded by temptations to stray from the true path of Islam by the practices of *yogis* and others. There were, furthermore, rivalries – between the various Sufi masters, and between them and the *ulama*. To cap it all, kingships under the Saltanat and the Mughals were inherently unstable. Succession struggles apart, the dynasties had to be sustained largely by the power of the sword. Medieval European kingships received vital support from the Church; the Chinese literati placed its own long tradition of governing at the service of every new dynasty; the caste order buoyed up kingships in the Indic world; but dynasties like the Saltanat and the Mughals could count on little by way of support from the society they governed, either in ideology or in institutions. The sense of insecurity in all this had multiple springs.

A recent, sensitive anthropological study from a cluster of villages in western Bihar shows us something of the manner in which social groups remember and recreate their sense of the past, of their multiple pasts, with or without written texts. Everyday conversations in everyday situations are central to this process of transmitting group memories. These memories fasten on certain enduring material features in the milieu, persisting reminders of the shifting of equations of power in the past: conspicuous ruins of forts, palaces, tombs, and the like; and the implanting of outsiders, agents of new rulers, who gained land rights that the erstwhile dominant groups lost (Gottschalk 2001). Around such material elements congeal the memories of conquests, of shifts of local power. Winners and losers both continue to live in the locality through their descendants who, recounting their ancestors' fortunes in times past, keep alive too the associated emotions and sentiments. And this happens even as both sides must, and do, weave fresh bonds of living and working in cooperation, overlaying the older memories and sentiments, in this palimpsest of many time horizons.

There were, besides, the religious specialists and their entourage: custodians of their respective traditions, some of whom would interpret ongoing episodes of conflict, here silent there violent, in terms of the frameworks of identities as they saw them. There were an Akbar's conciliatory gestures; and there were strong practical reasons for keeping the public arenas in good order; yet the contrary memories of the past, and interpretations of the present, could code a sense of opposition into the flow of everyday life. Thus were created the "historical structures" of the kind that shaped "interactional structures" – then, and in subsequent centuries (Denzin 1983: 137). Why the dominant schools of historians in late twentieth century India have resisted this elementary insight is a puzzle whose scrutiny would take us to their unstated ideological assumptions.

And yet they worked together, and people of various strata lived together reasonably amicably. This was not achieved by applying state power and force in everyday life; only the modern state has come to acquire potential capacities of that magnitude. It was achieved rather through *inertia*: once certain social and political arrangements are established, most people most of the time find good reasons to continue with public habits that have become familiar, whatever their reservations in private.

CR&O

The medieval centuries saw recurrent bouts of conquest and contention. There is no gainsaying the conquerors' dominance in the battlefields, transmuted later into the famous dynasties and their empires, large and small. A motley crew of immigrants followed in their train: men on horseback, refugees looking for patronage and work, maulvis, Sufis, artisans, and all the rest. Yet, their numbers remained small – and the urge to distinguish themselves from the ocean of indigenes strong. It helped to try to enlarge one's "own" side by persuading indigenes to take to the new faith – these processes we have seen. And the evengelists sought at times to make the converts commit themselves to their new community more or less irrevocably. A recent historian of the process in medieval Kashmir lists a long series of steps taken along this path: adopting Islamic names, performing circumcision, building mosques in place of temples, changing style of dress, eating beef, taking to Muslim ceremonies, fairs and festivals, and much else (Wani 2005: 278).

All this was "societal contention" – a process that will engage Chapter 7 – one no less disruptive in the thirteenth or the fifteenth century than it was in the twentieth. In responding to the traumatic effect of the horseborne conquerors from Central and West Asia, Sheldon Pollock (1993) has argued, key actors shaping the indigenous imagination discovered the possibility of putting the framework in the Ramayana story, and its central character, Rama, to do "powerful ideological work" (*ibid.*: 283). This was done through texts which praised indigenous rulers who resisted the invaders – their power and their virtues being compared with those of Rama himself. Kingship itself was being divinized, through the important new temples built with Rama as the presiding deity. It was done by equating the terrible conquerors with the demons whom Rama, the divine king, had slain. And it was done by rendering the Ramayana into the several vernaculars (*ibid.*: 286f). From these early codings, elements would be revived, off and on, down the centuries in various contexts. While Cynthia Talbot finds no support for Pollock's thesis in her Andhran inscriptions between the fourteenth and the seventeenth centuries, she does find there a context for demonizing Muslims. Rising out of the debris of the Kakatiyas, a new indigenous warrior elite needed marks of legitimacy for itself urgently, and it summoned a variety of resources to that end. Among these was its claim to have allayed Brahminical anxieties about threats to their position, availing of "the rich symbolism of the age-old fight against demons and disorder" that went back a millennium and more (1995: 703; 696–99).

2

facing the future 1

> Human beings can be described as organisms whose peculiarity it is to construct and modify, slowly and laboriously, over centuries, very complicated sets of mazes for themselves and their posterity, with interconnecting doors and pathways; and also to construct complex rules for interaction and even mutual aid in operating the mazes, as 'the way' to satisfy their multifarious wants. ...
>
> ... the maze can be and is run in many different ways in the same community, and both maze and way are furthermore always being changed.
>
> Wallace 1957: 25f

Among the ambiguities of the medieval period, we have seen, was the simultaneous presence both of exclusivist religious specialists and their associates, and of several levels of integrative arrangements: governments, shared sacred localities, everyday life – say in caste organized localities, in commerce, in the performing arts, and in the emergence of shared languages. With the decline of the Mughal and Awadhi states in north India, the cement of power began to dissolve and what had been an integrated ruling class came apart partially, but other shared arrangements continued. The British takeover led into a triangle of ambivalences – between the British (including the missionaries), the legatees of the Muslim ruling class and its ideologues, and corresponding Hindu groups. Yet there was a widespread inching towards a *modus vivendi*: towards a new order around a different style of government, its different epistemologies, and the new communications – printing, the railways, the post office. The setting permitted the pursuit of a limited diversity of purposes.

Between the key groups among the Muslims and Hindus, there were some striking contrasts, apart from their distinctive religious complexes, scriptures, and styles of everyday piety. The remains of the Muslim ruling class were nostalgic about the empire that their ancestors had governed; and through the colonial period the religious men of Islam worked hard to summon the various elements in their flock to an active sense of community, the *umma*. A distinctive quality on the Hindu side was the numerous *jatis* and sects, which were somewhat intersecting since some sects had followers from many *jatis*. In the nineteenth century already in the new colonial cities – Bombay, Madras, Calcutta – the tasks of mediation between the British and the indigenes drew in upper castes like the Brahmins, who were quick to take to English, and the Hindu merchant castes who worked extensive commercial networks.

The implications of these differences will surface in the chapters that follow. We shall see that even somewhat similar initiatives turned all too often into very different institutional forms and propagated themselves in strikingly different ways. The impulses as well as the consequences of reform, and their rhythms and contents, were somewhat different as between Muslims and Hindus. On balance, some Hindu groups' resistance to European ideas and values was weaker, and their defiance of religious orthodoxy somewhat stronger, than that of their Muslim counterparts. It could be said, with good reason, that many Hindus found, in the inequities of the caste order, and in much else in the Brahminical tradition, urgent grounds for trying to reshape their society; the pressures felt among Muslims were of a different kind. This chapter and the next take stock of the kinds of resources that groups among Hindus and Muslims, respectively, mustered in the early colonial period as they prepared to face the future in this time of transition. In this chapter, I shall argue that reform efforts among Hindus found useful social capital in *jati* solidarities; and that the momenta of these social processes could later be turned to other purposes.

The Hindu Scene: Caste, Sect, Institution

In an earlier work, I considered some of the processes which built on resources available within the structure of traditional Indian society for coping with the colonial regime: *one*, the bonds of kinship and marriage, available within the *jati*, which could be extended, but only up to a point; and *two*, the possibility of still larger social mobilization through recourse to general symbols, like the cow or Ganapati, a Maharashtrian deity, or the Khalifa, and even a distinctive ideology, which sometimes added up to a new *sect*, like the Arya Samaj (Saberwal 2001). The following paragraphs review these triggers which served a great many as they faced up to their colonial future. In the process, we shall notice, many learned also the possibility and value of building institutions on the models becoming available in their experience of educational and other institutions, being established by the government or by Christian missionaries. These institutions were to become a third trigger for later generations.

The following paragraphs open with the *jati* and the sect, social forms that have long marked the Hindu space. Social forms arise in course of efforts at achieving a certain range of purposes; but forms once realized – and the corresponding social habits – become available for other purposes too. My argument is that, during the nineteenth and early twentieth centuries, the received forms began to be used differently: moments arose for acting towards new purposes, which might be wholly unrelated to purposes pursued earlier. In these paragraphs I shall look for such moments, alongside a general consideration of the *jati* and the sect as social forms.

Jati

In the shaping of Indian history, we have to understand the significance of the caste order. Of the several dimensions of that complex social form, the webs of close *jati* bonds, of kinship and marriage, turned out to be the most durable. Ranajit Guha cites Irfan Habib to the effect that if castes like Jats, Mewatis, Wattus, and Dogars took to arms in the late Mughal empire, their particular members could not easily keep out; and then Guha notes, for peasant uprisings in the nineteenth century, that the caste group "provided the anti-colonialist mass struggles of our people with some kind of an armature, however imperfect this might have been ..." (1983: 331).

This social grid could help sustain its members, and their sense of who they were, even in adversity; and when the tide turned, it could also serve as a flexible resource, being an all-purpose network, the repository of a kind of social capital. Along this network lay, ordinarily, familiar relationships, buttressed by the *jati*'s social controls; along these relationships would travel the skills of caste occupation, and information about threats and opportunities emerging. These ties could often be stretched and adapted to fit the settings in changing circumstances and their nascent purposes; these furnished a measure of social cushioning.

The availability of this social capital and its uses are well-known in the social sciences. Here are some instances from the precolonial period. Between the eleventh and the eighteenth centuries, at least in northern India, the caste order was crucial in enabling indigenous groups to hold their ground, even though defensively. This resilience had, for example, enabled merchant *jatis* to maintain their hold at least on inland commerce all through the Saltanat and Mughal and later periods (Subramanian and Ray 1991), though particular families and groups would of course rise and fall. *Jati* autonomy enabled its members to chart, and to change, their own course in some measure. In medieval Tamil Nadu, during the eleventh to the thirteenth centuries under the Cholas, some men of the weaver *jati* were merchants in textiles too, "transporting them among localities by bullock-loads and headloads" (Mines 1984: 13); but the security conditions were poor, and brigands active. To guard their caravans and warehouses, the weavers became armed warriors too.

At least among the upper castes, the effective *jati* networks were often spread widely, making them available for a variety of personal needs. Banarasi Das, the early seventeenth century Jain merchant, found welcome and support among his castemates whenever he went to another town (Lath 1981: iv–v). And there is the late case of Aminchand – a major merchant in mid-eighteenth century Calcutta – who was consumed by intrigues in 1758. His son, Fatahchand, surfaced in Benaras the next year, "rising rapidly to the position of one of the premier bankers" (Dalmia 1997: 120f). The long established habits of reorienting caste relationships to changing contexts were to continue into the colonial phase.

Previously I have reviewed the high costs that the Indic world has paid historically for its segmentation along the caste and other axes (Saberwal 1995: Chaps 2 and 7). The argument here is that *jati* relationships had their uses too, which carried over into the colonial period. In coping with the emergent threats and opportunities, the networks of relatively small caste groups, familiar social anchors, continued to be renewed through the ubiquitous ties of kinship and arranged marriages, and these social ties, circumscribed within the *jati*, could be used advantageously. I would nevertheless stop short of the occasional claim that precolonial India already had an active *civil society* by virtue of its numerous castes and sects, for these corporate groups commonly exercised coercive powers over their members.

I proceed now to amplify the general conception outlined above. Given *jati* autonomy, a major locus of their social control has been *within* each *jati*, largely independent of Brahminical authority. This latter was contingent, ultimately dependant on royal support – whether the rulers, including locally dominant castes, accepted Brahmins as counsellors, or otherwise thought it expedient to sustain the caste hierarchy. The *jatis*' internal controls could secure conformity with (adaptable) *jati practice* – regardless of what the scriptures might ordain. The *jati*'s autonomy enabled it to make its own choices, in howsoever modest a measure; and the range of choices exercised historically has sometimes included that of switching to a different occupation – or to another faith; much of this lay beyond Brahminical authority. In their role as family priests to upper castes, the Brahmins' ceremonial would add auspiciousness to what were basically family decisions, following the family's judgments and perceived interests.

Insofar as each *jati* was largely self-regulating, the profusion of *jatis* implied a multiplicity of points where small groups could make small-scale choices for the future, autonomously, within the group, in the light of their members' own perceptions. Many groups therefore found it relatively easy to try out something different, in ways small and large, tentatively, to see where it led. Even in times when, say, some Brahmins apprehended grave disorder, others, say traders and moneylenders, might notice an opportunity in the new political milieu. The orientation was pragmatic, situational, turning only on the interests of family and kin. Such exploration would enlarge somewhat the awareness, and the options, of the group that made such a move, moves which were in the main unspectacular. Their significance lay in the possibility of their extensive replication: as word spread along ties of kinship and marriage (and of sect, see below), others, similarly placed, could try to follow suit, with cumulative, diverse consequences.

I have outlined above a general model of the process whereby people could often deploy their *jati*-linked relationships and resources for diverse purposes in the colonial setting. I proceed now to illustrate the process with several instances: Brahmins' ability to gain influence and status through colonial governments; a range of anti-Brahmin revolts; and finally the securing of commercial, artisanal, and other opportunities during this period.

Brahmins in governments

Concerning the consequential case of the Brahmins, we have evidence from the Bombay Presidency, Tamil Nadu, and from the princely state of Mysore in latter day Karnataka. In early nineteenth century

Bombay, Brahmins found employment with Europeans and drew their castemates with them. It gave them a large lead in employment with Europeans and with the early colonial state in the Bombay Presidency. As the work of the government in Bombay switched to English, the Brahmins were quick to realize the importance of learning the language, and of studying in the new schools: for their customary privileges, it offerred the seal of a new kind of merit in the new order (Naregal 2001: 168, 172–74).

Brahmins in the princely state of Mysore too established a virtual monopoly in their control over the state administration (Bairy 2003: Chap. 3). While some Brahmin students could count on support from their own families, others had to turn to practices like *vaaraanna* and *bhikshaanna* to put themselves through the new schools:

> *Vaaraanna*, ... 'weekly food', refers to the arrangement among the Brahmins residing in cities and towns of feeding one or more poor Brahmin boys, ... on a particular day of the week, till the completion of their education. *Bhikshaanna* ... 'food collected through begging' ... [was less common] students used to go around with a vessel in their hands to local Brahmins' houses begging for food (Bairy 2003: 101).

Such support could take different forms. The home of Kashinath Chatre (1788–1830) "was known to have been an informal hostel for bright – of course brahmin – boys from families known to him, so that they could study in Bombay (Naregal 2001: 173)." Forms of support that had enabled poor Brahmin boys to pursue traditional Sanskrit learning became available also to help them through modern schools.

Veena Naregal narrates the circumstances, in mid-nineteenth century Bombay and Maharashtra, in which small numbers of Brahmins, and other traditionally literate castes, took to the English language. They built on their early presence in pivotal institutions in the field of education (Naregal 2001: 66f and elsewhere), and later in the publication of books and journals. Given the motivation, the caste links, and sometimes material support from the community (*ibid.*: 172–74), the Brahmins, and other literate *jatis*, were cornering government *jobs* early. These early leads have often had enduring, snowballing implications which reached well beyond the matter of government jobs alone. Similarly in late nineteenth and early twentieth century Tamil Nadu: Pandian has recently argued the welding together of the Brahmins' claims to, and assertion of, their cultural superiority with their influential and lucrative presence in the colonial government and the new professions, especially law. The Brahmins' dominance, and their social exclusiveness, especially in the matter of inter-dining, were formidable. Even when representing Tamils in the Indian National Congress, as late as 1917, they required special exclusive arrangements to be made for their meals (Pandian 2007: Chaps 2–3; also Radhakrishnan 1993: 1586–89).

The Brahmins' dominance in the new governments reasserted their prior dominance in some regions; but they had difficulties. They used to be able to suppress challenges in the past, thanks to the willingness of locally dominant castes, or the area's king, to enforce the caste hierarchy. The colonial dispensation would not bring state power to bear on defending the caste order in full measure. Brahmins could no longer count on the self-evident validity of the ideology of the caste order – and of their own place in it.

Revolts against Brahminism

Non-Brahmins were quick to challenge the old hierarchies in the new order. In the inequities of the caste order, the non-Brahmins found *reasons for protest* and for organizing resistance; in their particular *jatis*, or clusters thereof, they found *social bases*, marshalling their internal caste relationships for their actions. This support enabled them to stand up to the Brahminical routines for putting them down. Furthermore, insofar as Brahmins had been among the earliest to take to western learning, they could scarcely advise others not to follow suit; and in the western ideology one could find ammunition against entrenched social hierarchies. Powerful non-Brahmin movements sprang up in several regions: Phule, and then the Mahars in Maharashtra; Nadars, the Justice Party, and the Self-Respectors in Tamil Nadu; Ad Dharm in Punjab.[1] Several of the lower Hindu castes have contested their lowly status, and their social disabilities in the caste order, with dogged determination, over several generations.

The humiliations of the caste order had, for the lower castes, been systematic and pervasive, providing clear targets for public action.

---

[1] Omvedt 1976 on Phule and the non-Brahmin movement, especially Chap. 9; Zelliot 1992: Chap. 2 on the Mahars; Hardgrave 1969 on the Nadars; Pandian 2007: Chaps 4–6 on diverse cultural and political challenges in Tamil Nadu, including the Justice Party and the Self-Respect movement; Juergensmeyer 1982 on Ad Dharm. The gulf, and later the tension, between Brahmins and non-Brahmins in Maharashtra runs through Richard I. Cashman's study around Tilak (1975).

The Nadars, for example, pressed for rights to enter high caste temples and to let their women wear an upper garment publicly. The relatively egalitarian ideas came from the missionaries; resources for pressing the ideas, from castemates who had made good as merchants. Given the logic of the caste order, the well-to-do Nadar merchants were subject to the disabilities as much as their poorer castemen; and so they had reason to join their fellows in their common struggles.

While we cannot say that, already in the nineteenth century, the caste order was losing its legitimacy among the dominant castes, they were increasingly on the defensive about this form of social organization, or at least about its socially oppressive implications. Urban centres, especially, were too open for keeping the lower castes down effortlessly. A space for public life, including public debate, was emerging. The Brahminical ideology was facing challenges on a wide front, not limited to the caste order. When these disputes went to the colonial courts, the outcomes often depended on western ideas on what was acceptable. In late nineteenth century Bombay city, a young women could secure release from an unwanted marriage, thanks partly to public support (Chandra 1998). In this setting, there was no single fallback Brahminical ideology that could be presented – nor an authoritative forum where it might be commended – for general acceptance. There were numerous reformulations, of course, and some of these spawned new sects, as we shall see; but, with passing generations, these became less and less comfortable with the caste order.

Skills and mobility

In the colonial setting, a variety of skills, associated with one's traditional occupation, within one's *jati*, could serve as useful resources: artisanal (in constructing buildings, railways and the like); literary and clerical (in government and other offices and into the new professions); but, above all, *commercial* skills – dealing with money, that most fluid and flexible of commodities – which turned out to have a special edge. While most traders remained locked into cycles of reproduction within their local economies (as in Fox 1967), there were notable inter-regional movements: Bengalis, who were the first in service to European merchants in Calcutta in the eighteenth century, were later edged out, first by (Punjabi) Khatris, then by Marwaris (Timberg 1978: 56, 59; Mahadevan 1976 and Rudner 1989 on Chettiars).

Given the new communications and the consequent possibilities of moving around, caste networks have often helped in chain migration, directed at securing distant economic opportunities (in Punjab, Kessinger 1974 for Sikh Jats villagers; van den Dungen 1968 on several other groups; Bihari Noniyas moving to Bombay, Rowe 1973). Moving away from home, one could sometimes try out new, unaccustomed roles and learn new skills. Several Punjabi Sikh Ramgarhias, traditionally carpenters and blacksmiths, took to substantial contracting in Assam in the early twentieth century (Banerjee 2006). By the mid-century, there were several cases of members of a *jati* entering a new occupation on a large scale: weavers and leatherworkers turned to lathework in a Punjabi town (Saberwal 1976: Chap. 5); and Mahisya peasants became light engineering entrepreneurs in Howrah in West Bengal (Owens and Nandy 1978).

To sum up, *all jatis* are constituted of (relatively) passive networks continually renewed through the working of kinship and marriages. During the nineteenth and early twentieth centuries, some of these were pressed into activities which had public consequences: Brahmins in several regions – Bombay, Madras, Mysore, and elsewhere – used their *jati* networks to secure privileged access, and at times control, over the apparatus of state. In contesting that Brahminical *administrative* domination, several categories of non-Brahmins – professionals (as in Madras), alumni of missionary schools (Jotiba Phule in Pune) – learned to draw on their caste networks for support. The caste hierarchy was beginning to unravel a little, pointing the way to a social polycentrism – in which even some lower castes began to contest their lowly status actively. In an early initiative in 1851–52, Phule, with diverse support, established in Pune three schools each for girls and for lower caste boys – Mahars and Mangs (Naregal 2001: 93–100). This growing social polycentrism would underlie the ability of later generations to summon political support on caste bases (Kothari 1970).

The foregoing calls for several caveats. First, our discussion of challenges from the lower castes overstates their successes implicitly. It is their success stories that have engaged scholarly interest much more than the continuing, overwhelming dominance of the upper and middle castes which, in fact, has been far more widespread. Second, it should be remembered that *jati* has been only one of the frames in which people have acted. Other frames have included individual effort, as in education, the sect, or patronage from the powerful, including governments. Some of this diversity can be seen for Bengal in the late nineteenth and early twentieth centuries (Bandyopadhyay 1990: Chap. 3).

Needless to say, different *jatis* felt impelled to activate their networks at varying times in diverse contexts, depending on local motives and opportunities. To take a negative instance, the Rajput marriage rules, which often required that spouses be found between previously unrelated lineages, gave them exceptionally widespread *jati* networks; but they were slow to draw on them for public activity during the colonial period. Their historic orientation was that of warriors and rulers; but the road to the colonial (and later) ruling arrangements lay through unwarriorlike activities like studying and passing examinations, or through seeking electoral support. Warriorhood could not always be an asset for them; and the Rajput population is relatively small (Chakravarti 1975). Their experience has been somewhat similar to that of the legatees of the Mughal ruling class, whom we meet later.

Sect

Granting the ubiquity of the bonds of family and *jati*, these could not extend indefinitely; for any particular person, these links used to be confined within fairly close limits, given the slow means of communications of the time. A social form that could escape this limitation was that of a sect, whose leader, a *guru*, would draw his followers into another order of relationships among themselves. The emergence of new sects has been virtually a "cottage industry" in the "Hindu" space. The link between *jati* and sect has been variable: a sect could be formed within a *jati*; or, starting off with members from more than one *jati*, a sect could demolish the marriage barriers among its members and turn them all into one *jati*; or the sect may remain open, with members from several *jatis* each of which continue to be endogamous, that is separate marriage groups (Eschmann 1997 offers an overview on sects in Hinduism).

Sect within a jati. Between the late nineteenth and early twentieth centuries, a group of Saraswat Brahmins, affiliated with their guru's centre, *matha*, at Chitrapur, near the border between South and North Canara (in latter day Karnataka), took a complex social trajectory: from a background of scribal services and non-cultivating landownership in north Canara, they moved to the growing metropolis of Bombay, and to modern professional lives there, recreating for themselves a milieu of caste neighbourhoods and numerous caste-based associations for mutual social support amidst the enveloping flux (Conlon 1977). Similarly, Sri Narayan Dharma Paripalana (SNDP) in Kerala, in the late nineteenth century came to be limited to the Ezhavas (Rao 1979: Chaps 2–3); and *ad dharm* in Punjab by the mid-twentieth century to the weaver–leatherworker *jati*s (Saberwal 1976: 68–70). In such cases, the shared ideology of the sect, and its leadership, symbolism, and social focus may help energize the *jati* in its pursuits.

Sect becomes an endogamous jati. Saurabh Dube (1998) has tracked the course of the Satnami sect in Chhatisgarh through nearly two centuries. Predominantly of *chamar*, "leatherworker", membership, it drew in others of "low" castes too. Its evolving internal structure of authority and control managed, however, to make the sect endogamous, obliterating internal caste differences and blocking marriages with former castemates outside the sect.

The open sect. The form of a sect can reach beyond the limits of family and *jati*. A sect's founder and its core message, its ideology, may have a wider appeal, perhaps turning around a sacred text and a set of symbols and principles. Rajat K. Ray sees the open Hindu sect as associated with a vernacularization of devotionalism. Starting in about the fifteenth century, this form of the sect was centred on the "Guru", who "need not be a Brahman" (2003: 107). Perhaps the most extraordinary case of recent times has been that of the Brahmo Samaj, initiated in early nineteenth century Calcutta by Ram Mohan Roy,[2] with a strong affinity with the Unitarians, a sect then emerging out of Christianity. Its membership in early decades came from the Bengali upper castes – Brahmin, Baidya, Kayastha – though its ideology and practice have been remarkably open-ended. The ideological impulse in the Brahmo Samaj was in many ways radical enough to arouse acute anxieties: at the mid-nineteenth century, numerous young men who chose, for example, to discard their sacred thread, were expelled from their homes, and excommunicated. Brahmos in several Bengali cities had to move to all-Brahmo neighbourhoods. At times they functioned as a separate *jati*; and they persuaded the government to promulgate the Brahmo Marriage Act (1872) to validate their marriages (Kopf 1979: 103f). All this was a passing phase: the non-Brahmo

---

[2] Razi Aquil has reminded me of the great importance of Ram Mohan Roy's early grounding in "the Perso-Islamicate intellectual tradition" – one that his followers sought to purge from his writings that they preserved, to fit him into the mould of "a colonial Hindu figure and not an early modern intellectual who drew on a much bigger pool of non-western ideas ..." (e-mail 21 July 2007).

antagonisms abated with time, as did the Brahmo momentum, and in any case their overall vision would not let them become a distinctive *jati* permanently.

The Brahmo Samaj was a point of reference for the Arya Samaj in Punjab, as well as the Ramakrishna Mission, later in the century. The ideologies at issue have had various sources: charismatic founders (as in SNDP in Kerala, Rao 1979: Chap. 2; Swaminarayan sect in Gujarat, Williams 1984; Ramakrishna Mission in Bengal and elsewhere, Beckerlegge 2006); or the new faith could be anchored to texts claimed to be ancient revelations (the Vedas, in the case of the Arya Samaj, Jones 1976: 31–33). These sects have been notable for the influence that their members could often exercise over the sect's ideology; and they have been notable too for the large pools of ideas upon which they could draw to justify their choices, which might, in fact, be made for other reasons.

Lay influence

Especially in a new or a small sect, its members would be able to influence its ideology, inflecting it to suit their own interests in changing times. Their bargaining power with the sect's religious leaders would be greater than it would be with religious authorities seen as custodians of an ancient tradition and its eternal truths, scriptures, and sanctions. For instance, the Chitrapur *guru* until 1915 had been adamant about excommunicating any follower who went abroad; but his successor waived the rule in line with his twentieth century followers' needs. These sects and their social networks too could thus become resources in their lay members' proactive coping with their life spaces.

Lay men, that is, would share in the sect's leadership. Members in a supra-caste sect could work up an extensive social network, of reach larger than possible for *jati*-based networks. These larger networks have sometimes served various purposes unrelated to the sect's core beliefs. The Arya Samaj has been the best known instance. Though the ancient Vedas formed its scriptural core, its lay leaders – merchants and the new professionals in Lahore – carried their scriptures lightly, exercising a remarkable freedom of maneuver (Jones 1976: 38, 43–45). Its agenda for "social reform" apart, it became, in effect, a wide-ranging social field within which to pursue a variety of purposes: build mainline educational institutions, start a bank, persuade those whose ancestors had moved to other religious traditions to return to Hinduism (*shuddhi*), and much else. In late nineteenth century Banaras, the author, publisher, and public man Harishchandra, of Aggarwal merchant background, was a leading figure in the newly formed, orthodox Dharma Sabha; and he founded the Vaishnavite Tadiya Samaj. His writings and journals influenced not only the forms of literature but also the criteria for defining the category "Hindu", especially in relation to the reform movements, Brahmo Samaj and Arya Samaj (Dalmia 1997: Chap. 6).

Nonica Datta has explored the appropriation of the Arya Samaj framework, its ideological and organizational forms, by Jats in Haryana, especially between 1879 and 1912. Being settled on canal irrigated lands, and taken favourably into the colonial army, they had done well economically; but Brahmins and other upper castes continued to rank them low down – as Shudras – much to the Jat unhappiness. Then they came across Dayananda, founder of the Arya Samaj, whose text *Satyarthaprakash* had said positive things about Jats, and provided scriptural support for their familial arrangements, especially regarding their pattern of widows' customary remarriage (N. Datta 1999: 22f). Jat leadership proceeded then to draw upon the Arya Samaj to give themselves an exalted religious routine and symbols – the sacred thread, Sanskrit and Vedas, and cow protection – to buttress their claims to higher caste status, to form Jat organizations, and to establish educational institutions roughly according to Arya models (*ibid.*: 82f). It was almost wholly a Jat effort – they were always in control over what happened in Jat society; so it was a case more of Jats appropriating the Arya repertoire for their own ambitions than of the Arya Samaj remaking Jats into a demanding Arya mould, though the Arya "reformism" did pull the Jats out of their earlier ambience that had included multiple religious traditions (*ibid.*: 56f).

Pools of ideas

Granting the subcontinental spread of a scriptural tradition, the caste order, pilgrimage centres and the like, the Brahminical tradition has been polycentric historically, comfortable with regional and sectarian differences. In each region, diverse local beliefs and practices came to be interlinked with the texts, symbols, and assumptions of the high tradition (for Bengal, Chakrabarti 2001). Consequently, the wider tradition came to be associated with a plurality of scriptural texts and symbols, available for varied interpretations. We may speak of a certain *ideological* laissez-faire – once the overall framework of the caste order itself was accepted. "Changes in beliefs there might not evoke a whisper whereas even the most minor change in a social practice might provoke a revolt (Parekh 1989: 15)." Correspondingly, the tradition could carry a wide range of symbols – the cow, Vedas, Ganapati, Shivaji, particular *jati* traditions, India as "mother", and indeed anti-Brahminism; around these, the various social entities could congeal as impulses moved them. The tradition gives at times the impression of featuring a chaos of symbols and ideas.

It turned out then that the nineteenth century reformers had access to a large stock of traditional texts, which maintained a variety of positions on particular issues. These could often be cited in support of a direction that a group might want to take. For choices influenced by a menu of western practices, justifications would be found in indigenous texts. Here is an instance from Ishwar Chandra Sarma, better known as Vidyasagar (b. 1820): "Bengal's most learned Sanskrit scholar [but not a Brahmo], but also her most successful social reformer; he was an ardent rationalist, but spent most of his time justifying that rationalism from Hindu texts ... – yet was known to be a dedicated humanist and a professed atheist" (Kopf 1979: 47):

> In 1853, Vidyasagar discovered a sloka or verse from the *Parashara Samhita*, an ancient legal text in Sanskrit, which favored widow remarriage. Parashara had stated three alternatives for the widow – remarriage, sati, and an ascetic life. Since sati had been abolished by law in 1830 and the rigors of asceticism were no longer feasible, remarriage was the only suitable alternative. This was only part of Vidyasagar's technique for changing social values from within the system . ... he also sought to demonstrate on ethical grounds that it was inhuman to prohibit child widows from remarrying. Vidyasagar was extremely effective. His ideas were incorporated into a Widow Remarriage Bill that became law on July 26, 1856. In the same way, Vidyasagar attacked the evils of Kulin polygamy, the denial of female education, and child marriage. Throughout he implied that evil and unscrupulous Brahmins had probably falsified the ancient texts to satisfy their own brutal inclinations (*ibid.*: 57).

In mid-nineteenth century Maharashtra, "intellectuals [with western education] engaged in frequent public debates on exegetical issues to 'demonstrate' that the high Hindu texts implicitly approved of specific issues on the reform agenda." Later in the century, however, Veena Naregal notices a shift in their attitudes. As they sensed the prospect of gaining power through public support, their "reform" interests shifted from an egalitarian vision to 'secondary' issues like "widow-remarriage, the issue of the appropriate education for girls, and the age of consent"

(Naregal 2001: 226f). In Bengal at the end of the century, Vivekananda juggled with several strands from the Vedantic tradition, and from other influences then in the air, to advance a doctrine of organized social service, *seva*, as a form of worship that went into the making of Ramakrishna Mission (Beckerlegge 2006: Part 3). Gandhi in South Africa at about the same time was making a "commitment to a life of compassionate caring", which translated into a wide range of "constructive work" in India in later decades (Brown 1989: 83).

As for the Brahmos, the range of ideas they imbibed was so vast as to make them into a class apart. In the main, from the West they drew on Unitarian ideas (which had dropped such stock Christian notions as the trinity of the Father, the Son, and the Holy Ghost), though some Brahmos tried the trinitarian option too; and within the Hindu tradition, they shifted between the abstract, philosophic, Vedantic thought and the Vaishnana forms of *bhakti*, especially as a vehicle for carrying Brahmo ideas to mass audiences. And then there was the climactic phase led by Keshub Chandra Sen, 1875–80, when Keshub and his close associates explored also the foundational contexts of Islam, Christianity, Hinduism, Sikhism, and Buddhism – trying out a wide gamut of symbols and ritual forms in quest of a universal religion, transcending all denominational differences (Kopf 1979: Chap. 9).

Multiple affiliations

Choosing between available alternatives may have been facilitated by the possibility of maintaining multiple affiliations simultaneously. As Burton Stein said for non-Brahmin Tamilians:

> [For] most non-Brahmans, exclusive sectarianism appears to be rare if the sectarian information provided of the eighteenth century and later is credited. These eighteenth century reports and later ethnographic evidence ... suggest that most non-Brahman Tamilians maintained multiplex sectarian affiliations, seldom shifting from one to another, but more often adding to their affiliational connections through time (Stein 1977: 27).

Ralph Nicholas suggests that, in Bengali culture, a variety of beliefs and opinions can flourish together, each being evaluated not for being right/wrong, or true/false, but for "its appropriateness to a person endowed by birth with his qualities" (1981: 89).

We have a general process here. The compact social bonding within family and *jati* was an important potential resource. While one's inner life could be sustained within the family, or within a network of families – bonded by common neighbourhoods, marriages, perhaps a shared preceptor – it was possible to go beyond them somewhat. One could take in, tentatively, a body of ideas and practices, unrelated to the family tradition, following older habits of subscribing to multiple traditions simultaneously. One could maintain an exploratory stance, taking in bits, say, of western ideas, entertaining them as if on a trial basis. A. K. Ramanujan, poet and scholar, recalled his father: "a mathematician, an astronomer ... also a Sanskrit scholar, an expert astrologer":

> My father's clothes represented his inner life very well. He was a south Indian Brahmin gentleman. He wore neat white turbans, a Sri Vaisnava caste mark (in his earlier pictures, a diamond earring), yet wore Tootal ties, Kromentz buttons and collar studs, and donned English serge jackets over his muslin *dhotis* which he wore draped in traditional Brahmin style. He often wore tartan-patterned socks and silent well-polished leather shoes when he went to the university, but he carefully took them off before he entered the inner quarters of the house (1989: 42; see Pandian 2007: 63–66 for the Tamil lawyer, P. S. Sivaswamy Aiyer, 1864–1946).

Ideas from another tradition could be entertained – while one's sense of the self stayed anchored to an indigenous lifestyle and values, and family networks. Successive generations could often make adjustments between what was old and what was new relatively unhurriedly.

Importance of resources

Granted the profusion of sects, their historical fortunes have been highly uneven, and a key variable influencing their prospects has been that of resources available to them: resources both of ideas and of the more material sorts. The Satnamis were short of both kinds of resources; and their struggles over more than a century and a half made little difference to their members' life space (Dube 1998). Lush with Gujarati financial support and managerial abilities, the Swaminarayan sect has evolved a complex, expansive, relatively stable institutional structure, and its members appear to be comfortable with familiar Brahminical virtues (Williams 1984). The Brahmo saga sprang from pockets of wealth in early colonial Bengal: *zamindars*, a major entrepreneur (Dwarkanath Tagore), high level colonial employment, and the professions of law and medicine. We have already noted their precocious churning of the world of ideas. Their ideology inspired numerous young men to live simple lives and to spread the Brahmo message throughout the subcontinent, generating waves of social thought, independent institutional initiatives, and ideas of social reform, which left their mark on every aspect of society and of the life of the mind (Kopf 1979).

Institution

In the diverse agendas at work from the late nineteenth century onwards, a major theme was to create facilities – schools, colleges, hostels, and the like – in support of the new, mainline education whose framework was being defined under colonial auspices. Hindu College in Calcutta was a pioneering institution, "established [1816], financed, and managed by the Calcutta *nouveaux riches* [who] owed much of their recently acquired wealth to European relationships". (It grew ultimately to be the Presidency College. Kopf 1969: 180.) The college curriculum included science, and it was equipped with scientific laboratories. Whatever the significance of these laboratories at Hindu College, however, its social vision was narrow and exclusive: "by its foundation charter the College could not admit any student who was not a Hindu" (Mujeeb 1967: 521n quoting Majumdar 1960: [26]).

Brahmo Samaj, the small but innovative nineteenth century sect rising in Calcutta, propelled a surge in institution-building. In Calcutta, this included the first women's school, started in 1873, which grew into Bethune College in 1878, and City College, which began as a secondary school for boys in 1879. Away from Calcutta,

> Wherever a Brahmo Samaj was established [within Bengal], there followed an institutional complex dedicated to social and religious reform. Whether in Mymensingh, Barisal, Chittagong, Comilla, or Sylhet, there was invariably the mandir or community prayer hall and meeting place, a girls' school and boys' school on various levels, possibly a college, Sangat Sabha or discussion society for the youth, a charitable hospital, a library, a printing press for newspapers and tracts, a night school for workers and peasants, and a ladies' society (Kopf 1979: 226f).

Two Brahmo missionaries in Bihar "worked tirelessly to build new schools, hospitals, clinics, community centres, cooperatives, libraries, night schools for workers, and orphanages ... outbursts of ascetic devotion on behalf of social service" (*ibid.*: 234). Brahmo ideas were also reaching the depths of the Bengal countryside through institutions built under other impulses.

Sumit Sarkar has noted the "impressive number of middle and high English schools and private colleges even in remote districts of Bengal", established by the local *bhadralok* – middle-class families, often receiving agricultural land rents, whose sons were taking to English education avidly (1973: 149). They had taken advantage of the government's grants-in-aid policy to establish these institutions (see below). We read of numerous students catching the Brahmo vision initially from their schoolteachers in these institutions in the 1860s and later (e.g., on Ramananda Chatterji, Kopf 1979: 149). This history of institution-building, going more than three generations back, no doubt inspired the flurry of initiatives in "national education" in Bengal during the Swadeshi movement (1903–08).[3] Enthusiasm in this phase far exceeded the resources available, but at least one significant initiative did survive: "the College of Engineering and Technology, the real institutional nucleus ... of the modern Jadavpur University" (Sarkar 1973: 167).

The Brahmo role in institution-building was manifold. An initiative emerging among Brahmos led to the founding, in Midnapore in 1866, of a "Society for the Promotion of National Feeling among the Educated Natives of Bengal". This "Society" morphed into the popular Hindu Mela in 1867, an annual event which did much to foster Hindu community consciousness in Calcutta (Prasad 1999: 224). At another level, the Brahmos dominated the Indian Association (IA), established a decade later, to represent the concerns of the "educated middle class" to the government (Kopf 1979: 144). The IA President was Surendranath Banerjea (1848–1925), non-Brahmo but a fellow traveller; shortly after his selection for the Indian Civil Service, he had been dismissed at his first posting, on a minor issue – and was subsequently denied admission to the bar too. Brahmos did most of

---

[3] Swadeshi literally means indigenous. It became the theme around which resistance was organized in Bengal in opposing a colonial attempt to split the Bengal Presidency into two. Publicly, the justification offered for the move was that it would make the vast territory administratively easier to govern; but confidential notings, which became public later, testified to a strong political motive: to hive off a predominantly Muslim eastern province, thereby denying a major economic and political base to the (predominantly Hindu) nationalist political leadership located in Calcutta. One plank to the resistance movement was to boycott foreign merchandise in favour of the indigenous. This Partition of Bengal was annulled in 1911, but the episode left many Muslims with the feeling of enduring Hindu opposition to any move that might help Muslim advance.

the IA work. Banerjea travelled around India, accompanying Brahmo missionaries in their visits to the various Samajes all over the country – or he would take the same route independently – setting up IA branches wherever he went (*ibid.*: 145). On this groundwork Banerjea founded the Indian National Conference in 1883 which, three years later, merged into the Indian National Congress. He became a major political figure and served as Congress President in 1895 and 1902.

In Punjab and nearby areas, it was the Arya Samaj that set the pace for educational institutions. It began in 1886 with the Dayanand Anglo-Vedic High School in Lahore, which would add Vedic studies to the prevailing curriculum of government schools; D. A. V. College opened its doors two years later (Jones 1976: 77, 85). These institutions became:

> models for others, both within the Samaj and without. Individual Samajists, local branches [of Arya Samaj], other reform groups and opponents of the Samaj began to organize schools throughout the province. ... During the 1890s Aryas would build an educational system throughout the entire province, from the primary grades through college (Jones 1976: 87f).

The Aryas were stepping into a space defined by prevailing government policies. T. N. Madan and B. G. Halbar (1972: 123) have noted that, after 1854, the colonial government and the missionaries held back from building educational institutions in India, leaving room for "private Indian enterprise". In a policy codified in the Education Despatch of 1854, the colonial government proposed a system of grants-in-aid: "This aid was to be given on the basis of complete religious neutrality to all schools imparting a good secular education under satisfactory local management and government inspection" (Ghosh 2000: 79).

By 1882, the number of institutions built and run by Indians had grown dramatically. Longohr (2001) calls this "educational 'subcontracting'" and sees these institutions as major vehicles for the spread of religious nationalism in colonial India. In my reading, the onset of these sentiments antedated the institutions; the link between the institutions and the growth of these sentiments was probably reciprocal. The point is not that students in institutions rising on caste or sect bases would have been free from prejudice – prejudices they would have imbibed from their social milieu anyway; the point rather is that the relative scarcity of such institutions on the Muslim side, which the next chapter will notice, put the Muslim youth under a handicap at least for a while.

Caste and sect relationships, then, often helped mobilize resources for these institutions, oriented towards, though not always reserved for, particular social constituencies. T. N. Madan and B. G. Halbar considered three districts in present-day Karnataka: Dharwar and Belgaum in the north, Mysore in the south, focussing on "prominent private educational societies". In the mid-twentieth century, they found the Brahmins, Lingayats, and Christians to be "the most active in educational private enterprise", establishing institutions – for primary, secondary, and collegiate education – which would then be controlled by the promoting community, though teachers, and especially students, came from diverse backgrounds.[4]

By the early twentieth century, it was already possible to stretch the field for mobilizing resources well beyond the limits of *jati* and sect. The founding of Banares Hindu University (BHU) in 1916 culminated a decade-long effort led by Madan Mohan Malaviya, then a leading public figure in UP. The Central Hindu College, established in 1898 by Annie Besant and the Theosophical Society of Banares, was absorbed in BHU; and Malaviya had toured all over India, raising funds, especially from the rulers of princely states (Lutt 1976). In passing we note that, in the 1910s, the Aligarh leadership was also demanding that its college be made into a university. The founding of a denominational university had become one more arena for rivalry between Muslim and Hindu leaderships, adding to the several others that we shall consider in later chapters.

In the nature of things, once an institution was established, annual cohorts of students would keep flowing through it, picking up a range of skills and competence. All this served, on one side, to spread the availability of this package called "education", which included a range of ideas, forms of thought, and skills (Chandra 1992: 18–22 on Vishnu Krishna Chiplunker in Marathi speaking areas); and, on the other, it spread the experience of building an institution – or a chain of them. An understanding of the large educational institution as a social

---

[4] Omvedt 1976: 171–73 has a brief review of the Deccan Maratha Education Association, established in Poona in 1884, and other Maratha educational organizations. Cashman 1975: 100, 102 notes a Brahmin-led Deccan Education Society, also established in 1884.

For late nineteenth and early twentieth century Kerala, see accounts of easy passages from traditional contexts of learning to new, university-linked institutions, in Wood (1985: Chaps 2, 3, and 6).

form, infinitely replicable and generally durable, was settling into the local repertoire.

Institutions, be it remembered, embody malleable blocks of resources for attaining flexible objectives, recurrently, on a continuing basis. Elsewhere I have charted the route that Europe took so that, by the thirteenth century, one could say that Europe had mastered the art of building institutions (Saberwal 1995: Chap. 4). In parts of Indian society one can see a movement in that direction by the end of the nineteenth century. We have seen that *jati* and sect often served as proto-institutions, their networks being mobilized to raise resources for the newer kinds of institutions – these were modest efforts initially, yet their builders were learning skills at another level.

The new educational institutions offered experience of relatively "open-ended" relationships, compared with what would have been familiar within the family and the caste order; this experience could subsequently be carried into larger public spaces. The prevailing social arrangements, and the ideology of the caste order, were too entrenched to be changed much easily; but here and there the practices could be softened, and the limits of the possible began to be stretched. The experience of building such institutions could, furthermore, be carried into other fields. Strong on trading castes, the Arya Samaji networks in late nineteenth century Lahore provided social fields supportive of other kinds of institutions too, especially commercial ones, among them the Punjab National Bank and Bharat Insurance Co. (Jones 1976: 177f).[5] These various institutions became a third kind of resource, alongside those of caste and sect, available in the search for advantage.

Additional motivations for mastering western knowledge and scholarly skills came from several different directions. By the early nineteenth century, the Bengali literate castes' greater engagement with western learning, and with colonial institutions, introduced them to Orientalist scholarship. The work of William Jones, H. T. Colebrooke, H. H. Wilson, and James Princep, successively, proposed the family connections between Sanskrit, Greek, and Latin and the corresponding philosophies; identified a monotheistic stance in the Vedas; mapped the

---

[5] Punjab National Bank was a joint stock company, and other companies – institutions of another kind – were rising then in Bombay and Ahmedabad, partly to establish textile mills (e.g., Gillion 1968: Chap. 3 on Ahmedabad). *The Tribune*, the daily newspaper from Lahore, was not an Arya enterprise, but Arya Samajis had easy access to its columns.

Maurya and Gupta periods and their textual traditions; and, decoding the Brahmi script, rediscovered Buddhist India (Kopf 1969: Chaps. 2, 11, and 15). This was part of the backdrop for the Bengali enthusiasm for establishing the Hindu College in Calcutta in 1816.[6] They were drawn to the power of western epistemologies, in ways that made them proud of their own past; the Urdu-speaking Muslim elites in Calcutta, in contrast, found little of interest in the new scholarship (Ahmed 1981: 6; Kopf 1969: 164). At about the same time, archeology revealed Harappa and much else (Singh 2004). Ancient traditions which had long dropped out of awareness became available again.

Around *jati*, sect, and modern institution, the decades preceding and following the end of the nineteenth century saw all manner of contestation – between Brahmo factions, and between Brahmos and the orthodox (and similarly with the Arya Samajis); between Brahmins and their lower caste challengers like Phule in Pune; the various intra-caste contests in Bombay city; the non-Brahmin challengers in south India; and so on. Yet these were rarely violent, thanks partly to colonial agencies for "law and order". This contestation proceeded through mobilizing support, and through diverse movements for social "reform" – both within *jati*s and in inter-*jati* relationships at various levels.[7] In the process, something new was being learned: how to rally people around shared concerns, on social bases whose scale tended to grow over time; how to pursue this contestation in a relatively orderly manner; and how to function in public spaces. Skills honed in this social politics in the regions would carry into wider arenas in later decades.

---

[6] Two generations later, the same feeling found a particular inflexion in Bankim Chatterji's novel *Anandamath*, set in the 1770s, though written a century later. Bankim's ambivalence to colonial rule is well-known; but in the last chapter, a character who may be seen as his *alter ego* tells Satyananda, the novel's great monk, "The English are very knowledgeable in the outward knowledge, and they're very good at instructing people." With that outward knowledge "our people [will] be ready to understand the inner [knowledge]" which would move them to become "wise and virtuous and strong once more" (Chatterji 1881–82/2005: 229). Bankim's larger vision, which informs the whole novel, made it a force in the national movement.

[7] On the Arya Samaj, Jones 1976; on Phule and the Satyashodhak Samaj in Maharashtra, Omvedt 1976; on intra-caste contests in Bombay, Dobbin 1972: Chaps 3 and 5; on the non-Brahmins' assertion in south India, Irschick 1969.

Through the nineteenth century and the early twentieth, in countless localities, we have seen that numerous clusters of Hindus were stretching their reach, along social networks large or small. These diverse initiatives found social bases in one's *jati* and sect, and in one's *jati*'s traditional learning, especially in commerce and in other scribal traditions. There was an edge here in *skills* – especially in large-scale trading, and in defensive capacities for coping with uncertainty from a position of political weakness. In the circumstances of late nineteenth century colonial India, this latter drew them to the potential of the new kind of education – which introduced them, incidentally but extensively, to the experience of western institutions. To caste and sect was thus added the format of the modern institution – and the skills associated with western learning, and something of western ideas concerning men and women and society. A slender bridge was thrown across – for travel out of the confines of *jati* and sect, and into somewhat more open-ended relationships. Greater familiarity with western learning, furthermore, would alert them to the emerging professional opportunities: lawyers, doctors, teachers, engineers, and so forth.

The task of institution-building, independently of governmental initiative, called for substantial liquid resources. The Brahmo initiatives in Calcutta were backed by Hindu *zamindars* and successful professionals; but Punjabis in the Arya Samaj struggled often to draw in small contributions, spreading thereby a sense of involvement in a vast collective enterprise: illustratively, appeals at public meetings, including those at the annual celebrations of each Samaj; monthly subscriptions from various Samajes; "Group donations ... from clerks and the staffs of various offices, from students, teachers, and businessmen"; the diversion to Arya projects of traditional gifts to Brahmins on important family occasions (Jones 1976: 76–84). In the absence of support from the very wealthy, the Aryas showed ingenuity in gathering small contributions – from a far-flung constituency, which they were themselves actively bringing into being.

3

facing the future 2

> It is a loss of orientation that most directly gives rise to ideological activity, an inability, for lack of usable models, to comprehend the universe of civic rights and responsibilities in which one finds oneself located.
>
> Geertz 1973: 219

Precolonial periods had seen the message of Islam reaching vast numbers in the subcontinent; and it had been the faith of dominant sections of the ruling classes in polities whose identities, number, sizes, and shapes stayed in flux. Their descendants, as well as those of the erstwhile Hindu ruling groups, were disempowered in British India. The religious elites, Muslim and Hindu, had always stood apart; with the passing of the Mughals and their successor regime in Awadh, the political elite too was bifurcated. Throughout northern and eastern India, furthermore, few merchants of note were Muslim; and therefore they could partake little of the commercial, or industrial wealth, limited as it was, generated during the colonial period. Finally, while the segmentation inherent in the caste order is well recognized, the following discussion will show that the social fragmentation of Muslims at this time may have been no less than that of Hindus (Hardy 1972: 1–2). Looking to the future in the nineteenth century, the magnitude of the difficulty Muslims faced will become clearer if we consider the social composition of the category at the time.

Social Composition of "Indian Muslims"

If we look back, say from the end of the nineteenth century, the ancestors of Muslims in India can be tracked in several directions. One fraction descended from immigrants: merchants along the coast in Kerala and Tamil Nadu; and in north India, members of ruling dynasties and others in the ruling class, their religious mentors and the like. Then there were the indigenous peasantries, especially numerous in Bengal, Punjab, and Kashmir; the tribes of Balochistan and North West Frontier Province (NWFP); and Hindu converts to Islam, some of whom were of upper caste backgrounds, including the Khoja and Bohra merchants in Gujarat. In this dispersed social space, I shall dwell especially on two categories: the literati and the merchants.

Descendants of immigrants. Their numbers were relatively small, with a concentration in northern India. As rulers, their ancestors had built open ruling coalitions, and promulgated policies of fair governance, whatever the lapses in practice. At least before Aurangzeb's wars, the Mughal dynasty, and its ruling class, had controlled fabulous wealth, thanks to its tax collection apparatus, and its officials' ability at times to use the strong arm in relation to merchants and their wealth (Subramanian and Ray 1991: 24–27).

Aristocracies in decline are fraught with anxiety. Their pride in the past gives them a sense of superiority; their declining hold on the present portends an uncertain future. In retrospect, the Mughal achievement had rested on the close cooperation between the immigrant ruling class and indigenous groups: leading Rajput families and administrators from various backgrounds, not to mention people in commerce, the fine arts, and other fields. The crumbling of that edifice revealed that the descendants of immigrant groups commanded, and transmitted in their families, rather a limited range of skills, and few resources of ideas, or modes of traditional action, that would energize them to reach out to the larger society.

In the pre-modern world, control over land was often the principal form for accumulating wealth. Continuing from their roles in the vanished dynasties, some of them had estates; and following the upheaval in Delhi in 1857, many shifted to these estates, or the small towns near the properties, creating there the lively *qasbati* culture (see below) about which Mushirul Hasan has written eloquently (2004a). Some found employment in princely states, especially Hyderabad and Bhopal. Some others projected large visions: Syed Ahmad Khan worked imaginatively at presenting a positive image of Muslims and, recognizing the importance of western learning, at building the institution at Aligarh (established as a school in 1875, upgraded to College in 1877, and to University in 1920–21); and a group of religious scholars, recognizing the widespread inadequacies in the knowledge, and practice, of Islam, established an influential *madrasa* at Deoband (1867) for training Islamic scholars rigorously.

One difficulty was that their principal ancestral skill was in a certain kind of governing – a function pre-empted by the British. They still had their estates, but also rather expansive lifestyles, that got some families into trouble. Some, though, like the Kidwais, who early recognized the value of the new education, moved confidently into a variety of modern occupations (Hasan 2004a: 41–46). They cultivated a literary creativity, and some found employment in the early colonial order: in the law courts, and as Urdu teachers. Of the several regions, Muslims in UP and Bihar held their own, and more, in higher education, professions, and government employment (Brass 1975; Ghosh 1997: 21f).

Given the change of political regimes, the heirs to the former ruling class saw themselves as sliding economically, and therefore socially. This followed partly from the division of properties in successive generations, and partly from their properties going to the market, passing slowly to Hindu moneylenders and others who commanded cash.[1] Immersed in an ocean of indigenes, they held to their marks of distinction emblematically: their lifestyle, their origins in west and central Asia, and Islam. By and large, they were anxious about the future individually. Few could raise the energy for new collective initiatives to build institutions that would serve the community in the future.

This is not the place to dilate on the versatility of the Islamic intellectual tradition, as it flourished under the Abbasids and immediately following, between the eighth and the tenth centuries. Leaving aside the systematizing of Islamic law, and poetry and literary criticism, the philosophers built on the old Greek tradition; and there was much "discussion of points of religious belief on the basis of rational criteria" (Hodgson 1974: vol. 1, 438). The Saltanat, Mughal, and other Muslim dynasties' central concern, however, was to maintain their kingships and empires and their revenues. The central Asian background of the Turks and the Mughals had been nomadic, and "in spite of all their architectural ambitions and achievements," tents continued to be the

---

[1] Robinson 1975: 62–65 on western UP where landholdings were not protected by primogeniture, as *taluqdari* lands were in Awadh; Hasan 2004a: 42–45. In Oudh, that is the region around Lucknow and Fyzabad, the large landholding *taluqdars* had the integrity of their lands protected through primogeniture, established through legislation in 1869; next year, the Court of Wards was established for managing estates that got into financial distress (Robinson 1975: 17).

mark of royal camps (Mujeeb 1967: 373). The rulers were generous to *madrasas*, centred on learned families, and to religious learning there. Learned men, coming from west Asia, or cultivating their learning within family circles, often graced the royal courts. They had come without their libraries, however, and therefore had to abstain from activities that would require access to such collections. No great institutions of Islamic learning, such as those at Baghdad or Cairo, could arise in medieval India (Ikram 1964: 113).

> ... even Akhar failed to see the possibilities in the introduction of printing. The scarcity of books resulted in comparative ignorance, low standards of education, and limitation of the subjects of study. Because of this, the governing classes were ignorant of the affairs of the outside world (*ibid*.: 273).

Aurangzeb made an endowment towards the famous Farangi Mahall *madrasa* in Lucknow. Its instruction was relatively secular, being oriented towards administrative employment (Robinson 2001). Systematic fresh thought, like that of the philosophers just noted, however, had faded long ago. By the nineteenth century, the Muslim literati were concentrated substantially in religious learning, and in literary activity, like the poet Ghalib. Effort to promote the use of secular reason and scientific observation, even by Syed Ahmad Khan, had to retreat before the grip of religious orthodoxy.

Regional diversity. The vast majority of Muslims in India have, of course, been indi-genous in their ancestry – whatever the lure of such appellations as Sayyid, Shaikh, Qureshi, and Ansari as tokens of status within Islamic space. We have seen the making of the large blocks of Muslim populations in Bengal and Punjab. In both regions they were overwhelmingly rural cultivators. A series of Sufi establishments in western Punjab had sizable landholdings. The colonial regime took local leaders into its apparatus in its lower ranks, rewarding its loyal servants with honours, grants of land, opportunities to rise in government, and the like (Gilmartin 1988: 13ff).

The need to market their produce led Punjabi Muslim landowners to market towns and to Hindu and Sikh merchants (who would double as moneylenders), giving Muslim landholders a distinctive identity – and a sense of class opposition to the merchants. The British solicitude for Punjabi cultivators, the backbone of the imperial army, led to the Land Alienation Act (LAA), 1900. It excluded non-cultivating castes, like the merchants, from buying agricultural land – thereby defending the cultivators against the moneylenders, who could no longer foreclose on mortgages against land. The class opposition built into LAA provided the basis for a cross-communal political alliance between Muslim and Hindu agriculturalists, under the banner of the Unionist Party, for a generation immediately before Partition (Gilmartin 1988: 26–38).

The Dogra Hindu rulership in Kashmir had emerged in the wake of the Sikh–British wars, in the mid-1800s. Its administration was manned principally by men drawn from the Hindu Pandits who were substantial land controllers too. Early in the twentieth century, opposition to the dominant Pandits began to rise around a growing Islamic consciousness in the tenantry, aided by Kashmiri Muslim migrants in Punjab (Rao and Chowdhary 2006).

In eastern Bengal, the nineteenth century wave of Islamic revival is generally traced to Haji Shariatullah (1781–1840) who spent nearly two decades of his youth at the sacred sites of Islam in Arabia. There he encountered religiosity in forms contrasting starkly with those back home. Upon returning to Bengal in 1818, Shariatullah embarked upon a lifetime of travelling through the Bengal countryside, imparting to the faithful his ideas on the true Islamic way of life, and exhorting them to shed their pre-Islamic legacy of ideas and practices and to abide, instead, by the "fundamental obligations of Islam (*farz*, pl. *faraiz*: an obligatory duty)", hence the name of his movement, Faraizi (Metcalf 1982: 68f; Eaton 1994: 282; Ahmed 1981: 39–49). The villagers were slow to respond, but Shariatullah's message continued to be carried by his son and several others in later decades; and Rafiuddin Ahmed (1981) shows something of the depth of the polarization that followed by the last quarter of the century.

Another Haji, Titu Mir, underwent a remarkable transformation during his pilgrimage shortly thereafter. In 1830–31 he led a peasant rebellion in Barasat in western Bengal, which started as being anti-landlords and ended as being against the Raj (Guha 1983: 94). In the relations between Muslims and Hindus in eastern Bengal, there was often also an opposition of interests: the Hindus were absentee landlords, moneylenders, and educated government officials, whom the Muslim peasants often faced from a position of weakness. In embracing the nineteenth century Islamizing movements, therefore, they were also distancing themselves from their high caste Hindu neighbours and landlords, and even, in some measure, from their Bengali legacy (p. 122f).

Pradip Kumar Datta (1999: Chap. 2) and Ranabir Samaddar (2006) have written of the leaders of Bengali Muslims in the first half of the twentieth century: of their writings and efforts at mobilizing along diverse axes, and at building capacities through education. They were shaping a distinctive identity around Islam, and in opposition to the domination of Hindu landowners, whose children had been taking over the new professions too.

Merchants. Nineteenth century North India had few important Muslim merchants.[2] The Mughals had had no difficulties in establishing satisfactory relationships with indigenous merchants; and, later, when the Mughal and their successor regimes faced difficulties, they called in Hindu financiers. Hindu, Sikh, and Jain merchants' commercial skills were augmented by their ramifying, established networks of caste and kinship, which underwrote their commerce (see below). All this gave them an edge over newcomers, presenting the latter with formidable "entry barriers". In their comprehensive survey of western, northern, and eastern India, Lakshmi Subramanian and Rajat K. Ray (1991: 27–37) found substantial ship-owning Muslim merchants in seventeenth century Surat, their oceanic trade with west Asia favoured somewhat by the Mughal regime; but they began to lose ground as the English company edged the indigenous regime out, thanks to help from Hindu merchants. Since the eighteenth century, the Calcutta region too has had a few major Muslim merchants here and there (Markovits 1991: 289 and later; Subramanian and Ray 1991: 40f; Minault 1982: 39f).

Though major Muslim merchants have been scarce in the north, Narayani Gupta (1981: 54, 61) has identified two clusters of substantial Punjabi Muslim merchants in Delhi in the later nineteenth century. The earlier cluster had built on an extensive shoe trade – a commodity that Hindu merchants may then have avoided – and a later group of

---

[2] One searches in vain for a significant Muslim merchant in Bayly's study of north India (1983). Mohammad Mujeeb's wide-ranging *The Indian Muslims* (1967) is centered on northern India, with its Saltanat and Mughal regimes. In its 19 page index, the categories "traders", "merchants", and "commerce" are missing – though there are references to "trade routes" and to Arabs trading along the west coast.

While considering the 1911 Census data, Bimal Prasad is in error in saying that "In commerce and industry ..., the Muslims of UP occupied a leading position (1999: 110)". In the same data, Francis Robinson (1975: 15) separates "one or two trading and moneylending communities such as the Pathans of Shahjahanpur and the Syeds of Jansath" and the "pedlars, stall-holders and shopkeepers" from "all the middling and all the big trading and banking concerns [which] were Hindu-owned."

wholesalers who grew to dominate Delhi's Sadar Bazar. For the early twentieth century, Markovits (1991: 291) notes Sir Syed Maratib Ali, whose company "became the largest contractor of military canteens in the Punjab, a hugely profitable activity... ." Between the two World Wars, D. E. U. Baker (1979: 117, 129) notices only two Muslims in substantial commerce in the then Central Provinces.

Arab and Persian commerce, it will be remembered, had a long history; indeed, merchants had been central to the Abbasids, 750–945 CE (Hodgson 1974: vol. 1), and Arab and Persian merchants had flourished in the Indian Ocean from the eighth to the fifteenth centuries (Wink 1990: Chap. 3, 1997: 274–93). Consequently, the relative scarcity of merchants among north Indian Muslims is somewhat puzzling. The key to the puzzle lies in two complementary elements. On one side was the ethos of the ruling class. To express his displeasure at his grandson, then governor of Bengal, "who had made a monopoly of several items of export," Aurangzeb sent him a verse:

> Those who purchase – sell;
> We neither purchase nor sell.

(Ray 2003: 238f)

"We" here, of course referred to the ruling class and its descendants. A style that befitted a ruling class was, however, unhelpful when it ceased to rule. On the other side, any among them who might have ventured into commerce would have faced difficulty in breaking into the tight world of credit and trust among the Hindu merchant *jati*s. Illustratively, Leighton W. Hazelhurst (1966: Chap. 7) has described the socio-religious rituals, especially at weddings, that served to validate commercial credit among north Indian *baniya*s in a town near Ambala (probably Jagadhri), in present day Haryana (see Rudner 1989 on Nattukottai Chettiar bankers). These traditions had underwritten their formidable commercial capabilities down the centuries.[3]

In the nineteenth century, what remained of the wealth of the erstwhile Muslim nobility in UP could be seen in their landholdings;

---

[3] In an unusual case, in Kanpur, the most successful Muslim merchants, dealers in foreign goods, had moved in the late 1920s "to large shops located prominently on one of the main roads"; but they found themselves pitted against Hindu networks that dominated the Municipality. In the 1931 Riots, to be noticed later, they suffered at the hands of street gangs too (Freitag 1989: 233f).

but where the indivisibility of their holdings, and their ownership, was not protected by legislation (see fn. 1), the lands were passing gradually to men of several Hindu castes. Elsewhere, too, the Hindu merchant castes were spreading in trade and moneylending and the new industry. The 56 cotton textile mills in Bombay in 1880 were owned by Parsis and Hindu Bhatias; the first to be owned by a Muslim was "projected in 1886" (Prasad 1999: 127). Always weak in northern India, Muslim commercial presence remained so through the colonial period; and it did not gain in industrial wealth either.

Western India had Khoja, Bohra, and other Muslim merchant communities. In 1759, in collusion with Hindu trading castes in Surat, the English company merchants forced their way into the city and declared "a monopoly over shipping to the Gulfs, delivering thereby a body-blow to the Muslim ship-owning merchants of Surat" (Subramanian and Ray 1991: 27). Diverse Muslim groups remained significant parts of mid-nineteenth century Bombay's commerce. In the late nineteenth century, following several legal contests, the Aga Khan secured formal control over Khojas in India; subsequently, they have prospered, especially in East Africa (Masselos 1973; Dobbin 1972: 119, 154, and elsewhere; Mallison 1997).

As is well known, Muslims in south India have, by and large, been comfortable in their regional languages and social contexts. They have descended partly from Arab and Persian traders who married local women and settled down, and partly from those who came under the influence of Sufis, seen as holy men. Many of them have been changing gradually to conform to the tenets of Islam more closely (Bayly 1989: Part 1). In northern Kerala, Muslim peasants, known as Moplah, had found their land rights reduced sharply by the colonial regime, setting them against powerful (Hindu) landlords who were allied with the government. Thanks to devoted religious leaders, they were able to translate their agrarian discontent into organized action. During the Khilafat and Non-cooperation movements, the local tenancy issues also cropped up as part of the agitation; and a long assertive tradition came to be directed against the Hindu landlords (Panikkar 1989: 49, 58, 121).

In sum, Islam in India had appealed to indigenous warrior groups only in modest measure; it was not short of soldiers in any case. Of literati, too, at least in the religious and literary fields, Muslims had enough in many parts of the country. A sparsity of merchants, at least among Sunnis, remained. Together, these categories, principally descendants of immigrants, the *ashraf*, carried the dual legacy of a formidable ruling class and a world religion. The associated pride and expectations shaped many of the arguments in later generations. Then there were the large blocks of indigenes that had been drawn to Islam: peasantries and small landholders, and the pastoral and forest and hill peoples. There was a kind of tension in the situation: indigenes who had "become" Muslim had continued, by and large, to live and function within their local caste orders, often with only a hazy sense of the meaning of becoming a Muslim. The following paragraphs consider the social "reform" campaigns during the nineteenth and early twentieth centuries that sought to resolve this tension.

Gathering the *umma*, Forging the Community

By the early twentieth century, a sense of community, the *umma*, and a corresponding body of consensual opinion, were emerging in the Muslim space, and we can track the process with some precision. The making of that consensus has been pivotal to the social history of modern India. The processes converging upon it, and its long-term consequences, have both been complex. Here we consider the processes that led to the *umma* and the consensus.

One can argue that the eighteenth century Muslim space in the subcontinent was even more diverse, and unorganized, than the then Hindu social space. Before the nineteenth century, the effort to draw the Muslims into a distinctive social organization had been modest at best. Islam's experience elsewhere, from west Africa to central and southeast Asia, had been one of people in a region taking to the new faith wholesale: such Islamic forms as the mosque, the prayer, the Sufi's tomb, the maulvi, and the pilgrimage would settle into the prevailing social arrangements seamlessly. India was more difficult: its ancient religious traditions were entrenched socially in the caste order. In that milieu, Islam could also find a place; though, at least in north India, religious specialists on both sides saw the arrangements as provisional, weak on justifications.

Most Muslims in the subcontinent – in Sind, Punjab, Delhi and its vicinity, Rajasthan, Gujarat, Bengal, Tamil Nadu, Malabar and elsewhere – were indigenes, spoke the local language, and were part of their respective regional societies. Urban centres like Calcutta, Hyderabad, and Madras had Urdu-speaking Muslim immigrants. For Calcutta, we learn from Rafiuddin Ahmed (1981: 22f) that the Urdu-speaking, Shia elite who saw themselves as high status *ashraf*, took little interest in the rural Bengali-speaking Muslims, whom they saw as low status *ajlaf* (*atrap* in Bengali), at least until after the results of the first Census (1872). Until then the Urdu-speaking *ashraf* sought British patronage to advance themselves, rather like the Brahmins in Maharashtra (Naregal 2001). The Census revealed a surprising majority of Muslims in Bengal, concentrated in the eastern parts. Subsequently, the *ulama* in rural Bengal helped mediate across the *ashraf-ajlaf* disconnect, helping Muslims emerge as a political entity, sharing interests, as Muslims, against Bengali Hindus (Ahmed 1981: 28–32, 72).

Similarly among the Moplahs in northern Kerala, in course of frequent uprisings against their landlords, between 1836 and 1854, the number of mosques grew dramatically, and the "hitherto inconspicuous Thangals [priests]" gained "key local influence. The consequence of this mediation by mosques and Thangals was to promote a vertical alliance between the Moplah poor and their more affluent co-religionists and thus help in modifying the class antagonism of the peasantry by Islamic ideology" (Guha 1983: 171). Their religious men were helping Muslims transcend these social cleavages. The *madrasa* at Deoband and its graduates were to promulgate an ideology that carried a similar vision for the entire subcontinent. We shall return to this theme shortly.

In north India, the lives of the medieval Muslim elite – religious or political – had turned significantly on their access to Muslim dynasts. That had ended by the early nineteenth century; yet the various Muslim groups could function on reasonable terms under British auspices. "In 1825, the East India Company took over an existing *madrasa* ..." in Delhi, renaming it Delhi College. Its new curriculum included Persian, Arabic, Sanskrit, and English as languages, and the Western sciences, taught in "the medium of Urdu"; supported by a major programme of translations from Arabic, Persian and English into Urdu. The relaxed social milieu and the vigorous activity at Delhi College seemed to augur a future of productive cooperation between Muslims, Europeans, and Hindus (Naim 2004a: 262–64; also Minault 2000, Hasan 2005: 115–25). After the disruption of 1857, Delhi College lingered for a while as a shell of an institution. Yet the experience of its peak years survived in diverse ways in the lives of its teachers and students: in Delhi's cosmopolitan culture later in the century, explored at length by Mushirul Hasan (see below), and also in providing a model for a significant institution of religious instruction, the *madrasa* at Deoband (Metcalf 1982: 71–75).

1857, however, saw an assault, especially in Delhi, in which Muslims, religious or lay, often found themselves defenceless. In the heat of the moment, the British took them to be guilty of rebellion unless they could prove otherwise. As the dust of the uprising settled, a difficult situation could be seen to be emerging for Muslims. Seen from above, from the viewpoint of the *ashraf*, principally the descendants of the immigrants, they were probably less than a tenth of all Muslims in the subcontinent, and the great bulk of the non-*ashraf*, especially in rural areas, often merged with their neighbours, who were not Muslim, more or less indistinguishably.

It was a time of insecurity, especially for the Muslim elite, as we shall see at length. A sense of security arises from a comfortably established social order, and one's confidence in a support group, not to mention power and wealth. In times of social disorder, individuals may still be able to count on their support groups; but larger social categories need leadership that can point confidently to a way out of the besetting troubles. A major response to the post-1857 situation was inspired by the thought of the eighteenth century Islamic scholar in Delhi, Waliullah, living in the lengthening shadows of the Mughal rule. Islam had reached large numbers in the subcontinent, however imperfect their observance, and awareness, of Islamic obligations. Assured the guidance of religious preceptors, Waliullah proposed, the community of Islam in India could yet be fostered, bringing the *umma* together, providing the conditions for pious lives, shaped according to the *shariat*, Islamic law (Metcalf 1982: 35f).

Perhaps the most influential expression of that purpose took the form of an unusually large, and well-organized, *madrasa* at Deoband, founded in 1867, and the many others that it inspired (Metcalf 1982; Chap. 6 will present the Deoband story at some length). UP had long carried, or been close to, the seats of power; and among Muslims, the *ulama*, religious scholars, had become a dominant voice in the social leadership in the mid-nineteenth century, influencing social choices significantly. Deoband would train men who would be knowledgeable in the scriptures and in the *shariat*; and the *ulama* at Deoband were affiliating with the Sufi traditions too, appropriating the Sufi charisma to their own teaching. Fired with a vision of a thoroughly Islamic community, the products of Deoband would push forward from the ubiquitous mosques.

Shortly thereafter, Syed Ahmad Khan promoted another institution also expressing the vision of a community of Muslims: the College at

Aligarh, which became the University in the 1920s. The college would equip *ashraf* men with western education for working in government and the new occupations. It became the cradle for generations of Muslim students to establish social networks, which provided Muslims with political leadership until 1947, but it did *not* lead to a chain of similar institutions; the resources requisite were not easy to come by. Aligarh had been critically dependent on government support right from the beginning (Lelyveld 1978: 139–42).

The *ulama* at Deoband (and also at Farangi Mahall; see Chap. 5, p. 124) stood proudly aloof from the colonial government (and, by implication, the West). Aligarh and Deoband both drew support from Muslim landlords and the princely states of Hyderabad, Bhopal, and Rampur (now in UP), and the officials working there and elsewhere; Metcalf has analyzed the pattern of support for Deoband carefully (1982: 248–52, 263). Among its 2, 658 contributors between 1867 and 1897, 7 per cent were "Traders and businessmen", almost entirely in north India; but nothing is said on how much they contributed. Gujarat and Bombay, where the Shia Bohras and Khojas were concentrated, were not significant sources of support. Deoband and Syed Ahmad Khan were firmly Sunni. Their networks then may have stopped short of the Shias in western India.

In these attempts at remaking the social order, Ayesha Jalal has noted that the messages gained inspirational quality through widespread recourse to poetry. "A conscious recasting of poetry for communitarian purposes in the late nineteenth century had an electrifying effect on psyches – be it the literate or the illiterate, the aristocratic or the lowly, in urban or rural areas (2001: 47)." Illustratively, Altaf Husain Hali's *Musaddas*, first published in 1879, sang of Islam's potently civilizing influence in its early generations, a proud influence ranging from Spain to Malaya; and it contrasted that past with the present of his contemporary Muslims in India: Hali was particularly harsh on the practices of the Muslim upper classes, the poets, and men of religion. Christopher Shackle and Javed Majeed, who have translated *Musaddas* into English, have reviewed the quick, far-flung responses to the major poem, drawing applause, emulation, and ridicule in equal measure (Shackle and Majeed 1997). Sabyasachi Bhattacharya (2003) has recently tracked the extraordinary fortunes of the Sanskrit–Bengali song, *bande mataram*, published initially by Bankim Chandra Chatterji in his novel *Anandamath* (1881–82/2005). The song caught on in Bengal during the Swadeshi movement (1905–08), and it was soon translated into

Marathi, Tamil, and other Indian languages and became a vehicle for nationalist defiance of colonial rulers. Parts of the song, however, struck some Muslims as idolatrous, so it came to acquire a singularly contentious set of associations: something to resist, as offending Islamic sensibility; something to recite, in celebrating (Hindu) nationalism.

Solidarity amidst conflicts

Deoband has maintained a relatively high profile since the late nineteenth century; but several other sectarian tendencies have also been active. Sectarian differences within Islam have been taken seriously, to the point that rivals may be declared *kafir*, misguided, or even denied the status of being Muslims at all. Contestation between even the various Sunni schools has at times been acute enough that they find it difficult to cooperate – as in the case of the Nadwatul Ulama, Nadwa in short, an institution launched in the 1890s. Founded with the explicit intention of promoting doctrinal rapprochement between the several Islamic sects, nearly all but the Deobandi walked out of Nadwa's councils in less than two decades (Hartung 2006).

Yet, conducted within a broadly shared field of ideas and assumptions, doctrinal contestation can help raise an awareness of that tradition, of Islamic consciousness and the *umma*. Apropos "Islamic unity", at least the preponderant Sunni schools – Ahl-i Hadis, Deobandi, Barelwi – have all shared a commitment to the Prophet, the Quran, and *hadis*. To this core Deoband added the *shariat*, the historically emerging "laws of Islam"; and the Barelwi doctrine went further, recognizing the importance of the intercession of saints, of visits to their tombs to partake of their sanctity, and the like (Metcalf 1982; Sanyal 1996).

By the nineteenth century, the old Sufi saints' tombs – like Hazarat Nizamuddin's in New Delhi – remained as dispensers of *baraka*, grace, and they remain, in music and in public culture, symbols of a gentle, open-ended, religious search. In Punjab, the colonial regime, and the Unionist governments, had relied on support from the custodians of the Sufis' tombs and establishments; and, by the elections of 1945–46, the Muslim League rallied some of them to its own banner (Gilmartin 1988: 213–22). As to seeking fresh religious experience, however, the Sufi tradition seems to have declined in a milieu of resurgent, scripturalist Islam, a generally critical ambience, and abrasive Hindutva.

Despite the disputes between all the Muslim sects and schools, the several groups have shared aspirations towards achieving a purer Islamic way of life, partly by modelling one's life on that of the Prophet; and distantiating, differentiating, from Hindus through de-casteing, abandoning folk deities, and the like. (For the Sunnis, the edge of difference has been no less sharp against the Shias and the Ahmediyas.) Yet *all* the sects and schools have promoted a sense of Islamic consciousness, of *umma*, the great community of Islam (Shaikh 1989).

It must not be thought that Islamic religious leadership has always been limited to fostering the *umma* only. In his work on peasant insurgency, Ranajit Guha noted that "the leaders of some of the mightiest peasant revolts spoke in the inspired language of prophets and reformers – [e.g.] Titu Mir of an Islamic kingdom to come [in the Barasat revolt, 1830–31, in western Bengal] ... (1983: 251)"; similarly, the Thangals, Moplah priests in northern Kerala, during numerous uprisings against Hindu landlords between 1836 and 1854. In these stock examples in Marxist interpretations of communalism, oppressed peasantries found leadership among religiously inspired men, so that what is incontestably class struggle in Marxist eyes may seem to others as sectarian conflict (*ibid.*: 74).

To resume our earlier discussion, the spread of a shared ideology influences the prevailing "common sense" – which, then, shapes choices in terms of "what the neighbours will think". Rafiuddin Ahmed (1981: 161f) illustrated the process in late nineteenth century eastern Bengal: widespread debates between rival Islamic *anjumans*, religio-political associations, that propagated somewhat divergent interpretations of Islam. Intra-mural disagreements and debates, and multiple contestations, may well serve to *reinforce* a consciousness of shared, distinctive religious identity. For UP, Sandra B. Freitag has documented this nexus – sectarian-contention-heightens-consciousness-of-larger-tradition – between Deobandis and Barelwis among Muslims in Bareilly in the 1870s, and between Arya Samajis and Sanatan Dharmis among Hindus in Agra in the next decade (1989: 117, 141f).

The sense of community, the *umma*, then, gained strength despite, even because of, all the doctrinal contestation; and it drew energy from other sources. What with Afghani and *pan-Islamism*, at least some Muslims felt the call of a global solidarity (Hasan 1991; Ahmed 1981: 107f); that unity one could also experience during the Hajj, the pilgrimage to the sacred sites of Mecca and Madina, or in any mosque during *namaz*. Those who realized, furthermore, how numbers would count in *electoral politics*, saw the unity of the *umma* as vital in yet another context.

Above all, however, the sense of the *umma* grew from a sense of opposition to Hindus. We shall see below that, from the early nineteenth century on, the relations between Muslims and Hindus, at least in north India, were changing, owing to a slowly rising spiral of social contention, which over the decades turned into social aggression: symbolic (as in provocative religious processions), societal (as in conversions and *shuddhi*), and physical (as in communal violence). Recurrent conflicts and persistent animosity across the religious line, pressed from both sides, helped strengthen oppositional identities (and, for Muslims, the sense of the *umma*) – which, of course, was part of a dialectic: oppositional identities and mutual aggression fed on each other. In this milieu of continuing communal conflict, the sense of the *umma* did indeed gain ground, but perhaps not in the manner that the ideologues at Deoband had envisioned.

The social sciences in India are just beginning to discover the implications of the shared experience of collective violence; it helps cement identities, reflected partly in withdrawing into communally marked spaces (Mehta and Chatterji 2001; Robinson 2005); Chap. 7 will deal with this theme. Such relocations carry a variety of costs: physical and economic, of having to find another home; and the social and emotional, of having to reconfigure one's matrix of relationships. I shall argue that it was the ideological pulls from both sides converging with the reaction to the experiences, or threats, of collective violence that persuaded people to pay the costs.

Alternatives

We have reviewed something of the impulses that carried forward the ancient Islamic vision of *umma*, of the community of Islam, during the colonial period. This is the perspective from above, from the scripturalist, *ashraf* point of view; but there were, in principle, alternate perspectives: that of a *jati* or a new sect; that from below, an *ajlaf* point of view, the possibility, that is, of the lowly organizing along *jati* lines, a vital story on the Hindu side; and finally the vision that would relate with non-Muslims positively, and participate in the new modes of learning actively. Why these alternatives remained weak will engage us now.

Old Jatis and New Sects. Islamic ideologues have always looked upon the caste order with distaste, and this was conveyed in the ideologies they promulgated. Consequently, Muslims – scholars, politicians, others – have been uncomfortable with the kinds of uses to which the varieties of social capital embedded in particular *jati*s could be put. Deoband's core message was to obliterate allegiance to *jati*-like groups and sects in favour of its own mainline Sunni teachings.

For this submergence of old *jati*s and new sects for doctrinal purity, various groups may have paid a price; of those who did retain their distinctive identities, several have flourished. From their trading beginnings in Sindh, Khojas were drawn to the Shia Ismaili banner. In the nineteenth century, we saw that they got their own *imam*, religious leader, in the Aga Khan; and they have moved into large-scale commerce, especially outside south Asia. Even the Ahmediyas have blossomed internationally – though, in Pakistan, the Parliament legislated that they were not Muslim. Mushirul Hasan (2004a) has recently documented the remarkable Kidwai clan from Awadh in UP: many of its members have done well in a setting which other Muslims often find unfriendly. These groups' track records stand in contrast with those of groups which came under the spell of Deoband and the like.

The Ajlaf Option. We may try to account for the weakness of the *ajlaf* assertion, in a comparative frame, through comparison with the corresponding Hindu space, for the *ajlaf* had originated among pastoralists, forest people, peasants, artisans, and other service castes – relatively low in the caste hierarchy – and had carried their caste identities with them. The high status *ashraf* were the immigrants and their descendants.

> At the height of Turkish and Mughal rule, the court ulama seem to have displayed little concern for the vast majority of Indian Muslims who were of 'low' or ajlaf origin. ... [The former] wrote and spoke Persian and Arabic, languages almost completely foreign to the ajlaf. ... The near monopoly over the cultural capital of scripturalist, shariah-centred Islam that the ashraf exercised created an almost unbridgeable barrier between them and the ajlaf, thereby serving to bolster their own claims to higher social status (Sikand 2005: 53, also 36f).

Several of the field studies collected in Imtiaz Ahmad's edited volume (1973a) showed the complexity of the local caste-like hierarchy among Muslims in north India (as in papers by Zarina Bhatty and Ranjit Bhattacharya). Within the *ajlaf* category, there has been a further separation between the "clean" and the "unclean" groups. The latter are sometimes called *arzal*, though the term is missing in the Ahmad volume.

Between the *ashraf-ajlaf* hierarchy and the caste order, there were differences nevertheless. Islamic religious authorities deny any place in Islam for caste identities and hierarchy and the associated differences; and among Tamil Muslims it may have been absent altogether (Mines 1972: 25; More 1997: 24). Yet at least in UP and Bihar, there are more recent reports of the *ajlaf* – the lower "castes" among Muslims – having been dominated and exploited (Awadh in UP: Hasan 2004a: 14f; Bihar: Ghosh 1997: 26f; Bengal: Ahmed 1981: 22f). So the question remains: why have the *ajlaf* deferred to the religious orthodoxy, in contrast to the militancy of several lower Hindu castes?

Muslims have been stratified, to be sure, and have had their internal social separations. Papiya Ghosh (1997) showed that, in Bihar, both before and after 1947, Muslims identified as Momin, formerly weavers, sometimes called Ansari, and other similar occupational groups, have mobilized in politics actively, in explicit opposition to high status, *ashraf*, groups, alleging that the Muslim League had represented the interests only of the latter. The Momins have been effective in securing political representation – and all that flows from it. How widespread the pattern has been remains unclear.

Without a scripturally reinforced criterion of purity and pollution, however, these social separations were not as humiliating for the *ajlaf* as their analogues were for lower castes Hindus; and Muslim society was somewhat more open socially than the Hindu space. Late nineteenth century dyers in Bombay, says the historian Asiya Siddiqi, "reminisced that their ancestors had converted to Islam because they had had differences with the Hindu priests": dyers "used urine in the process of dyeing, and ... would most likely be considered ritually unclean by the orthodox." However repugnant the Islamic high tradition may find the practice, their local maulvis may have been indulgent towards what was an occupational necessity for them. In the 1870s, the family of Ayesha, the butcher's widow, belonged to a diverse social web, and a religious scholar supposedly from Baghdad was her preceptor, and he had prepared her husband's will according to Islamic law (Siddiqi 2001: 119–21).

For the organization of Muslim society, the implications of the Deoband *madrasa*, for all its limitations, have been not less than revolutionary in this regard. Whereas *ashraf* men had founded the institution, its students included men of lower status backgrounds, who found clear opportunities for upward mobility in careers as maulvis: the "cultural capital" of the scriptures and the *shariat* was being transmitted to *ajlaf* students. Indeed, in recent generations, the latter category has dominated *madrasa* enrolments, and consequently the profession of the maulvi in India (Metcalf 1982: 245f; similarly in Bengal, Ahmed 1981: 29; Sikand 2005: 99). A dramatic illustration of the openness of the profession of the maulvi comes from the Meos – who began to take the obligations of Islam seriously only after their genocidal experience of 1947. "[Meos] dominate the number of *imam*s in Delhi mosques (80 per cent, according to one estimate)" (Mayaram 1997: 245).

In Bengal, by the 1911 Census, and in children's school registration, *millions* were giving themselves *ashraf* appellations – Shaikh was especially popular. Such claims came from self-designation – and these did contribute to heightened self-esteem. The trend was strong enough to override the old *ashraf* resistance (Ahmed 1981: 113–19; similarly in Bhojpur, across the Bihar–UP border, Pandey 1983: 76). Reporting on fieldwork in 1966–67 in what became Bangladesh, Peter Bertocci noted "an absolute decline in the number of Muslim 'caste' or 'caste-like' groups", a weakening of the caste matrix, and "the emergence of a broadly homogeneous Muslim peasant class" (1976: 33).

Clearly a major transformation of the category "Muslim" has been in progress, and men in *ajlaf* ranks have found opportunities for upward social mobility, sometimes gaining assimilation in high status groups. When we speak of caste groups among Muslims, the primary reference is to a restrictive regulation of marriages; but that too has lacked scriptural support. For an upwardly mobile family to intermarry with higher status groups has been difficult, yet possible, among Muslims (e.g., Ahmed 1981: 13, 19, 118); it used to be virtually impossible among Hindus. In Ahmad Ali's *Twilight in Delhi*, set in the1930s, the Syed patriarch resists his son's wish to marry a girl of a Mughal family, but his main objection is not that the family is Mughal but that it had had a marriage involving a servant woman. His wife and daughter, however, proceed with arrangements for the marriage on which the son has set his heart, bypassing the father's resistance. Imtiaz Ahmad (1973b) considers the tactics used by Muslim families of Kayastha background to gain recognition as high status Sheikhs of ancient lineage: namely, to seek marriage relations with acknowledged Sheikh families, but to terminate negotiations if the other side tried to probe one's own credentials. Little reason among such men, then, to want to look back and join castemates in contesting caste-linked disabilities.

Caste-like disabilities among Muslims appear, then, not to have been harsh enough to set in motion caste-based revolts from below;

or it may be that those who suffered could not summon the will to rise in protest. A major spur for a certain kind of "social reform" among Hindus was virtually absent among Muslims in India. They have had many different kinds of social struggle, but little of consequence over caste issues. A caste identity has been something to live down, not play up, among Muslims. Religious identity has trumped caste differences. Consequently, the Muslim elites – and even more so, India's ruling elites – have been able simply to ignore these caste-like differences as a non-issue.

Liberal Muslims

Mushirul Hasan has recently explored another alternative to forging the *umma*: a cluster of liberal Muslims in late nineteenth century Delhi, and the diverse activities around *qasbas*, small towns in Awadh that had grown around garrisons. The leading lights in Delhi were Nazir Ahmad, the pioneering novelist in Urdu, and Zakaullah (the prolific author of modern textbooks, and friend of C. F. Andrews, his biographer). These men were remarkable for their wide circles of friends, extensive curiosity, and diverse pursuits. They had shared the experience of Delhi College before 1857, but their number overall was small. And while they remain interesting individuals, apart from Syed Ahmad Khan's College at Aligarh, and possibly Nazir Ahmed's novels, their work did not make a lasting mark, possibly because many of their social class had migrated to the *qasba* towns in the wake of 1857 (Hasan 2005; Prasad 1999: 140–59 for a different view).

The *qasbas*, small urban centres dotting Awadh, the area around Lucknow, and led by large land-controllers, were "heirs of the once-powerful Indo-Persian culture" and "centres of Islamic piety, and of literary and cultural effervescence". These could boast of an unusually active intelligentsia. Even as their landed properties contracted, their energies flowed into literary effort, especially around poetry, biography, and journalism, into political activity, and into bureaucratic careers. A college proposed for Dehra Dun could, in the event, not be built there (Hasan 1991: 160; 2004a: 17, 44, 140, 156, and elsewhere).

There was also the remarkable figure of Shibli Numani (1857–1914), a religious scholar of stature, even though his independent ways brought him marginalization at the hands of mainline *ulama*. Mehr Afroz Murad, a scholar in Karachi, offers a concise exposition of Shibli's ambitious effort at rethinking the elements of Islamic theology and laws, and of Muslim politics, in late nineteenth and early twentieth century India. In her reading, Shibli's primary concern was to define the core of Islam, showing that the faith was not incompatible with modern scientific accounts of the nature of reality, and that the *shariat* was open to revision in course of responding to changing social needs and circumstances. In her discussion of Shibli's handling of the *shariat*, Murad says that his "selection of the cases as well as the criteria on which he judged them are both influenced, if not exactly determined, by the priorities and values of Western liberalism"; the same holds for his strategies concerning matters of faith. All this was broadly similar to what Hindu reformers like Ishwar Chandra Vidyasagar were doing, as seen in the previous chapter (p. 145).

Put briefly, in his effort at "building up a case for a ... greater role of reason in Islamic theology, Shibli's one and only obsession", he made several major sets of moves (Murad 1996: 31). One was to define the core of the faith, and demonstrate its reasonableness; and to locate a minimal core of the law, leaving the rest to respond to changing circumstances. To this end, he delved into the medieval period for the thought of the then theologians and authorities on Islamic law. In this corpus he looked for rational explanations for key elements in the Islamic religious tradition, so that, say, Shibli's understanding of Prophet Muhammad's altered states of consciousness would not be very different from that, say, of Maxime Rodinson (1971). On the legal side, Shibli separated "beliefs and matters which constitute the universal principles of religion" from a people's "rules and practices" for meeting their specific, local conditions (Murad 1996: 71). Insofar as the latter had evolved at a particular juncture in Arabia and other parts of west Asia, it cleared the way for modifying these "rules and practices" for peoples elsewhere. However striking the range, the depth, and the originality of Shibli's thought, it appealed to the *ulama* no more than had Syed Ahmad Khan's theology (see p. 123). Though Shibli was associated for long spells with two major institutions – the college at Aligarh, and the Nadwatul Ulama in Lucknow – his ideas did not find an adequate institutional base. He had personal difficulties too, among them that of his family's Rathod Rajput background which could seem to be a "low origin" in an Ashraf milieu (Murad 1996: 121, 125; Metcalf 1982: 340f).

"Social reform" has been a major theme in Indian history since the nineteenth century. Reforms in the Muslim space, however, have gone slow on secular debate, struggle, and breaks with traditional arrangements. In all the social and ideological flux, the weightier moves have tended rather to reinforce religious and social orthodoxy and to foster a more rigorous Islamization, anchored to mosque, *madrasa*, and – in eastern Bengal – *anjuman*, religious associations. Given the strength of orthodoxy, the range of ways of life, experiences, and choices available to Muslims became more limited than might otherwise have been the case. In the matter of reforming women's place in society, the *ulama*, acting in alliance with "Muslim social reformers in the late nineteenth and early twentieth centuries", promoted a regime which "increasingly asserted male control and values over women's lives" in educational, social, and legal arenas (Minault 1998: 306, 307).[4]

Since studying in mainline institutions was necessary for getting jobs, the *ulama* authorized such study. Ranabir Samaddar (2006) writes of famous preachers in early twentieth century Bengal urging Muslims to get a modern education. For engaging with the western tradition more thoroughly, however, there have been fewer takers. In his survey of nineteenth century Indians engaging with the western presence in India and articulating their reactions to it, K. N. Panikkar noted more than 20 men; Syed Ahmad Khan was the lone Muslim, in his reckoning, willing to engage vigorously with the western tradition (1975). (Another selection might include Shibli Numani and the other, less influential, men in Delhi; see Hasan 2005.) Why this was so will concern us below.

AIMEC

The All India Muslim Educational Conference (AIMEC) was founded in 1886 as another project of Syed Ahmad Khan: intended to encourage "the study of western sciences and literature" carrying the Aligarh message to Muslims throughout the subcontinent (Khan 2001: 1). Its annual sessions, held fairly regularly from 1886 to 1945, usually found Muslim notables to preside over them. It was a useful strand in the Muslim notables' networks, drawing in especially men who were active more in education than in politics; one among them was Shaikh Abdullah, founder of the women's school at Aligarh (see below). At its annual meeting in 1906, in Dacca, the All India Muslim League was founded. Between 1905 and 1926, AIMEC appointed full-time

---

[4] C. M. Naim (2004b) has an autobiographical account of a how a young Muslim girl became literate in the mid-1800s against strong resistance in her landed family.

agents too, who travelled a great deal, their tasks including that of gathering funds for AIMEC's activities. The organization received grants for its various projects from the princely states of Bhopal, Hyderabad, and Bahawalpur (*ibid.*: 49). These included lobbying to upgrade the M. A. O. College, Aligarh, into a University; and starting a women's school at Aligarh, in a small way in 1906, which ultimately became a Women's College (*ibid.*: Chaps 4–5).

AIMEC actively promoted various regional associatons, also devoted to Muslim education, among them the Anjuman-i-Himayat-i-Islam (AHI) in Lahore. The latter again was largely a forum for discussion, concerned "with problems of education and the development of the Urdu language, and also with the spreading of English education and English literature among the Muslims" (Gordon-Polonskaya 1971: 111). Between 1899 and 1904, the recital of his poems at AHI's annual meetings helped make the young poet Mohammad Iqbal famous. AIMEC's ambitions were considerable; but the task of embodying them in institutions was doubly strapped: by *ulama* opposition to western learning, and by sparsity of material resources. Bombay city in the nineteenth century had affluent Muslim merchants but, in the 1870s and 1880s, they were riven by too many rivalries to be much help, though a generation later AIMEC had established productive links with the Sulaimani Bohra and Ismaili leadership there (Dobbin 1972: 229–46; Khan 2001: 51).

Institutions

The previous chapter noted the importance of varied institutions for society. An institution may be built to a particular mandate; and the experience of building it can be carried to other purposes. The T. N. Madan and B. G. Halbar study (1972) traced a part of the pattern of "educational private enterprise" in India since the mid-nineteenth century. The variety of promoters has included religious sects (like the Arya Samaj: Jones 1976: Chap. 2), castes (like the Nadars in Madurai: Templeman 1996: 171f), and successful merchants or industrialists in the philanthropic mode (see Kudaisya 2003: 393 on activities supported by Birla Education Trust; Harris 1958: Chaps 6 and 7 on the Indian Institute of Science, Bangalore, supported by J. N. Tata).

Whatever the importance of caste-like identities for orienting personal, intimate relationships, at least Muslims in north India have overlooked their potential for sustaining certain kinds of public effort.

Nor has such effort found nurture in the numerous sects. We have seen why, from the mid-nineteenth century on, in India's diverse, subcontinental society, institution-building among Muslims sought primarily to strengthen the believers' allegiance and religious knowledge and observances. Significant social capital was tending to get recycled into realizing a religiously rooted Islamic community. Groups large and small, which had been marginal historically, were brought into a closer religious identification. The reach of these growing networks, and the sentiments of community, found varied expressions later, as we shall see.

Syed Ahmad Khan is well-known for the independent path he charted: his interest in western science, learning, and social practices; and his initiative for the college at Aligarh. Indeed, Syed Ahmad Khan was ahead of the Arya Samaji institution-building in Punjab, though he had to lean on the government for his college. In Punjab, "By the turn of the [nineteenth] century, [Anjuman Himayat-i-Islam] managed an Islamia College in Lahore and several Islamia high schools" (Gilmartin 1988: 77). Despite the deficit in resources, Jamia Milia Islamia was initiated in the 1920s, as a nationalist project, first in Aligarh, then in Delhi. The two great physicians, Ajmal Khan and M. A. Ansari, and Gandhi, are reported to have secured its initial funds (Talib 1998).

In south India, voluntary effort did lead to a stock of institutions. In their study of private institution in three districts in Karnataka, T. N. Madan and B. G. Halbar (1972) found that – alongside Brahmins, Lingayats, and Christians – Muslim enterprise had also been notable. The Anjuman-e-Islam of Hubli had built several *secondary* schools. Its activity may have been limited because its institutions' medium of instruction was Urdu, as against Kannada and English in the others. Only Christians and Brahmins exceeded the Muslim literacy level, but overall the authors judged the latter as educationally backward (*ibid.*: 133–36). In Tamil Nadu, while the response to modern education among Muslims has been similar, several organizations in Madras city launched institutions for their education, 1880s onwards (More 1997: 50–87, Radhakrishnan 1993: 1591f). Given the vigorous Left politics in Kerala in recent decades, Muslims there have built modern educational institutions vigorously (Miller 1976: 204–21; Sikand 2005: Chaps 4 and 5; Hasan 2004b for the wider current scene).

To return to the colonial period, Anil Seal (1968: Chaps 2 and 8) considered, for the late nineteenth century, the Muslim–Hindu differential in taking to western education. In latter day UP, Muslims were doing at least as well as Hindus. In the three Presidencies, however – Bengal, Madras, Bombay – they lagged behind (Seal 1968: 306, Tables 11, 18, 25, 33). In Bombay Presidency, though strong in commerce, Muslims held back from the new education because it was unrelated to their range of occupations (*ibid.*: 86). In Bengal, it was poverty that held the predominantly peasant Muslims back; and both Urdu-speaking *ashraf* and the *ulama* opposed modern education for the *ajlaf* initially. By the early twentieth century, however, Bengali Muslim religious public men were promoting aspirations to modern education, alongside the religious ideals (Ahmad 1981: 23–31, 102, 141–50; Samaddar 2006).

At the end of 1911, the Viceroy, visiting Dacca in eastern Bengal in the wake of the revocation of the first Partition of Bengal, announced that a university would be established in the city. Though a majority of its teachers were Hindu until 1947, the number of Muslim students grew, and they would contribute significantly to the later Muslim political leadership of Bengal. From 1921, Bengal and Punjab had, as Ministers of Education, Fazlul Huq and Fazl-i Husain respectively, and they were to demonstrate the use of state power to enable Muslims to improve their educational levels markedly; and there was substantial governmental support in Bombay and Sind too. In British India overall, "the number of Muslim pupils in educational institutions recognized by the government" grews rapidly between 1917 and 1927; by the end of that decade, at 4.7 per cent, the Muslims' enrollment was a bit higher than that of all others at 4.3 per cent (Basu 1980: 229). Many more educated Muslim men were entering the job market but the job situation was unhelpful. Apart from whatever government jobs came their way, there was also the private sector; there the Hindu merchants' and industrialists' control was growing. In that sector, Muslims would face a double barrier to employment: to the owners' general preference for close kin and castemates were added the implications of growing communal antagonisms, which will engage us in later chapters.

The two chapters on "Facing the future" have been implicitly comparative. In an entity by itself, we notice something of the attributes that it has. In considering entities comparatively, we may also notice attributes *missing* in particular entities. To ask, then, why particular attributes are present or absent in given cases sets up further questions for enquiry. A great deal has been shared between Muslims and Hindus historically; and therefore, in the limited areas of difference, the contrastive processes may be considered, comparatively, to advantage.

A search for links between causes and consequences, in these areas of difference, points towards connections between characteristic institutions, say the caste order, and the beliefs and practices of their respective traditional intelligentsia.

Drawing on the work of both sociologists and historians, these chapters have sought to locate the kinds of resources summoned by Hindus and Muslims, during the nineteenth century and beyond, to cope with shifting colonial sands. I have suggested that many Hindus were able to draw on their social networks in castes and sects to mediate their efforts at institution-building, whose importance for societies I have stressed. Muslims, in contrast, found it un-Islamic to put *jati* bonds to public uses; and the principal Islamic sects' defining focus on the Prophet complex (p. 119f) inhibited their generating small packets of local charisma – around which might grow modest, freshly energized social networks. The Sufis had had charisma, but their orientation was otherworldly.

The immigrants' descendants apart, the nineteenth century found a large, dispersed, unorganized category of persons who might be identified as Muslim, but whose prevailing beliefs and practices were often un-Islamic, given their overwhelmingly indigenous origins. Leaving aside the Shias, the Sunni tradition in nineteenth century India tended to evolve towards religious centralism of a certain kind, turning around the Prophet, the Quran, the *hadis*, the *shariat*, the *Hajj*, prayers directed towards Mecca, and the like. Veneration of Sufi saints and their tombs has, in addition, been respected in the Barelwi sect. In any case, it was the protagonists of a sterner, more exclusive vision of an Islamic community, radiating from the seminary at Deoband, who were able to appropriate the Sufi halo to their own practice; and to define the Sufi openness to other religious traditions as a deviance – of which the high road of Islam had to be purged. In the various Islamic reform movements including that initiated by Deoband, Rafiuddin Ahmed sees "essentially the response of the *ulama* to the loss of their old world – gone with the decline of Muslim power in India – which they sought to regain by a return to the primitive purity of Islam" (1981: 41).

Opening under a new political rule, the nineteenth century grew to be a rather contentious time: in some regions, the local social and political equations had to be reset, with much pushing, and resisting, of rival claims. The early vocabularies of this contention – music before a mosque, cow sacrifice at *Id* – stoked religious embers of long standing.

The scale and the depth of the contention followed a rising spiral in later generations, aided by the printing presses and new institutional forms, and spurred by one's rivals' own ambitious moves. Altogether, we shall see that these processes had momentous consequences.

The century and a half leading to the Partition revealed some deficits in the Muslim space. One concerned merchants, especially away from the coasts. Another deficit lay in the area of a certain *critical* tradition – notwithstanding the distinguished past under the Abbasids and in the Maghreb – so that the movement for Islamic purism, led by the *shariat*-oriented *ulama* of Deoband, did not meet much effective resistance. Deoband did foster the *umma*, the solidarity around a sense of community, but it also made Muslims wary of others: of the West, and its institutions and forms of knowledge, and of the emerging, changing Hindus around them; wary, that is, of appropriating all that was creative and forward looking in the larger world, wary of appropriating the resources needed for doing the work of the world. These two deficits combined to produce a third. Even as the colonial government left the field of educational institutions to private initiative, Muslims appeared, at times, to be cool to mainline schooling, let alone actively building institutions for the purpose. As the decades passed, these deficits over a mercantile, and later, an entrepreneurial class, over an open-minded appreciation of the diverse forms of knowledge, science, and technology, and in the cumulative experience of building institutions independently of the government, would influence the Muslim responses to emerging social and political issues. The implications of these divergent processes will engage us in the chapters ahead.

4

nineteenth century anxieties

> In the late nineteenth and early twentieth centuries, men in India – Hindus, Muslims, and British – made choices which ultimately led to the partition of India ... [though the idea was not publicly canvassed in India] before the late 1930s, no political organization adopted it as its goal until the Muslim League did so in 1940, and the idea had no chance of success until the Muslim League demonstrated its persuasive power in the elections of 1946.
>
> Brass 1975: 124

Change of Phase

The eighteenth and nineteenth centuries saw several major processes converging: the unravelling of the old ruling social alliance, the flow of power to the British, the new logic that would inform the changing economy, the (slow) waves of new technology, a continuing churning of the body social. The cumulative effect of all this was acute enough that we see here a change of phase in the history of south Asia. One element in the picture concerned *horses*, or their fading significance.

The fading of the horse made a difference. Over the millennia – since the coming of the "Aryans" and long before that – polities in India had had no answer to horse-borne conquerors from the north. We have seen that when these latter men found effective leadership, they could recurrently put irresistible pressure on the sedentary civilizations of China, India, and Iran and its neighbours (pp. 3–4). The secret of their power lay in the stock of warhorses raised on the central Asian savannah – horses of extraordinary speed and stamina. Medieval Indian kingdoms spent fortunes on trying to import these horses from central Asia but could never get enough. Such were the facts of ecology.

The medieval period brought to north India new sets of men on horseback; and the Mughal political structure was reckoned in terms of *mansabdari*, its ranks graded by the number of horseborne men an official had to maintain – and his corresponding *jagir*, fief, to sustain that force. By the mid-eighteenth century, however, the horse – and privileged access to central Asia – had virtually dropped out of the equations of power. The East India Company rode to power in Bengal, and elsewhere, on its firearms (Ray 2003: 256, 295ff). In Indian political life, however, Central Asian horse-borne warriors continued to have an afterlife until the early twentieth century: a 1922 Annie Besant text saw them as a potential danger; and three years later, a speech in Lahore by Saifuddin Kitchlu held them out as a threat (Prasad 2000: 220).

The Mughal – and later the Awadhi – ruling class had been "open". With a political arrangement at stake, the social organization had evolved pragmatically. Man Singh, Akbar's Rajput wife's nephew, had led the Mughal troops that brought Bengal into the empire. Yet the indigenous, or at least non-Muslim, elements in this ruling class had come from, and maintained their bonds within, their particular *jatis*. As the imperial – in Awadh, Nawabi – hold on power shrank, the sons of the indigenes, Rajput, Kayastha, Khatri, Brahmin, ceased to look up to the erstwhile ruling class. They stayed back within their *jatis*, returning to their ancestors' continuing rounds of life and occupations.

The immigrants' descendants had no local *jati* anchors; they identified rather with their region of origin, and they had more reason to continue to identify with the former ruling class. Many settled into small towns, *qasba*s, around Lucknow. Rather like the Rajputs, their primary skill lay with force and power. During the nineteenth century, they alone would press claims to links with the Mughal ruling class. That ruling class had featured both immigrants and indigenes. As the century advanced, the shared political legacy would count for less and less.

The colonial arrangements, imposed by alien rulers, went far beyond the merely political. The nineteenth century already was a time of changing *material* conditions, the conditions of life generally, including of course the "relations of production" too. It was a time of a changing economic regime, sometimes called capitalism. It was a time of new technologies with growing social impacts, with printing presses which made possible the printing of pamphlets and books and journals addressed to lay readers: "a laicised literate order radically altered the means and modes of social contestation" (Naregal 2001: 4). It was a time of railways and factories which drew workers from distant areas, and the post office. It was a time of new metropolitan centres like Bombay and Calcutta, of western education, and of new rules of the social game.

It was a time of altered structures and loci of power, and of new needs for mobilizing – mobilizing people for political competition, mobilizing capital for diverse purposes; and a time for dredging the past in search of visions for the future. Multiple agencies were pursuing diverse agendas, some of which turned out to have greater staying power than others. Among the more strident and durable voices, at least in northern India, using the new communications vigorously, were those of exclusive *religious* identities (and therefore differences). Society was being churned many times over. The social geography was getting redrawn, and altogether new social landscapes were beginning to emerge. Indians were authoring much of that churning – but they also had to cope with it, with whatever stocks of ideas and other cultural resources they could command.

The following pages will continue with our strategy of considering the categories "Muslim" and "Hindu" in terms both of their (sometimes adversarial) *relationships* and of the *contrast* between the two social spaces: spaces which had shared much in historical experience, culture, language, and social arrangement, yet where the social processes have taken somewhat contrastive courses. In several settings Muslims felt, rightly or wrongly, that they were outplayed by their Hindu neighbours. Reviewing these settings will give us a feel for the experiences, and the consequent attitudes, which defined the ground realities, and which shaped their leaders' later public stances that loom so large in the historians' analyses.

Attributing Responsibility

It was part of this churning that shared spaces – such as those of Gujarati Rajput villagers, the Haryanvi Jats, the Meos, and the eastern Bengali villagers – began to cleave along the Muslim: Hindu interface. Medieval social arrangements had included various points of separation; in the colonial context, several of these began to come into sharper relief. A common explanation for the growing separation attributes it to the British policy of "divide and rule". To be sure, the British played a part in the growing consciousness of a sense of difference, but the complex subcontinental theatre featured several sets of actors, with their own evolving scripts; and we have to be careful in apportioning responsibility for the rise of separativeness.

Earlier studies have identified numerous moments when British actions can be seen directly to set Muslims apart from Hindus, and reviewing them quickly will help size up the issues:

- Some seventeenth and eighteenth century Europeans coming to India carried adverse images of "Muslims", drawn from earlier, historic contestations in southern Europe and west Asia since the eleventh century. Some of them did so; but the attitudes that various colonial figures displayed in India through the generations were much too diverse. No simple original prejudice can account for much.
- Already in the late eighteenth and early nineteenth centuries, as the new rulers, the British had to settle all manner of disputes among their new subjects. To this end, they needed a handle on indigenous "laws", in oral and/or written texts; and the effort to codify these led separately into "Hindu" and "Muslim" streams (Cohn 1996: 65–75). This reified a difference; but would an alternative course have been more practicable?
- In the early nineteenth century, fresh Company recruits from Britain received their initial orientation to India at College of Fort William (CFW), Calcutta. CFW was organised with separate departments for Urdu and Hindi, following the different scripts. What had been a double-scripted, shared, common language of use, Hindustani, came to be separated – which "may be viewed as the beginnings of the Hindu–Muslim rivalry in microcosm but without Hindu and Muslim participants" (Kopf 1969: 162). A sense of their being separate languages received institutional stamp. Later in the century, anxieties over lower level government employment in UP ran into contrary considerations: on one side, the case for Urdu in the Persian script, established in administrative practice, indeed a symbol of inter-communal cooperation, given the political equations of an earlier era; on the other, the demand for switching to Hindi in the Devanagari script: literacy in the latter was far more extensive. Jobs were certainly at stake but the passions aroused were relatively modest. These could never match those over, say, the cow: assimilated to the image of the milk-giving mother; as against an object both for everyday food and for meeting a religious obligation, to sacrifice at Bakr Id (Pandey 1983).
- To be sure, the colonial regime, and its friends, did at times play one group against another. Mushirul Hasan has shown how Theodore Beck, the English Principal of the College at Aligarh, 1884 on, who was close both to the colonial establishment in India and to Syed Ahmad Khan, kept persuading Syed to keep

his distance from the Congress (Hasan 1991: 33–35). Curzon's clear, divisive intention behind the Partition of Bengal in 1905 is well known (Sarkar 1973: Chap. 1). All this may be granted; yet, as Rabindranath Tagore wrote in response to the communal riots in Bengal in 1906–07:

> That Muslims could be used against Hindus is the really worrying fact, who used them is not as important. Satan cannot enter till he finds a flaw... (*ibid.*: 83).

The following analysis will show that, once the principal indigenous political structures had ceased to matter, the effective channels for acting socially tended to spread along lines of *jati* and faith. Numerous indigenous actors, pursuing their own agendas, were at work; and we shall see how the forces of separation and contention became ascendant.

- Nineteenth century British historians' representations of India's past directed attention towards recurring instances of oppression of Hindus during the medieval period, contrasting them with the alleged blessings of the Raj (Elliott and Dawson 1867–77; Chatterjee 1994: 100f). Christian missionaries, on the other hand, targeted the beliefs and practices of "Hindu" and "Muslim", disregarding all the diversity within them. Indian repostes tended to bifurcate correspondingly. Writing of Punjab and UP in the nineteenth century, for example, John Webster notes the Presbytarians' criticisms of Hindu and Muslim texts, which elicited separate responses from Swami Dayananda on behalf of Hindus, and from Ghulam Ahmad of Qadian on behalf of Muslims (1976: Chap. 4). As we will see, however, other powerful impulses were at work too; and while the historians' and the missionaries' role in queering the pitch is well taken, their share in the overall process was modest at best.
- The decenniel census is often cited as evidence of colonial culpability for sharpening the communal divide. The first major Census in Bengal in 1872, for instance, reported an unexpected Muslim majority in the eastern districts, which opened up new political possibilities there (Ahmed 1981: 6, 15). Contention along lines of religious difference, however, had antedated the Census. Later on, the Census report came to be recognized as an arbiter of a *jati*'s rank in the caste hierarchy; but the Census

tables for other personal characteristics – language, occupation, age, gender – excited little interest. The Census, that is to say, was a neutral bureaucratic operation; which of its findings became public issues depended on which social anxieties were currently active, and these clearly originated elsewhere.

The whole lot of elements mentioned above still cover only a corner of our staggeringly complex field. Can we characterize that "whole" field, even for the nineteenth century by itself? Nothing more than a rough approximation can be attempted. There was colonial mischief, of course, but there was more. If my earlier argument about the bifurcation of the former ruling class holds, the early British observers of Indian society would have encountered a ruling class that was *already bifurcating* – after some five centuries of participating in a shared space, in what has been called the "composite culture". When the British tried "divide and rule", it would work along the grain of processes whose springs lay embedded within India's social and political history. In the emerging course of the relationship between "Muslims" and "Hindus" during the period, furthermore, we shall meet actors and institutions – who would claim to speak on behalf of, and would seek to mobilize, these categories in a consolidated manner, sliding into contentious modes – which tended to become self-aggravating. Much of the force of their impact derived, finally, from the seismic political, economic, and technological changes of the time.

However well the British earned their reputation of being troublemakers, we have to consider also the independently conceived agendas of those active on the Hindu and the Muslim sides – as well as the epochal changes engulfing the period. In opening his three volume search for the "foundations and supports" of Muslim nationalism, Bimal Prasad assigns only a supplementary place to "British policy in dealing with the communal problem" (1999: 19, 241–52). His second volume, however, cites chapter and verse to document the divisive British role, for instance in instituting separate electorates (2000: 100–18). In an earlier chapter, we considered the medieval legacy concerning the relations between Muslims and Hindus. By and large, the less we think of that legacy, the weightier becomes the British culpability for the communal separation – and vice versa. Taken as a whole, then, the "responsibility" for the growth of separativeness between Hindus and Muslims may be attributed four ways, roughly equally. There were those who acted contentiously on behalf of these two categories, there were the colonial rulers, and there also were the changing circumstances of the nineteenth century. This study brackets off the colonial role by and large; it foregrounds, rather, the dynamic of the relations between Muslims and Hindus.

As we explore the changing scene in the pages below, we shall notice the consequences of the Indians' virtual exclusion from competing for, and exercising, power. The cement of power had disappeared, and hence, too, the need to cooperate in managing it. Their competitive energies found other channels; it was the *religious* networks, symbols, and sentiments that fell into place more quickly than any other. Ayesha Jalal argues a sharp contrast between the then British practice at home, of playing religious identities down in public life, and that in India of tolerating "some debate and dissent as long as these related to the religious and cultural concerns of Indians" – but not matters political (2001: 37). They used the religious categories for praise and blame, say, for the 1857 uprising; and for managing – or manipulating – the public space, once Indians began to challenge the colonial rule. Put otherwise, it was the advocates of exclusivist identities, continuing from an earlier era, who were quick to recognize the possibilities in the new regime. Religious leaders were circulating alternate lifestyles and (discordant) social maps for orienting one's social existence. The choices made on the two sides led to divergent chains of consequences.

In the life of complex societies it is important to try to anticipate the likely consequences of the choices we make, or refuse to make; but, for anticipating the likely consequences in novel milieux, we are hostage to our prior sense of history and our own stocks of ideas with which to interpret what is unfamiliar. Nineteenth century Indians were face to face with difficult choices: whether or not to go for western education, to take recourse to colonial law, to go back to ancient scriptures, to give women more space, to tinker with the caste order. For making radical choices on such novel issues, their prior historical experience and contemporary knowledge could help them in only a limited way.

Anxieties' Spiral

From the Mughals, who ceased to matter, except symbolically, after 1707, to the British, who let the Mughal line reign, if not rule, in Delhi until 1857, it was a century and a half of drift and transition: inevitably a time of uncertainty and anxiety – at least for those whose interests and visions reached beyond the short term and their own localities. With the coming of the colonial order, the *primary* changes were political.

In the larger arenas, the use of force became a British monopoly. By the early 1800s, numerous localities felt a double rupture: the old officialdom had to give way to the British whose perceptions were sharply different; and the old hierarchical ideology governing localities was displaced by "assumptions about 'equity' and 'precedent'" (Bayly 1983: 336). In the late nineteenth century Tamil Brahmins' perception, the beef-eating Englishman was conceptually equal to the scavenger; and "The inability to exercise power over the scavenger/ Englishman was for the Brahmin a most humiliating loss of power (Pandian 2007: 32)" even though, as we saw earlier, some Tamil Brahmins attained power, influence, and wealth in the colonial regime. Colonial rule brought new modes of governance, new laws, new courts of justice and, we shall see, it changed the rules governing the use of public spaces.

Muslims and Hindus were both disempowered and humiliated, yet the loss of power stung no one more than the Muslim descendants of north India's ruling elite (see for some details Ray 2003: 354–64, *passim*). This disempowerment and humiliation, as we shall see, came to have large implications. As we saw in Chapters 2 and 3, the uncertainties set off searches for alternatives, on which a group might lay anchor for the future. Memories of conquest and rulership apart, the Muslim elite's ancestors had in many ways been luminously creative; yet a sense of siege, of multiple vulnerabilities, came to haunt it by the late nineteenth century.

Hafeez Malik has reviewed the acute, widespread, sense of loss, at least among the leading Muslim groups of the time (1963: Chap. 5). Northern India had strong challengers, "the Marathas in the south, Sikhs in the Punjab and the British who were to overthrow all"; Malik quotes poems by Shah Abdul Aziz, the famous *alim* of Delhi, depicting "the lacerated feelings of the Moslems in the middle of the eighteenth century". Dynastic ups and downs may be routine on the giant wheels of history; what hurt Abdul Aziz, however, was his perception that Sikhs and Marathas were targeting "multitudes of Moslems" *as* Muslims (*ibid.*: 141f). Then the colonial hold spread until the mid-1800s; and 1857 was a watershed: a humiliating, traumatic watershed in north Indian centres like Delhi and Kanpur, given the colonial reprisals for revolt. These moments were not easily forgotten. For those at the receiving end, anxieties remained sharp.

Muslim difficulties were considerable in Bengal too, and Malik attributes them directly to British policies. "Under the Moghul rule the [*ashraf*] Moslems had almost monopolized government employment. However, under the British they were gradually excluded altogether from state patronage" (Malik 1963: 145). Formerly, they had been army officers; now they could not "enter a British regiment". Muslims, holding "the higher fiscal posts", had overseen "the collection of land revenue"; after Cornwallis and the Permanent Settlement, the role passed to the English Collector. In the new tenurial system, much of the landownership passed to Hindus, who had earlier "staffed the subordinate revenue service" only. Muslim presence in other government jobs fell sharply when Persian, as the official language, gave way to English and Bengali (*ibid.*: 145ff).

The older Muslim educational system got into serious trouble too: it had rested on lands endowed by Muslim notables for maintaining educational institutions – "one fourth of all the land in the province of Bengal". Starting in 1828, the East India Company began to confiscate most of these lands, depriving the old institutions of their wherewithal (Malik 1963: 150). The "descendants of the rulers" – says Malik, for Bengali peasants! – were reluctant to take to the new educational institutions because "the teachers in the government schools were Hindu and the language Bengali (*ibid.*: 149)." To Malik's roster, Sumit Sarkar adds the implications of English education. Just "when Hindu bhadralok castes were eagerly making the switchover from Persian to English education with a confidence buttressed by rising rent-receipts from zamindari or tenure-holding", Muslims stayed away, owing to "economic distress as well as a conservative distrust of an alien and irreligious system of learning" (1973: 410). This had consequences for competing for the few relatively senior government jobs. (Much in these paras on Bengal is contested by Bimal Prasad who leans on a different body of research (1999: Chap. 2).

Farzana Shaikh has examined closely the political ideologies prevailing among the Muslims, then and later: that it was right and natural for them to be rulers, so at least some believed, for the last, and the final, revelation had been made to Muslims through the Prophet: hence their intrinsic moral superiority; and the exercise of power ought to follow from moral worth, not from numbers. Hence, too, the insistence, later, that Muslims were a "nation", not a "minority" (Shaikh 1989: 114–18). Some of the difficulty turned on variable implications of the Urdu word *qaum*, sometimes used for "nation" (see Sikand 2005: 90).

Political ideologies apart, many of the defining institutions for the identity of the Indian Muslim were located in Delhi and UP: Agra

90 *spirals of contention*

and Delhi had been capitals of empires, which had left behind major monumental remains and numerous mosques great and small. Renowned Sufi saints had lived in the region, like Shah Abdur Razzaq at Bansa in Awadh (see p. 9), and their tombs commanded widespread veneration. The Muslim elite which had dispersed into the landed estates and small towns of the region constituted the largest concentration of Urdu speakers, and they cultivated a proud cultural style. Firangi Mahall in Lucknow had educated generations of men who had served the governments of the day; at Deoband, in western UP, the notable new Islamic seminary was established in the 1860s; and in the same region emerged the College at Aligarh, the ambitious institution for the new, western education – which later became the university.

There was a *disjunction* between UP's elite Muslims' wide-ranging stature in the present, as in the past, and their relatively small numbers in UP. Only about a seventh of UP's population was Muslim, and the logic of numbers in a society headed for electoral politics was plain. Hence the anxieties that spurred them into political activity: "Throughout the development of Muslim separatism in British India, whenever the politics of All-India Muslim organisations were vigorous they were more the politics of UP Muslims than those of any other groups of Indian Muslims (Robinson 1975: 5, 40–46, 71–81)."

The passing of rulership to the British released a barrage of *secondary* changes, ramifying through social, economic, and political spaces – which we shall now explore. Various urban centres in nineteenth century UP had had their own established social hierarchies of urban power, wealth, and status. The Muslim elites, connected socially and politically with the Nawabi regime in Lucknow, in Awadh, regional successors to the Mughals, controlled land and exercised local social power in the numerous small towns; their cultural preferences would prevail in the towns they dominated. Other groups in town had their place, but if they wished to build a temple or organize a celebration, they had to clear the matter with the dominant gentry. Likewise, in commercial centres like Banaras, it was the Hindu merchants who called the shots. Generalizing on the less urbanized Bhojpur, the region across the Bihar–UP border, Gyan Pandey wrote:

> [In several localities] there was an insistence [over a long period] that the assent of the local zamindars was required for all religious, if not social, innovations. ... [Dominant communities, whether Muslim or Hindu]

demonstrated their continued and often increased readiness to rise in defence of institutions and practices that had come to symbolize for them their ascendancy and/or their self-respect. Frequently the consequences were bloody (1983: 124).

The colonial regime, in effect, was changing the *rules of the game* of public life. The insertion of colonial notions of legal equality in localities, where historically created hierarchies had prevailed, offered room for pursuing novel agendas, especially by newcomers into the towns. The older elites would have to cope with these men pursuing their diverse agendas, defying the erstwhile hierarchies. Various equations had to be renegotiated for a new social order but, as we shall see shortly, there were no clear arenas – councils or legislatures – in which to engage in this renegotiation, and it happened in the streets in rather disorderly ways. Indeed, these skirmishes inaugurated an early phase in the game of social contention whose stakes were to grow over the generations (Chap. 6).

Nineteenth century agendas in UP's towns were often collective, not individual. The period seems, on balance, to have favoured some of the Hindu upper castes which were building up economic, social, and even political pressure in a limited way. The Muslim elite, proud descendants of a ruling class, had little taste for the marketplace; and we saw that substantial Muslim merchants in north India were scarce (pp. 60–62). As commerce revived in north India in the colonial peace, it was the (Hindu) merchant castes that stole the show, and they sought to leverage their new wealth to challenge the established *social* hierarchies in north India's small towns:

> Newcomers and newly rich men in the towns who had little connection with the patronage of the earlier Muslim rulers were often unwilling to acquiesce in a continued ceremonial inferiority which their new rulers were disinclined to enforce. Thus in a town like Rewari, north of Delhi, it was the Hindu commercial community led by about 300 'wealthy and influential persons' who tried in 1838 to coerce the Muslims into giving up the slaughter of meat in the town by operating a *hartal* against them and denying them food (Bayly 1983: 337).

Then there was the old elite, smarting under its loss of power:

> In several ... riots, the old law officers were seen taking leading parts in riots by the Muslim population against what they regarded as modifications of custom and precedence in religious practice. In Kashipur in 1833, for

instance, the *kazi* [a Muslim law officer] of the division had to be removed. He had denounced a Muslim police officer as a heretic and threatened to pollute the town with cow-slaughter after an unpopular compromise with the Hindus over the location of a temple (Bayly 1983: 336).

In the less urbanized Bhojpur region, at Bihar–UP border, similar anxieties prevailed, for similar reasons (Pandey 1983: 73f, 77).

These were local skirmishes. Underlying them were the personal influence that the local *kazi* had wielded, and the personal networks of *kinship and marriage*, renewed continually during family visiting and ceremonies. We have considered these networks within the caste order (see p. 34ff); but these were important among Muslims too (see Metcalf 1982: 98ff, on the backdrop to Deoband; Robinson 2001: Chaps 3–4 for Firangi Mahall). Rival links could spread some along diverse personal networks, as of priest and patron, mosque and maulvi, and the *akhara* – a community centre where young men would engage in body-building activities (Freitag 1989: 121–23 and elsewhere).

The reach of such personal networks was necessarily limited; at the edge of the *jati* or a patronage group, the network would taper off. Asserting oneself in the new situation was beginning to need the strength of numbers; and the nineteenth century found the key in *religious symbols*. Invoking symbols of wide range one could reach out to mobilize, well beyond the confines of a particular *jati* or other interest group. Religious beliefs, symbols, and practices had spread through society over the centuries, becoming embedded in everyday life; and corresponding stocks of *memories* meant different things to different groups. These memories were available for invoking variously.

We have seen earlier the extraordinary spread of Bankim Chandra Chatterji's Sanskrit–Bengali song, *bande mataram*, which appeared first in his novel *Anandamath* (1881–82/2005). Sabyasachi Bhattacharya has explored the context in which Bankim chose to personify the country, India, first "as the mother" and then as "'Durga holding her ten weapons of war', the destroyer of foes, as well as the goddess of wealth, Kamala, and the goddess of learning, Vani": why did Bankim employ these metaphors, and why did this kind of representation strike a chord among such vast numbers? Bhattacharya sees these representations as Jungian archetypes "collectively shared by those who have a shared history, real or imagined": "The text of Vande Mataram is basically a series of evocations of the memory of a discourse that had been part of the world outlook of Bankim and his audience" (2003: 77, 85, 92, 93). By the early 1900s, as "Vande Mataram" gained an emblematical quality among Hindus, beginning in Bengal, it became a potent, if ambiguous, weapon: the phrase was becoming a war cry, first of nationalist challenge to colonial rule, initially in the Swadeshi movement (1903–08), and then of Hindus against Muslims (Lipner 2005: 75–79). The Muslim elite took offence at the aggressive cry, at the song's "idolatrous" tenor, and at the novel's adverse allusions to Muslims recurrently – making the song an abiding focus of contention along communal lines.

It turned out that the possibility of working with cultural and religious symbols and shared memories would pass muster with the colonial regime too. Ever watchful over possible challenges to colonial authority, we have noted earlier that the regime was indulgent towards "religious" and "cultural" activities. In processions, and later in public meetings, associations, and the like, the colonial regime did permit competition – implicitly, by way of mobilizing numbers. This opened a window for challenging old privileges with impunity; hitherto quiescent groups could press their claims through street action (Bayly 1983: 336f; Freitag 1989). These were long familiar moves around symbols: innocent actions that get under the other side's skin.

By the late nineteenth century, the possibility of enlarging the scale of mobilization around impersonal symbols was being worked through: the cow in late nineteenth century UP, Ganapati and Shivaji in Maharashtra in the 1890s (Chap. 5, p. 127) were only the first of a long series. To pass from kinship, caste, and personal networks to symbols of wide span, say, for anchoring mobilization, is to shift levels – to "shift gears" (Saberwal 2001). Recourse to symbols helped awaken dormant wider identities, enabling social and political mobilization, and the din of competitiveness, to grow in unprecedented measure. Such mobilization had implications which were separative, serving to weaken, if not abrogate, what had been mutual arrangements on the shared middle ground. These themes, from two centuries ago, continue to echo in conflicts and violence in the early twenty-first century.

Networks of kinship and marriage, religious and other symbols and establishments, pools of memories, and colonial perceptions and actions: all these were part of the scene, their implications for the emerging social categorization somewhat convergent. Yet these were far from decisive for the communal consolidations that followed. Of greater moment were: the possibility of building on nascent *ideologies* being conceived in exclusive religious terms; the *anxieties* that motivated men to propagate these exclusive visions; the new *institutional models*, through which to

94 *spirals of contention*

coordinate and indoctrinate, and the *technologies*, like printing, which slashed the costs of reaching relatively large numbers speedily.

These were elite initiatives, led by the late nineteenth century religious specialists. Communication between the Muslim and Hindu religious elites in earlier centuries had in any case been sparse, being limited to such groups as Sufis, Nath Jogis, and Ismailis. The new initiatives would seek to make the principle of separation more pervasive; but meanwhile there were other elements adding particularly to Muslim anxieties. The last chapter took note of their weakness in commerce and industry. Subcontinentally, Muslims were about a quarter of the overall population, but there were concentrations in the areas that are now Pakistan and Bangladesh; elsewhere their *numbers* were more modest, being about a seventh in UP. This made them wary of a plain one-man-one-vote electoral system, as we shall see below; but the pressure of numbers was felt in other ways too. There was, for instance, the demand for the use of Hindi, in place of Urdu, in courts of law and in schools. Under the pressure of numbers, Hindi gained ground over Urdu in Bihar and UP, in 1881 and 1900 respectively. This would mean fewer opportunities for work for Muslims – for whom Urdu was the first language. Muslims had the strength of numbers in Bengal and Punjab, but there they found themselves up against Hindu landlords and merchants respectively; and Hindus spread into the new professions almost everywhere.

Sometimes Muslims felt that it was the combined weight of wealth and numbers that bore down on them. Take the cow protection campaign in eastern UP at the turn of the century. Apart from the urban publicity and related activity, the cow protectionists set up a framework for gathering resources in small packets from individual households, using these to buy up cattle being taken to the slaughter house; the resources would also be used for sheltering old cows and the like. In 1893, large numbers of Hindus of certain castes gathered and attacked Muslim localities where they thought cows were going to be sacrificed for the festival of Id. The mob was at times too large for the local police picket to control (Pandey 1983). By the late nineteenth century, a palpable bar of separation was forming between Muslims and Hindus, especially in northern and eastern India. These efforts took roughly parallel courses among "Hindus" and "Muslims" – which the next chapter will explore. Here we pause and ask: why did the shared spaces offer so little resistance to these drives at social reconfiguration?

The Softness of Shared Spaces

If the precolonial society had had substantial shared spaces, how could the assaults on them carry the day so easily? To answer this question, we have to scrutinize each of the domains wherein this sharing used to be manifest: the imperatives of governance, commerce, everyday neighbourliness, and the search for supernatural aid. We have already commented on the bifurcation of the Mughal ruling class with the waning of empire, and on the scarcity of Muslims in large-scale commerce in northern India. The great Muslim merchant groups lived along the coast, many tracing their origins to seafaring Arabs and Persians of yore (Wink 1997). Their social and cultural traditions of shared commercial mutuality were reflected in the political stances of Badruddin Tyabji in the late nineteenth century and M. A. Jinnah in the early twentieth (Seal 1968: 327–38; Wolpert 1984: Chaps 2–4). In Punjab, UP and Bengal, this strand was weaker, separative tugs stronger.

There remains everyday life, the sharing between neighbours, and the shared sources for supernatural succour. These domains of everyday coping arise situationally; and their strength comes from the persistence of habits, and from their grounding in local bonds and practices which may be more or less well-entrenched. These local bonds, as in the Meo case, have had to contend with contrary, persistent pressures – pressures arising in the subcontinental theatre of multiple initiatives: on one side, the call to abide by the true, eternal path ordained by the Islamic tradition; on the other, hostile attention from Hindu zealots, including at times calls to return to Hinduism. Harjot Oberoi (1994) considers similar pressures, in the late nineteenth century Punjab, for practising an exclusive Sikh identity where religious practices had earlier been eclectic.

Arrangements which had been integrative at these various levels had not had much systematic ideological or institutional cover. Through the nineteenth century, with the old order passing, there were scarcely any political arrangements in which different groups of Indians had shared stakes. Impulses to pull apart, on the other hand, sprang from different directions. In Sumit Sarkar's blunt view:

> Syncretist tendencies all too often took the form of irrational devotionalism and superstitions shared in common; religious reform movements in the nineteenth century – both Hindu and Muslim – were bound to regard such cults and rites as a debasement of the pristine purity of their respective faiths (1973: 409).

96 *spirals of contention*

The following reviews the sources of separativeness briefly: as inherent to the logic of major religious traditions; as spurred by the anxieties of the eighteenth and nineteenth centuries; and as exacerbated by recurring social aggression.

A "great" religious tradition commonly has inherent processes to renew the faith for those whose observances have become lax, and even to carry its vision and truth and way of life to those who live beyond its pale. It is its ability to generate and sustain these processes that helps make it "great": think of the Sufi orders in Islam and the missions in Christianity. Among the most striking illustrations of this process in nineteenth century India was that of Haji Shariatullah (1781–1840), whom we met in the last chapter, the man who, returning from two decades in Hajj country, spent his life preaching the true Islamic life in rural Bengal.

Apart from the inherent tendencies of major religious traditions to expand, and to be exclusive, we have seen that the eighteenth and nineteenth centuries were a time of wide-ranging anxieties, arising respectively in the displacement of power, in Christian missionary activity, and in the increased possibilities of physical mobility. In concluding Chapter 2, we noted the multiple sources of anxiety that had haunted leading Muslim groups even under the Saltanat and the Mughals; these did not disappear with loss of political power. Following the trauma of 1857, their descendants, in their estates, or *qasba* towns, in western UP, could continue to cultivate an inherited cultural style, indeed come to prize it, a mark of civilizational perfection. Yet as the estates were divided, or sold, as the new political process of elections was introduced, as the Muslims sensed a loss of British sympathy around the Khilafat – through all this, Muslim anxieties continued to grow.

Among the urbanized Hindus, especially in Punjab, the anxiety levels rose in the late nineteenth century, as the colonial regime sought to bind to itself key rural groups, a crucial stratum where to recruit for the army. The clan and tribal leaders who were allotted lands in western Punjab, along with the heads of Sufi establishments, were principally Muslim; and the official solicitousness for them made the urban, Hindu merchants anxious. The official vision saw a need to protect rural landholders from the grasp of urban merchant-moneylenders' calculation; and the official efforts at drawing Muslims into government jobs struck the merchants' sons as a denial of opportunity to them. These anxieties persuaded at least upper caste urban Hindus to respond to the Gujarati *sanyasi*, Dayananda, and his vision of a religious community that would be committed to the ancient truths of the Vedas; it would be shorn of what were seen as the countless debilitating accretions, of belief and practice, then prevailing in the Hindu space.

The apprehensions prevailing had other sources too. The manner of the Christian missionary challenge in north India during the nineteenth century was far more aggressive than had been the case in the South in earlier centuries (cf. Webster 1976: Chap. 4 on north India with Bayly 1989: Part 2). This challenge, in the form of propagating a "gospel", was directed not at *jatis*, say Khatris or Afghans, which had been important units of social organization in the erstwhile social order, but at religious entities – Islam, Hinduism, Sikhism; and it attacked the religious entities separately for their particular texts, beliefs, and practices. Indigenous responses were correspondingly segmented: Muslim and Hindu publicists found ways to stress the glories of their respective traditions – and exchanged rude barbs with Christian missionaries, and with each other. Consciousness of distinctive, respective *religious* identities was growing.

New Differentials: Western Learning

We saw earlier that although Muslims were rather slower than the Hindus in taking to modern schooling, they were catching up, and surpassing Hindus in school enrollments and the like by the 1930s. A certain orientational difference, however, remained. The Muslims' engagement with this western learning was job-oriented a little more than on the Hindu side, and I wish to explore here both the sources and the consequences of this difference.

As the nineteenth century had advanced, colonial offices had turned increasingly to the use of the English language, and we have seen the speed with which sections of the Hindu literati castes appropriated the language (p. 37f). In late eighteenth century Bengal, the initial indigenous associates of European merchants were principally Bengali upper caste Hindu merchants. This association had several chains of consequences. After the Permanent Settlement, as *zamindari*s came up for sale, some owned by Muslims, these men had the cash for buying up. Out of their ranks came, too, the early Bengali entrepreneurship. Steam power had reached Bengal by 1830. Over the next two decades, Dwarkanath Tagore (1794–1846), scion of a leading Bengali landholding and commercial family of Calcutta, built a commercial empire spanning *zamindari*, indigo, tea, coalmining, steamships, banking, and much else. That empire disintegrated later, in Dwarkanath's own lifetime, poor management converging with the hostility of Europeans in Calcutta (Kling 1976).

This early commercial wealth was meanwhile setting another chain off. Learning the English language apart, its bearers were familiarizing themselves with the European forms of learning, and deepening their familiarity with western ideology and historical experience – in Bengal, and later in Bombay (Raychaudhuri 1988; Dobbin 1972: Chaps 3–5, 8). Referring to the scene in Bengal, D. P. Mukerji, the sociologist, wrote:

> Bengali literature owes a geat deal to the disgruntled [Bengali] Babu. The fact of the matter about him was this; he was meant to be a clerk with the possession of a fair smattering of the English language, a good handwriting, and loyal manners, but he started reading John Sturart Mill, Burke, Milton, Paine, Godwin, Comte, Kant, Hegel, and the rest of them (Mukerji 1948: 91f).

This was something of a historic accident. It so happened that some of the ideas being absorbed from the West had been formulated at a high level of generality; and these included various hints for reconstituting society in a somewhat different key: ideas, that is, for a certain kind of "social reform", one that questioned the entrenched beliefs and practices received from the past. The rise of the Brahmo Samaj in Bengal, which we met earlier, was only one expression of an inter-civilizational process of considerable depth. Given the diversity of indigenous traditions to which these men were heir, their absorption of bits and pieces of western traditions led to a variety of "reform" movements in different parts of India, each usually able to claim internal religious validity for whatever agenda it pursued (see p. 45f), without needing the approval of a canonical religious authority.

We can think of several men on the Muslim side who took the European experience seriously: Syed Ahmad Khan, Shibli Numani, and, in the early twentieth century, Iqbal. On balance, however, the nineteenth century Muslims' inter-civilizational engagement with the West was weaker (Metcalf 1982: 317–35, 339–41). Muzaffar Alam has offered an interesting explanation:

> ... There might perhaps have been more of an eclectic culture of borrowing and exchanging from the Western world if the Muslim world had felt more secure.... In [the] older examples of cultural exchange, Muslims had been the conquerors (2004: 17). ...

It is necessary to remember, however, that from Akbar to Aurangzeb, from the mid-sixteenth to the end of seventeenth century, the Mughals felt secure enough in relation to the western world. Mughal curiosity about the West did yield some activity, as seen in Sikand's collation:

- sixteenth century governor of Gujarat, under Akbar, studied Latin from Catholic priests, and wrote a book on Greek philosophy;
- seventeenth century Mughal nobleman, under Aurangzeb, travelled to Portugal to study, and translated a Latin book on mathematics into Arabic;
- seventeenth century maulvi in Jaunpur wrote two books on western philosophy;
- eighteenth (?) century ambassador of Nawab of Awadh in Calcutta, learnt several European languages, wrote texts on engineering and logarithms and translated Newton's *Principia*;
- late eighteenth century hakim in Delhi wrote an essay in English on elephantiasis, and published it in a journal in London;
- late eighteenth century French and Muslim scholars together translated European scientific treatises at the college in Srirangapatnam set up by Tipu Sultan (Sikand 2005: 51).

To all this, Sikand adds the work done at the College of Fort William, Calcutta, which reminds us also of what came later at Delhi College and in Baranas – all of this, of course, was under colonial auspices. Only the first three of the instances above concern the period from Akbar to Aurangzeb; and there was also Akbar's own curiosity about the Christian faith. Each of them expresses an individual's personal interest and initiative over some element of western learning. For an encounter with a major civilization, this is a bit thin.

None of these, it will be noticed, sought to assess either what could be learned from the West, or the threats that could be expected from that direction. Concerning threats, there was the Portuguese conquest of Goa and the European control over the Arabian Sea. But also there was much to learn, as in European technologies like the printing press and timekeeping devices. Clearly, the Mughals lacked the mechanisms for gathering and processing the information that might have alerted them to such threats and possibilities; or, rather, they lacked the institutions which might have nurtured the men who could have such competence. More might have been noticed, for instance, if the Mughals had sent to Europe emissaries in search of the sources of Europe's vigour, of its ability to make its presence felt across the oceans: someone, that is, like Syed Ahmad Khan who, during his 17 months in England in 1869–70, sought to ascertain "the foundations of British achievement and British power" (Lelyveld 1978: 108).

We may contrast this Mughal passivity with a somewhat comparable situation in Europe in the thirteenth century. Faced with the threat from the Mongols in the east, first the Pope in 1245 and then the King of France in 1249 despatched Franciscan friars on missions of enquiry, seeking information on the Mongols and on their attitudes to and intentions towards the Christian West (Southern 1962: 47–51). These friars, it will be recalled, were heirs to a tradition, going back some eight centuries, of the complex intertwining of churchmen with governance in Europe. As to Europe's growing awareness of the world outside, and the skills and technologies available there, there were the exploits of the Venetian and Genoese merchants, like Marco Polo. Genoese merchants opened a route to China through central Asian territories controlled by the Mongols (Scammell 1981: Chaps. 3 and 4, esp. pp. 162–63) – a channel that would convey technologies whose subsequent influence on Europe was transformative. The Mughal rulers, in contrast, had come recently from among central Asian pastoralists. With their combat skills astride warhorses they conquered complex, sedentary civilizations, but these did little to prepare them for appraising the possibilities and the threats that lay in distant lands, beyond the seas.

Had the Mughals sent emissaries to Europe, mandated to bring back critical appraisals of societies there, they might have been impressed with one thing – provided they had the conceptual resources requisite for reaching such conclusions: that Europe had devised a great variety of institutions and institutional forms. The joint stock company, like the companies coming to trade in India, was only one of these; by the end of the *thirteenth* century, in fact, Europe was already working with diverse, evolving forms of institutions in such realms as religion, state, knowledge, and commerce (see Saberwal 1995: Chap. 4).

In hindsight, the contrast with the Mughal scene was striking. Once the homelands of Islam – the latter day Iraq, Iran, and adjacent areas – had been ravished repeatedly, initially by Turki and decisively by Mongol conquerors, Muslim society stood substantially denuded of many of its erstwhile institutions (Hodgson 2004: vol. 2, 57, 64, 66, 398, 403; Iqbal 2003: 13, 121–23). Two sets of consequences followed. Institutionally, the principal resource that survived turned around the *ulama*, and the basis of their authority and influence, the *shariat*. Beyond that, there was the willingness to improvise. The institutional sway of the *ulama*, however, had an ideological consequence. T. N. Madan cites Fazlur Rahman's *Islam and modernity* (1982) to the effect that "a 'most fateful distinction' came to be made between the religious or traditional sciences, on the one hand, and the secular or rational sciences, on the other, to the detriment of the latter. Sufism too was inimical to the rational sciences and intellectualism generally" (Madan 1997: 155). These tendencies were to cast their shadow down the centuries to our time.

The Saltanat and the Mughal regimes in India had their ruling apparatus, into which they incorporated indigenous skills, say, the Rajputs' in governance or the merchants' in commerce. It was a land-based "nobility", organized for combat to gain control over territories. There were also the *ulama* skilled in the *shariat*, some of whom served as state functionaries like the *kazi*; and there was the Sufi complex. That was about all. Indigenous converts, whose numbers grew slowly, were devoid of any notable, institutional bases on which to bank for ambitious initiatives for their times. Put otherwise, the Mughals at their peak had an apparatus for gathering in the revenues and for continuing military expansion; but there were limits to the cultural baggage that they had brought with them, had appropriated in India, or could continue to access in western or central Asia. The Mughal authorities lacked the institutional means, and the skilled manpower needed, for probing, let alone monitoring, societies beyond the oceans: societies which were beginning to impinge on Mughal affairs with growing confidence and to increasing effect.

This thinness of intellectual and institutional resources for comprehending the unfamiliar was becoming manifest already in the eighteenth century (Mujeeb 1965: 314, 507). By the mid-nineteenth century, as we shall see, the *ulama* alone could muster a relatively comprehensive, if myopic, vision for the future. They could draw upon their networks to establish a large institution, the *madrasa* at Deoband (Chap. 5). They were committed to Islamic learning, in both form and substance: the bearer of what I have called Islam's second, scripturalist cultural style. All their commitment and all their labours could do little, however, to augment their flock's capacity for confronting the unfamiliar. The corpus crucial in the nineteenth century was that of western learning – and the civilizational setting that had spawned that learning. The *ulama*'s single-minded labours did manage to persuade many in their flock to distantiate, and to differentiate, themselves from their non-Muslim neighbours. This major reconfiguration had consequences that will engage us.

New Differentials: The Past in Imagining the Future

We have been examining the nineteenth century largely by asking what happened to social groups, to their identities, interests, social bonds and animosities, in a context of enormous changes – in communications, in the forms and substance of available learning, in the cutting edges of the economy. Activity at another level mattered at least as much in shaping the course of events: the imaginative responses to colonial subordination, galling for Muslim and Hindu alike. Authors on both sides delved into the past in search of ground on which to imagine for themselves futures more worthy than their present. These efforts of imagination, it turned out, put Muslims and Hindus on somewhat divergent tracks. The nineteenth century sense of colonial humiliations merged with memories of earlier centuries; the sense of the past, too, took forms that were often exclusive, mutually opposed.

I begin with Bankimchandra Chattopadhyaya (or Chatterji, 1838–94), the mid-nineteenth century figure whose literary output gave new turns to thought in Bengali literature and far beyond (Kaviraj 1995). Bankim had imbibed the western tradition extensively but found colonial subjugation humiliating; he was a colonial administrator too. Colonial arrangements were intrinsically unequal, and Bankim was acutely aware of how indigenous traditions and practices had been abased, both in colonial institutional routines (as in the courts), and in the attitudes of people around him. A key element in the prevailing image of the Bengali was that of being submissive, and short on physical strength. To generate self-images of greater worth, Bankim made several moves, especially in his later novels.

One set of moves centred on questions of identity and of the will to resist highhandedness. He looked for several different kinds of social spaces, and for *identities* on which to fasten his vision for the future: caste, Bengali, Hindu, Indian, all covered by the term *jati* (Kaviraj 1995: 128, 145). At the last level, Indian, he found that he could make a second move, namely, to locate in the past symbols of resistance that would serve as models, for the present and for the future, even though he wrapped them in the fiction of his historical novels. Locating the paradigms of resistance in these fictional accounts of the past reflected his judgment that he could not afford to challenge the colonial regime, his employer, frontally, especially since he had heavy debts to repay on behalf of his father and brother. (Even then, his novel, *Anandamath*, attracted the government's displeasure; and it did later become a major inspiration for activists against the Partition of Bengal, 1905. Lipner 2005: 47; Raychaudhuri 1988: 117–20.) Whatever be the defence for Bankim, Sumit Sarkar's comment remains pertinent:

> If true, this explanation only reveals all the more clearly the unconscious but almost universal bhadralok assumption that the sentiments of Muslim contemporaries were not worthy of serious notice, since the English-educated among them (who alone could be – and were usually – treated as social equals) were just a handful while the vast majority were 'ignorant' peasants. Patriotism tended to be identified with Hindu revivalism, 'Hindu' and 'national' came to be used as almost synonymous terms ... (1973: 411).

The agents of resistance in these Bankim texts can be seen to be "Hindu"; in one case the hero is a Rajput chief, up against Aurangzeb. Sudipta Kaviraj sees Bankim's thought on the relations between Muslims and Hindus "as a circuit of tension ..., a question whose urgency he obviously felt, but to which he could give only unclear and troubled answers" (Kaviraj 1995: 130). "The question of subjection is often asked (by Bankim) in terms of a long seven centuries, though what to do with the residue if Hindus constitute the possible nation is never asked" (*ibid.*: 129). Parts of his work have earned Bankim a reputation for being hostile to Muslims, and for contributing to the rise of communal consciousness, a reputation that Kaviraj insists is undeserved (*ibid.*: 1995: 186f, n62). However Bankim fares at the bar of history ultimately, the responses to his writings have taken two tracks: inspiring much anti-colonial sentiment and activity, while many Muslims saw these as hostile to them.

Sudhir Chandra notes a similar ambivalence in a wide range of nineteenth century regional literature: on one side, a sense of "Muslims as foreigners", which was yet "restrained by pragmatic considerations of Hindu–Muslim unity" and, on the other, "a ... larger view of the Indian nation in which Muslims were integral": "both these views were parts of a complex attitude characterized by ambiguities, contradictions and unresolved tensions" (1992: Chap. 3). The writing of Harishchandra (1850–85) – poet, writer, influential Hindi journal editor, and lay religious leader in Banaras – Vasudha Dalmia sees him recurring to the categories "we" or "us". In his early writings, the conception of Hindustan is that of a territorial entity, in a manner that "Hindu" would include Muslims and others living in India. Later in his short life, he veered towards a more exclusive conception of India as Bharatvarsh, defined by the heritage of Vedas and other indigenous scriptures – while continuing to make bows towards Muslims until the end (1997: Chap. 5; also Chandra 1992: 117–25). These nineteenth century authors were ahead of their times, if one may say so; their "creative" writings helped aggravate relationships as the levels of contestation rose in later generations.

A different window on the past was opened by the Orientalists working in Calcutta and elsewhere between the late eighteenth and the mid-nineteenth centuries. In these texts Hindu revivalists found much of interest concerning their own sense of the past (Kopf 1969). Harishchandra in Banaras, in the 1870s, also found a use for the evolving Orientalist corpus. He offered influential formulations concerning interlinkages between, and the historical evolution of, the various sects lying in the Hindu space (Dalmia 1995: 195–203). In Tamil Nadu, non-Brahmins as well as Brahmins harnessed Orientalist scholarship in support of their respective, Dravidian and Brahminical, interpretations of the past – and their claims on the present (Pandian 2007: Chaps. 2, 4, and 5). Vivekananda was in contact with several contemporary interpreters of Vedanta in Europe (Beckerlegge 2006: 223–26, 249). All these protagonists found much of interest in this European scholarship; but some Arya Samajis in Lahore were dismissive of that work since its appreciation of the Vedic tradition fell short of their own claims for it (Jones 1976: 164–66).

The ancient past uncovered by this body of Orientalist scholarship was, inevitably, wholly non-Islamic. The visions and aspirations on the Muslim side built, instead, on the wider political and civilizational record of Islam. The Central and West Asian origins apart, some Muslim ideologues celebrated, nostalgically, the symbols and ideas and achievements associated with the Abbasids, Iran, southern Spain, the Ottomans, and the like (for instance, Hali's *Musaddas*, in Shackle and Majeed 1997, and, later, Iqbal's famous poem, 'The Mosque of Cordoba': Metcalf 2004: Chap. 12). Iqbal went much further.

Iqbal's great asset lay in his considerable familiarity with modern western philosophy as well as the Islamic tradition. In his 1930 lectures in Madras, he examined the sources of what he regarded as the stasis in Islamic religious thought in "the last five hundred years" (2003: 13, 121-23). His attempt at its "reconstruction" turned on (*a*) asking why this stasis, (*b*) pointing to the periods of great creativity to say that a creative, open-ended, forward-looking style has been natural to Islam at certain junctures, and (*c*) showing that much in modern western thought, like empiricism, was already anticipated, and developed, in the Quran and other elements in the Islamic tradition (*ibid*.: Chap. 5). (His style is reminiscent of the efforts of men like Vidyasagar, noted in Chapter 3: to scan the tradition one considers one's own for justifications – and anticipations – for ideas and practices that one considers worthy of emulation from the West.) Iqbal's poetry secured him a stellar place among the makers of Pakistan, but his 1930 Madras lectures could not pass muster with the orthodoxy (Faruqi 1981: 336).

The implications of the distant peaks of Islamic achievement turned out to be rather thinner for Muslim society in India than happened on the Hindu side; and we might ask why. It will be remembered that Islam's refulgent climaxes in the past had been associated with moments of what I have earlier called Islam's expansive, outgoing cultural style (pp. 2-3). These were times when the bearers of several other traditions – Jewish, Christian, Hellenistic – had joined the Arabs under the banner of Islam; and with this open social stance, "Persian administrative and political thinking, Hellenistic techniques of philosophizing and of secular science, Indian mathematics and medicine were mastered effortlessly" (von Grunebaum 1955: 23). The question that was seldom asked is: what would be the consequences of letting Islam's other, scripturalist, backward-looking, cultural style gain ascendence, as began to happen in India in the late nineteenth century under the leadership of Deoband?

ය≫

All the foregoing were, in any case, elite enterprises which, as we shall see, came to affect the shared everyday life on the ground only gradually. It was the religious confrontation, however, that aroused the stronger passions. In his *Satyarthaprakash*, Dayananda was venomous both on the orthodox Hindu religious tradition, Sanatana Dharma, and on the scriptures of Islam and Christianity; it was the sparks from his attack on Islam that turned out to be lethal (see Chap. 6, esp. p. 148).

New differentials: Elective bodies

Did the Muslim lags in commerce and industry, and in western education, have *political* fallouts? Given the structure of Indian society historically, the advantages of knowledge, skills, networks, capital, and the like have tended to be transmitted, informally or formally, along the channels of family, kinship, *jati*, and sometimes sect. Consequently, in the limited framework of colonial education and economy, these advantages tended to snowball in favour of small groups which entered these activities early, leaving a sense of relative deprivation among several others. In everyday Muslim perception in many regions however, it was the larger category "Hindu" that was socially and economically ascendant. Then there was power. Even though sovereign power had passed to the British, there remained bits of power at other levels for which Indians could compete.

In positions of subordinate power, as in government jobs, it seemed in the late nineteenth century that Hindus were gaining the upper hand in several areas. There were also the institutions of local self-government; and elections to them, introduced in 1883, foreshadowed the new basis of political legitimacy: electoral success. These elective bodies could decide on matters like levying local taxes, awarding local contracts, and deciding between rival claims to public spaces in favour of one side or the other. Franchise in elections for these bodies was limited by income and property; and therefore in several regions Hindus tended to be over-represented in these bodies – even where Muslims were in a majority, which was one more ground for contention (Ahmed 1981: 161f on Bengal; Robinson 1975: 65 on UP). With the spread of the elective principle to more arenas – Provincial Councils, University Senates – the same difficulty kept reappearing (Robinson 1975: 48, 142)

In wider arenas, "Explicitly political action [in formal settings in the nineteenth century] was limited to the associations of educated men" (Seal 1968: 15). Leading lawyers among them, especially, made money, gained status, emerged as spokesmen for others (at times their clients), and got to know each other as *public men* (*ibid.*: Chap. 3). The newly educated men loomed large in "the politics of the associations" from the 1820s on, and it is the networks active in these diverse associations that foreshadowed the Indian National Congress which first met in 1885 (*ibid.*: Chaps 5 and 6). We have seen earlier the proto-political role of the Indian Association, supported by the Brahmos, since the mid-1870s (p. 49f).

Ostensibly for the sake of administrative efficiency, a key element in Curzon's decision to partition the Bengal Presidency in 1905 was the wish to clip the wings of the articulate, restive Bengali (principally Hindu) *bhadralok* in Calcutta – and to draw Bengali Muslims in the east to a larger share of the opportunities there. The extent, and the intensity, of (the overwhelmingly Hindu) "nationalist" resistance to this decision relied heavily on Hindu themes and religious symbolism. Given the intensity of this opposition, the Partition was annulled in 1911. For Bengali Muslims the setback was bitter; the whole episode served to aggravate Muslim apprehensions for the future (Sarkar 1973).

For the lags in education and government employment, Muslim leadership had earlier sought redress through political means: that is through demands addressed to the colonial regime for *separate* facilities where Muslims would be protected from Hindu competition. Their growing sense of a distinctive identity persuaded them to demand an extension of the principle to separate electorates, to ensure that Muslim representatives in electoral bodies would be at least proportionate, and elected by Muslim voters alone. As the separation of electorates was accepted in several arenas, between 1909 and 1919, the mega-categories "Muslim" and "Hindu" became a major axis around which the politics of the subcontinent would henceforth turn (Robinson 1975: 144–73 and elsewhere).

We have separated these several processes into the economic, the social, and the political but, of course, all these lay mixed together in social reality. Resources arising in landholdings, commerce, or political patronage funded various social and political moves; professional incomes, especially as lawyers, launched political careers; and Indian officials in the early colonial period would use privileged information and cash resources to aggrandize their landholdings (see p. 27, n14).

The feeling of vulnerability is subjective, psychological; and anyone, certainly any anxious group, can worry itself stiff. And where two or more such groups see each other as the source of their troubles, each may act in ways that put the others on edge. Both sides can thus lock each other into spirals of rising anxiety and a sense of vulnerability – in a manner such that each would, in retrospect, have reasons enough to wallow in its own long sense of injury and feelings of victimhood.

Nineteenth and early twentieth century Hindus too could worry themselves into feeling vulnerable. That the principal north Indian thrones since the thirteenth century had gone to immigrant conquerors, and their descendants, worried many. Hindus – for Bankimchandra

Chatterji, Bengali Hindus – have been physically weak, it was often said, and their segmentation into all manner of *jatis* made it difficult for them to coordinate in resistance, making them weak socially and politically (Kaviraj 1995: Chap. 4, pp. 126 on). Would the past repeat itself? Pradip Kumar Datta discusses U. N. Mukherji's *Hindus – a dying race* (1909), which raised the spectre of Hindus' imminent extinction owing to their numerous alleged weaknesses compared with Muslims. Late in the twentieth century, the "dying race" text was still being pressed to stoke Hindu anxieties (P. K. Datta 1999: 22–35). These worries preyed later on V. D. Savarkar and the RSS ideologues, among others. In the new circumstances, these men tied their ideologies to the Hindus' alleged indigenousness; and with the confidence of numbers, and of growing wealth, an urge to get even began to focus on Muslims (Datta 2006).

These indigenous responses arose partly from the fact of disempowerment in the colonial ambience. There was the colonial humiliation; and, being disempowered, a sense of being absolved of responsibility for the larger whole. Consequently, by the turn of the century, various zealots felt free to push to the hilt the cause of their own groups, which they defined in terms of religious identities. Their campaigns could arouse the fervours for one or another holy cause – and generate conflicts; but law and order, it was assumed, could be left to the colonial administration. There was nothing in their knowledge and experience to warn them of the likely long-term consequences of their visions and their campaigns.

The ambiguous legacy from the medieval period had included older traditions of thought, articulation, and public discussion in terms of the interests of the categories "Hindu" and "Muslim" explicitly. For instance, Eknath, famous Marathi bhakti poet (1553–99), composed a debate between a Hindu and a Turk (Muslim), illustrating "the intensity of religious tensions and polemics between the two communities in sixteenth century Maharashtra" (Wagle 1997: 139–41). The principal religious traditions remained fortified with their religious specialists, focal places (temples/mosques; hallowed pilgrimages), scriptures made venerable by their antiquity, systematic ideologies, and much else that made them durable. This kind of apparatus was scant for the alternate, irenic traditions in the spirit of a Kabir or a Nanak: traditions which were disparaging of exclusivism and supportive, rather, of shared space. Nanak's case is an instructive exception. His influence did acquire staying power – by becoming institutionalized as a distinctive religious tradition itself. Subsequent echoes from his disparagement of sectarianism have been fainter. In the circumstances of the nineteenth century, it was the protagonists of the major religious traditions that found advocates relatively quickly.

We have noted the sharp limits to the room for mobilizing through the embedded social bonds, say of family or *jati*. These limits have been transcended along two axes. We have discussed a *positive* axis, which lay through religious symbols and traditions: traditions that had been broadcast through the centuries. The next chapter will continue with this axis. There has also been a *negative* axis: the perception, that is, of an adversary who can be resisted only through a larger alliance or solidarity. In Bankim, Arya Samaj, Tilak, V. D. Savarkar, and the like (as well as in Deoband), there was the implicit search for larger solidarities, and a sense of agency, the confidence that societies can be reconstituted; and therefore they sought to identify internal weaknesses, and to project alternate visions to undo the weaknesses. Chapter 6 will show that the spiral of contention, whose beginnings we have seen, strengthened this axis for the growth of solidarities, separately, for both Muslims and Hindus. For both these axes, positive and negative, we have seen that there were precedents in the ambiguous legacy of earlier centuries.

Much of the new social capital – active social networks, with habits of rallying to shared purposes – arising during the nineteenth century, then, formed around exclusive religious identities. The associated habits of mind entered such new domains as those of western education, the modern professions, and electoral politics also. By the time sovereign power, through elections, loomed on the horizon, these clusters of social capital were in place, available for such purposes as would stir the imaginations of the time.

5

parallel processes

Institutions systematically direct individual memory and channel our perceptions into forms compatible with the relations they authorize. They fix processes that are essentially dynamic, they hide their influence, and they rouse our emotions to a standardized pitch on standardized issues. Add to all this that they endow themselves with rightness and send their mutual corroboration cascading through all the levels of our information system. No wonder they easily recruit us into joining their narcissistic self-contemplation.

Douglas, *How institutions think*[1]

Actor and Structure

During the nineteenth century, the very structure of Indian society was changing, separatively, in a way that sociologists and historians have had difficulty in grasping. The previous chapter noticed the several sources for the separative impulses. There were the tendencies internal to religious traditions, there were the situational anxieties, and there were the growing episodes – and experience – of communal violence. I have suggested earlier that we use the word "structure" to refer to "the totality of conditions within which one acts" (p. xxvi); these conditions include the society's patterns of relationships, differences, oppositions, and identities. A complex society can also carry several ideologies that are active simultaneously, seeking to maintain or to change the prevailing arrangements, often in contrary ways.

The ideologies and arrangements, then, may or may not be mutually consistent and, in any case, these are not self-propelling. Complex societies

[1] Epigraph in Chowdhury 2006.

are usually thick with conflicts, not only between persons and groups, as they pursue their diverse interests, but also between the various ideologies: the alternate visions of the kinds of arrangements that their protagonists would like to see prevail. For example, Akbar's vision of a multi-religious polity competed with some Islamic scholars' vision of Islamic supremacy. Akbar used his control over the imperial political apparatus to advance his vision of the polity; the *ulama* used their influence over members of the nobility to try to inflect imperial practice to conform to *their* vision. Insofar as Akbar, or the *ulama*, had their way, their society and polity changed somewhat. Using the theatre as a metaphor for society, we may speak of Akbar, the *ulama*, and everyone else as "actors" or "agents" in a "social drama". Insofar as they seek to influence, to alter, the prevailing state of affairs, they exercise their *agency* in relation to their society. Early seventeenth century north Indian society showed the marks of both these visions – and those of others, say Pratap's, who would not submit to the Mughal order (Taft 1994: 227ff).

A society – or the structure of a society – is in continual flux, then, as its members try to bend the prevailing arrangements to their own interests and purposes and ideologies. Thanks to their labours, the prevailing arrangements may change a little; successful revolutionaries change these arrangements radically. When their labours are done, what you find is a somewhat different structure. The process continues in time. There will always be other agents, pursuing their interests and purposes, and continuing to modify the structure further. If these various agents follow a particular ideology, and, even more, belong to an effective organization that is committed to the ideology, the changes they generate will have a cumulative character, these can have a certain direction, as our discussion in this chapter will demonstrate.

The exercise of *agency* is not limited to effecting immediate changes in society. It covers also the process of drawing together ideas – the work of shaping an ideology – that visualize the future in one or another key. Those who "do ideological work" are also agents, contributing to the reshaping of the structure, by inspiring other actors, then and later, to act in particular ways.[2]

---

[2] These paragraphs simplify a theme that I considered at length in Saberwal 2004b.

Memories and Contrasting Choices

Key events and processes since the nineteenth century have been recounted often enough to have become something of a catechism, one of the several that encapsulate one or another version of shared, at times stereotyped, memory. On one side is the seventeenth century figure of Shivaji, intrepid founder of a major Hindu kingdom, on whom a reviving Hindu consciousness was to fasten throughout northern India. Next to him in this hall of memories stands the mid-nineteenth century Bankimchandra Chattopadhyaya, or Bankim Chatterji, whom we met earlier, writing to foment aspirations to greater physical strength, collective pride, and resoluteness – with his choice of heroic actors shifting between the Bengali, the Hindu, and the Indian. Some of his writings, and some of the activity these inspired – as in the Swadeshi movement in the early twentieth century – are often interpreted as having been directed against Muslims (Lipner 2005: 60–104 has a candid, balanced appraisal).

If Bankim's influence came from the power of his imagination, expressed in his creative writing, that of the Arya Samaj came from its new form for a religious organization: a string of member-managed local congregations. In course of his travels earlier, Dayananda, the ascetic of Gujarati Brahmin background, had spent four months in 1872 in Calcutta with the Brahmo leaders; later he found a receptive audience among Hindu merchants and professionals in Lahore in Punjab (Jones 1976: 34f). He presented his vision in what became the foundational text for the Arya Samaj, *Satyarthaprakash* (Light of Truth). Reacting to what he saw as the superstitious encrustations in current orthodox Hindu beliefs and practices, and the aggressive Christian missionaries, Dayananda proposed a faith resting on the pristine purity of the millennia old Vedas. His principal text commented scathingly on beliefs and practices in the Brahminical tradition – its cults and sects and Puranic texts, idol worship, bathing in sacred rivers, and caste differences – and summoned all Hindus into the Arya Samaj; but he saved his heaviest artillery for Christian and Islamic scriptures and beliefs. The early Aryas dominated the professions, and commerce and moneylending, in largely agrarian Punjab. The Samaj was untrammelled initially by much received dogma, and its members were able to respond to their setting as they thought fit. Their support for the Arya Samaj reflected their anxieties over the stance of the government. The colonial government was especially solicitous of the landed groups there, for its army recruitment depended heavily on the Punjabi peasantry. Its support for them included assured jobs in the government, and legal protection against what were thought to be wily urban, largely Hindu, merchants and moneylenders (Gilmartin 1988: 26–38).

The landed groups were spread over all of Punjab's religious categories; but the Hindu merchants' anxiety came to be channelled into the Arya Samaj, with its diverse agenda. It was central to that agenda to press an aggressive Arya/Hindu identity. In turning the late nineteenth century Punjab into a setting for contention between social categories defined by religion, the Arya Samaj made a significant contribution. Its emerging ideology made it an actor in the prehistory of Hindutva though its major achievements included the gathering of energies into a range of mainstream educational institutions, and critiquing of Hindu social practices, including the caste order (Jones 1976. On proto-Hindutva, see also Pandian 2007: 57 on Tamil Brahmin publicist, G. Subramania Iyer [1855–1916]; and Sharma 2003 on a series of influential figures in the late nineteenth and early twentieth centuries).

There were significant differences in the internal structuring of Hindu and Muslim social spaces in the late nineteenth century, and these differences were reflected in the processes active among them, as in the varied social "reform" movements. Where such movements among Muslims tended to spread far and wide, corresponding initiatives among Hindus ran into barriers associated with *jati* and region. Between the several regions there certainly were interactions, whose magnitudes grew with improving communications; in the 1860s already, Dayananda had visited the Brahmos in Calcutta and orthodox Brahmins in Banaras – before founding the Arya Samaj in Lahore. Hindu responses to these impulses, however, were and remained decentralized and diversified, even though major elements of this tradition – the caste order, a scriptural tradition, pilgrimage centres and the like – covered the subcontinent. Institutions like the Arya Samaj and the Ramakrishna Mission gained momentum within limited regions; despite their claims of universalistic ambitions, their impulses did not carry much beyond their initial regions. This diversity of responses may be tracked to the distinctive quality of each region with its own language and cultural tradition, its own patterns of caste dominance and conflict, long tradition of numerous *gurus*, each independent with his own flock, and the varying exposures to western ideas. While the Arya Samaj struck a response in Punjab, where Brahminical orthodoxy had been weak, the Brahmins of Banaras were quick to rebuff Dayananda (Dalmia 1997: 385). In Pune in 1876, even while reformists like Ranade welcomed him, their orthodox rivals lampooned him publicly (Naregal 2001: 257, 266).

Impulses for "reform" within the Hindu social space were also shaped by the reformers' diverse locations within the caste order. We saw that a *jati* was a corporate group; and in coping with the anxieties of the times, the Hindus seem to have found anchor and support within their *jati*s: at one level was the assurance of belonging within one's *jati*; at another, one could try to draw on networks within, and adjoining, one's *jati*, in pursuing a variety of purposes (see p. 34 on). The purposes canvassed ranged *from* that of using caste funds for support in educational institutions *to* that of the lower castes contesting their traditional caste disabilities.

The diversity associated with the numerous *jati*s and their varied locations in the caste hierarchy was sharpened further by a differential exposure to western ideas. It was basically within the family and the *jati* that decisions would be made over whether to send children to institutions of western education, and to risk other forms of exposure to the West, like travelling to England. So strong was the impulse in some families to advance in the new professions – law, medicine – that they were willing to defy the ritual prohibitions against crossing the oceans; and this defiance became frequent enough that religious authorities, seeing the writing on the wall, would drop the prohibition (Conlon 1977 has one case). Brahmins were among the earliest to take to western education; they did *not* exercise any general influence for, or against, others following suit. This combination of diverse motivations, arising from one's location in the caste order, and the varying measures of exposure to the West, led to dispersed – and diverse – social reform activity among Hindus. In some cases, this activity, especially among the lower castes, went alongside scorching critiques of the Brahminical tradition, wherein indigenous ideological strands and those taken from the West would reinforce each other (see p. 38f).

Responses to the colonial setting were not limited to the realm of the religious traditions. Among the issues being addressed was that of identities: who are "we"? That is to say, how should "our" social boundaries be drawn, who all should be included among "we" or "us"? The previous chapter noticed the shifting conceptions of the Banarsi litterateur, Harishchandra (p. 103f). Such authors took extensive recourse to *Hindu* religious symbolism in constructing their idea of

parallel processes 115

what the *Indian* nation was (van der Veer 1996: 12f). Later exponents in this vein were to include Savarkar, the several Hindu Sabhas, and the RSS ideologues (Hansen 1999: 75–84). As the separative messages spread out, what was taken as common sense was itself shifting.

Heading the hall of memories of Muslim consciousness is the outstanding mid-eighteenth century *alim*, Shah Waliullah (1703–62), meditating on the remains of the empire. Over the preceding centuries, the leading lights of Islam in the subcontinent in India had taken the cover of Muslim power for granted. Islam had reached large numbers, and its propagators counted on slow infusions of ritual and symbols over time to give the faith depth and intensity. This had suited the *political* establishments too: their eyes were focussed instead on power, territory, and revenues. It fell to Waliullah to think through the prospects even as the buttresses of power fell away. In looking for fresh bulwarks, he mounted:

> a major individual effort at intellectual synthesis and systematization, an unprecedented *tatbiq* [bringing together of religious approaches and interpretations]. Troubled by the disorder he saw around him, perhaps even sensing that he was at the end of an age, he sought to stem the tide of decline by consolidating and clarifying the entire body of the Islamic tradition. Knowledge of the truth would bring Muslims to religious obedience that would end the divisions and deviations he so greatly deplored. (Metcalf 1982: 36.)

Waliullah wished for, and encouraged, a strong Muslim ruler to take the throne. Independently, and regardless of that hope, however, he "sought an important role for the religious leadership, the kind of role he himself exemplified in advising rulers, guiding the [Islamic] community, and safeguarding the intellectual heritage" – even without the props of power (Metcalf 1982: 36). Subsequently, leaders of the movements for Islamic revival in nineteenth century India, who could not count on the support of a Muslim ruler, found continuing inspiration in the path Waliullah had charted. In the past, strong Muslim rulers might keep the *ulama* at arm's length but, with these rulers gone, and the other elites disoriented, the *ulama* could reclaim a public role, as interpreters of the *shariat* for the times. They had traditions of austerity, of piety, and of lifestyles that were dedicated to the faith and to Islamic learning. They had a history of involvement in government, especially on the judicial side, giving *fatawa* (sing *fatwa*), learned opinions, drawing on the corpus of the *shariat* going back to the ninth and tenth centuries; and they had other emblems of legitimacy to draw on, as we shall see. Of all the several *ashraf* categories, the leading *ulama* were placed best in the late nineteenth century to show the way among the Muslims. When complex civilizations get into difficulties, they can often fall back on resources that are supportive: with the fall of Rome, the Catholic Church stepped into the breach; when indigenous polities gave way in India, the caste order continued to function; when Chinese empires fell apart, the Confucian literati, who were potential officials of an empire, continued to oversee their localities, waiting to regroup around a new emperor. Among the late nineteenth century Muslims, the mantle fell on the *ulama*.

Waliullah's eighteenth century vision had responded to the anxieties that were then beginning to assail. His sons and successors in Delhi continued to nurse this vision. It took several generations for these anxieties to become acute and widespread enough to spur initiatives for trying to realize the vision; and, by then, novel institutional forms and technologies were also coming on line. The vision that emerged centred on the imperatives to foster the faith, to propagate a commitment to Islamic practices and to the *shariat*, religious law, and to strengthen the religious identity among the believers. Though largely bereft of supporting state power, a community of believers in Islam that would be guided by the *ulama* could be nurtured. For shaping that lifeway, clear templates were available in Quranic injunctions, in the example of the Prophet's own life, and in the principles of pure Islamic living enunciated in the long tradition of Islamic law.

We have already noted the turn that processes of reform took among Muslims. The eighteenth century Muslim space in the subcontinent was, if anything, even *more* disaggregated, diversified, than the Hindu social space. There had not been much effort in the subcontinent earlier, under Mughal auspices, to place Muslims in a unified social framework. Ishtiaq Husain Qureshi has a chapter entitled "Towards integration into a single community" (1985: Chap. 4). Aware of the Muslims' diverse social locations, he maintained that it was the hostility of their Hindu neighbours, especially that of local Hindu chiefs to Muslim power, that held the Muslims of the subcontinent together. (Qureshi overlooked the significance of all the Muslims who served Hindu rulers, and vice versa.) Apart from this, he dilated on Muslims from beyond the subcontinent being welcomed to strengthen the local (*ashraf*) ranks, and developments in Urdu and Hindi poetry, music, and architecture. How these latter made for the "integration" of Muslims "into a single community" remains, at the end, unclear.

Qureshi mentions, too, the spread of Urdu speakers into the various regions; and this could be seen in the nineteenth century in their presence in cities like Calcutta, Hyderabad, and Madras. Most Muslims in the subcontinent – Sind, Gujarat, Punjab, Delhi and vicinity, Bengal, Tamil Nadu, Malabar and elsewhere – spoke the local language, however, and were fully part of their regional societies, where they had originated. On the other hand, although Muslim society has had caste analogues, these social groups have been somewhat open, a tendency reinforced by conscious efforts at Islamization. These processes we have considered earlier.

A major impulse for change among Muslims came from the theological school at Deoband (founded 1867) and other leading *ulama*. It strove for a distinctive community whose members would abide by Islamic religious injunctions more thoroughly than hitherto. The ideal of a more exclusive social and religious ambience would be promulgated, one that would be conducive to a purer Islamic lifestyle. Subsequent decades saw concerted efforts to pull the numerous Muslim groups, located within the regional caste orders, away from other religious influences. The reach of this effort was comprehensive, covering in principle the totality of individual and social existence. What Gail Minault (1998: 307) says, in reviewing her account of reform concerning Muslim women's place in society at the turn of the nineteenth century, holds more generally: "Scriptural authority ... was asserted over customary practice."

Guided by religious preceptors, the *ulama*, the intention was to foster a community in which to live in accord with the injunctions in the Quran, with models from the Prophet's own life, his wife Khadija, daughter Fatima, and close companions, and their social relationships: sources from which had had been drawn the principles that underlay the *shariat*. The effort was to persuade their followers to shape their individual lives, and to reorder social relationships, following the principles of pure living as enunciated in the long tradition of Islamic law (Metcalf 1982: 150, 152, and elsewhere). They would be insulated as far as possible from the laws and the courts of the colonial regime on one side and, on the other, from the caste order, its ideology, and its tumult of deities.

By virtue of their distinctive beliefs, practices, and personal bearing, India's Muslims would then stand apart from their neighbours.

The moral authority over, and the guidance of, the subcontinent's Muslims would remain in Muslim hands, though these would not wield political authority. In the process the Muslims would acquire a sense of community, of shared existence. These "constructions of community", to use a phrase from Rajat K. Ray, relied not only on the actions of the religious leaders but also on "memories of the past" (2003: 101). Reinforcement for these identities would come from yet other directions, as the next chapter will show.

Deoband: Impetus, Vision, Strengths

The stinging aftermath of 1857, when the British picked on the Muslims for harsh reprisal, had included "the destruction of the *madrasa* started by Shah Waliullah" in Delhi in the previous century (Minault 1982: 25). This was part of the impetus for initiating the new *madrasa* at Deoband near Saharanpur in western UP, in 1867. This was a time when the old elite, which included leading *ulama* too, was finding itself cornered, its routes to power, status, and influence narrowing, or threatened (Chapter 4). A group of *ulama* saw here a historic opportunity to provide leadership as anticipated by Waliullah nearly a century back: to foster a true and authentic Islam, subcontinentally, among people, a great many of whom had been Muslim but nominally. They would launch an institution that would advance that vision vigorously. The institution took as model Delhi College, established in 1825, which we have seen earlier (p. 64).

The *ulama*'s project was backed by members of the erstwhile ruling class, which had dispersed through western UP. In reconfiguring the social space along lines of religious difference, the influence of Deoband has been far-reaching and durable. By the late nineteenth century, its alumni were active in Bengal (Ahmed 1981: 83f); and a century and a half after its founding, all South Asia still has to reckon with it (Metcalf 2004: Chap. 11). Where did its strengths arise?

The new *madrasa*, by far the largest institution of its kind in south Asia, was led by a substantial group of distinguished *ulama*, Islamic religious scholars, who had close bonds with the erstwhile ruling class. Their learning had centred on the *shariat*, which carried the halo of having been codified more than a thousand years ago, during and following Abbasid times; it proved to be a critical resource in seeking to fashion a distinctive way of life. Muzaffar Alam has argued that the *shariat* used to be flexible, given the possibility of multiple readings of the prophetic traditions. It acquired its latter day rigidity during the colonial period –since the British tended to interpret variant interpretations as evidence not of flexibility but of the *ulama*'s failings (2004: 8). The *ulama* who founded Deoband provided leadership for taking the training of Islamic religious scholars to a new intensity. One great advantage of the *madrasa* at Deoband lay in its being by far the largest institution, organized along modern lines, its students drawn from all over the subcontinent and beyond. "Between 1907 and 1912, enrolment at Deoband leapt from 267 to 600 and the [institution's] buildings were extended" (Robinson 1975: 274). By 1980, the enrollment appears to have reached 1821 (Saiyed and Talib 1985: 195).

The focus on the Prophet. The Islamic tradition has carried an intense focus on the person of the Prophet, a focus more intense than any other religious tradition has conferred on its central figure. The origins for this lie partly in the Prophet's extraordinary life. Founding a religious tradition is rare enough; Mohammad went on also, uniquely for a major religious visionary, to found a state in the hitherto stateless Arab world. No wonder the Prophet rose to so lofty a pedestal for his followers, though this heavy emphasis appears to have evolved "throughout the Muslim world in the nineteenth century" (Metcalf 1982: 350, citing Annemarie Schimmel). The Prophet's centrality to the tradition has found expression in diverse ways:

- Quran, the scripture: attributed to his authorship;
- *hadis*, accounts of his deeds and sayings: illustrating for all Muslims how the Prophet had himself lived. These beckon them all to live as he did. "Veneration of the Prophet plays a central role in Islamic mysticism", notes Francis Robinson (2001: 82f; Sanyal 1996: 151–63). Saintly men are remembered for having modelled their own lives on that of the Prophet in the minutest detail. "The ulama modeled themselves on the Prophet," notes Metcalf (1982: 350) concerning Deobandis, "and ordinary people modeled themselves on them".[3]
- the *shariat*, Islamic law, a comprehensive code for living pious lives along the path shown by the Prophet in the seventh century.

---

[3] von Grunebaum (1955: 22) noted that, in transforming the ancestral Arab culture, a key move in Islam lay in "the delineation of a new 'standard' type of life, that is, a new human ideal, and a detailed pattern for its realization in a model biography extending from conception to beyond the day of judgment."

It was initially formulated by Islamic scholars on the basis of the Quran and *hadis* between the eighth to tenth centuries (Hodgson 1974: vol. 1, book 2, Chaps 3 and 4);
- everyday *namaz*, as well as the *Hajj*, the most sacred of pilgrimages, are oriented towards Mecca, where the Prophet had lived and taught, and Medina, where he had built the first Islamic state, and where, some believe, he lives on in his tomb. The significance of the *Hajj* went far beyond a simple exaltation of the Prophet: "The institution of the Haj ... provided the members of this world community with an annual renewal of the contact with 'the central point' (Ray 2003: 91)." It also renewed their awareness of the world community itself; and;
- Sayyids' high status in Muslim society who, it is claimed, descend genealogically from the Prophet himself.

Ahmad Riza Khan, the central figure in the Barelwi sect, advised his followers that, in choosing for themselves a *pir*, Sufi teacher, a major consideration should be that "the chain of transmission (*silsila*) should reach back from him, without a single break, to the Prophet" (Sanyal 1996: 134). The links here would of course be those of discipleship, not genealogy.

The *ulama* of Deoband carried yet another string to their bow. The scriptural base apart, they were also bridging the historic cleavage between the *ulama*, the learned in religious law, and Sufis, the seekers of mystic experience. Individual Deobandis stood in, and practised, the Sufi tradition; indeed some of them had become disciples in multiple Sufi orders, *silsilas*, partaking of the aura surrounding them all (Metcalf 1982: 158f). They brought many of their students into bonds of Sufi *pir–murid*, master–disciple relationships, individually, giving themselves chains of influence wherever their students went in later life. The more open Sufi tradition, built around a personal search for religious experience, was reoriented to fit in with the more doctrinaire Deobandi style. It discarded the older Sufi openness to other traditions, which had included, at times, the urge to try their transgressive practices.

These personal and institutional links were especially dense in western UP. Amidst the uncertainties of the late nineteenth century, the *ulama* of Deoband were able to draw to themselves multiple, disparate threads of religious authority. They led personal lives of exemplary simplicity. They gathered the many strands originating in the Prophet: being learned in the Quran, *hadis*, and the *shariat*; performing *Hajj*;

bearing the Sayyid or other high social status; and their personal devotion to the Prophet evident in countless ways. Here they had a highly charged symbolic core – the Prophet himself, all alone, and the law rooted in his words and deeds – around which to summon the faithful (Metcalf 1982: Chaps 3–6). And they had the web of former students bound to them in personal ties of Sufi discipleship.

The Deobandi *ulama* had built a strategic platform from which to say: Here's the Way. Follow a purer Islam. You have nothing to learn from the West or the Hindus. All this enabled them to advance a relatively unified doctrine, with shared tenets and symbols; and, in the light of this doctrine, to promulgate a rather uniform social vision for what had been a disparate congeries of groups in the subcontinent. The effort was to recast the Indian Muslim space so that its indigenous, caste-based, beehive-like social form would yield to Islam's unitary social design (Ray 2003: 125–33); a key institution for this effort was the *madrasa*, wherein to transmit the basic teachings of the faith. The sharp cleavages between them and some of the clusters of *ulama* elsewhere would nevertheless persist. The Barelvi sect, for instance, continued to venerate Sufi saints and their tombs, practices that Deoband rejected. The Barelvis retained a distinctive, largely rural following; but by the late nineteenth century their stance too was exclusivist, at least in relation to Hindus (e.g., Sanyal 1996: 291).

In a Muslim dominated state, a *fatwa* would have been issued by the learned in the *shariat*, as an authoritative legal opinion for the guidance of the state's officers of justice. In the colonial situation, it was turned into a medium for religious scholars to advise believers on correct Islamic beliefs and social practices. The large numbers who were reminded that, though Muslim, their lives were soaked in un-Islamic practice, needed urgent, detailed guidance regarding rites, beliefs, and conduct worthy of their faith. To a steady flow of anxious queries from all over the subcontinent, over countless perplexities, Deoband's *ulama* responded with a strong, confident stream of *fatawa*, meant to be based on the *shariat* of long standing, guiding the faithful (Metcalf 1982: 146–53).

The enquirers wished to do the right Islamic thing in a milieu fraught with both un-Islamic neighbours and un-Islamic government. In quick replies they received *fatawa* calling them unambiguously to disengage from all the misguided beliefs and practices prevailing in their vicinity, assuring them that they had nothing to learn from their Hindu neighbours or from colonial rulers – and their new educational institutions. During Deoband's first 100 years, by its own count, it sent out over 260,000 *fatawa*: an average of more than seven a day for a hundred years! The more crucial of these rulings were assembled and published in compendia for general use (Metcalf 1982: 146). The emerging technology of printing helped produce numerous other publications too: cheap booklets for elementary religious instruction, Urdu translations of the Quran and other texts; periodical journals for Islamic themes. Instruments for shaping an active Islamic consciousness were at hand (*ibid.*: 198–234).

In the vast spread of Deoband's influence, the *fatawa* were only one channel. Others included the seminary's alumni, some of whom established their own *madrasa* later, transmitting Deoband's spirit as well as syllabus; some of its teachers travelled a good deal, and others wrote tirelessly, feeding the insatiable appetite of the printing presses, and striving to promote a subcontinental sense of community among Muslims. Deoband helped reshape Muslim social horizons significantly. Urdu was Deoband's functional language, and this helped spread familiarity with the language somewhat. By way of ideas, it meant an orientation towards a corpus of Islamic texts – and to their associated languages: apart from Urdu, towards Arabic, and in smaller measure Persian.

The working of the overall process in Bengal may be taken illustratively. We have seen that Bengali Muslim villagers had originated within the region. Well into the nineteenth century, they observed restrictions on inter-dining and intermarriage – in relation not only to Hindus but also to other Muslims (Ahmed 1981: 5). Thanks, meanwhile, to such activists as Shariatullah and Titu Mir, whom we met earlier, and spurred by hostility towards their landowners, most of whom were Hindu, the Islamic consciousness had been spreading. Reviewing the process in rural Bengal, Rafiuddin Ahmed sees here a "people" turning into a "community". Symbols and slogans helped generate consciousness of solidarity, and so did a reorientation of the patterns of social interaction, through the activities of diverse religious and other associations. "Extreme rigidity of doctrinal interpretations" often marked the various reform movements, and therefore their advocates would clash; but these conflicts too served to spread awareness of the religious themes in dispute, within and between the major traditions. Indeed, the ideology of separation, drawn from the caste order, was being turned upside down: by 1873, Muslims in Pabna in eastern Bengal were refusing to eat food touched by a Hindu; and others were beginning to recoil from physical touch by a Hindu (*ibid.*: 71–73, 83, 90, 107).

The choice of language was important, especially as a badge of identity. All Bengalis had of course shared their language; but in the late nineteenth century, as contrastive identities took hold, Bengali Muslims began to feel uncomfortable with the language:

> 'Sanskritization' of Bengali no doubt contributed to their alienation, but their prime motive was a desperate quest for an uncompromising Islamic identity free of all idolatrous accretions (Ahmed 1981: 131).

Some of them toyed with the idea of switching to Urdu; others' vocabulary drew in "hundreds of Arabic and Persian words" as the campaign for Islamization moved forward; yet others "set about discovering a new pride in the Islamic heritage", expounding its religious themes in Bengali (*ibid.*: 122, 130).

Whereas the early Deoband teachers had belonged to families within the erstwhile ruling class, the *madrasa* drew many pupils from much humbler social backgrounds, clearing a path of upward social mobility for them, but also quickening the channels for carrying the process of Islamization to strata that had so long been neglected (Metcalf 1982: 245f). The ideological anchor they offered held in principle for all Muslims, or at least all Sunni Muslims, since Deoband was a Sunni seminary. Deoband's pull came to be felt even in institutions grounded in different premises. First, the College at Aligarh (estd 1875), an institution promoted in the secular mode, with an emphasis on western learning. Such was Deoband's reach that Syed Ahmad Khan discovered that he had to cede to the *ulama* control over the theological side of the institution of his dreams[4] before he could persuade Muslims to loosen their purse-strings for his project (Metcalf 1982: 323–29). Deoband's weight was felt again in the course taken by the Nadwatul Ulama (Nadwa for short, estd 1893 in Lucknow). Nadwa had been conceived with the explicit intention of accommodating, and advancing mutual understanding between, all the various sects of Islam. Shibli Numani, its best known scholar, hoped that Nadwa would draw upon the resources of western scholarship also to promote Islamic learning. Over the next two decades, however, virtually every

---

[4] Syed Ahmad Khan had long advocated the study of nature, that is of modern science, as a mode of apprehending truth; and he intended Aligarh to be a place where Muslim youth would be introduced to western learning. In his moderately revisionist ideas the *ulama* smelt blasphemy.

tendency (Shibli included), other than Deobandi, had been shown the door (Hartung 2006).

Financially, the seminary at Deoband drew large contributions from high status *ashraf* Muslims – "[those in] government service, religious leadership, trade, and landholding" (Metcalf 1982: 248) – but also from a good many in modest circumstances, sometimes spurred by their superiors. In return they had the satisfaction of getting steady guidance from the religious scholars. Deoband's size, and its faculty's calibre, made it exceptionally influential, but it was not alone. Other groups of *ulama* too were active in their own, albeit less influential, institutions. The world of the *ulama* overall was often fractious; yet there was remarkable convergence, at least in the earlier phase, in the directions they promoted regarding the Muslims' distinctive identity, and the stance they should take towards non-Muslims.

To be sure, Deoband had rivals and challengers whose religious emphases were different: for example, Firangi Mahall and the Barelvis (Robinson 2001; Sanyal 1996). We have noted Deoband's many advantages. The much older *madrasa* in Lucknow, Firangi Mahall, had trained men for service in states like Awadh that had functioned to Persian political and administrative routines; demand for these skills was collapsing, and the influence of Firangi Mahall waned. In the late nineteenth century, Deoband reoriented the *madrasa* syllabus towards offering a socio-religious anchor for Muslims living under an un-Islamic regime (Robinson 2001: 9–37; Metcalf 1982: 100f; on Barelvis, see p. 121).

The remarkable rise of Deoband's influence among Muslims in India, and beyond, was a tribute to the reach of the new technologies, especially those for communication, which began to be available in the nineteenth century: the printing press, the railways, the post office. Translations of scriptures themselves could be published to help bond believers to their religious affiliations. Several groups of visionaries were turning to these channels, each pushing its own agenda. In the nineteenth century, it turned out, it was the men of strong anchor in particular religious traditions who spoke most clearly and confidently. They drew on what were believed to be the timeless truths of their scriptures, to show the faithful how to act amidst unprecedented uncertainties. The several Muslim and Hindu institutions were given to much competitive stridency – the shaping of their ideologies was dialogic, responding to what others did (Jalal 2001: 57). The wider influence of their activities has struck many observers as having been regressive for Muslims in India (for example, Mujeeb 1965: 522f); but these observers speak from hindsight. The late nineteenth century actors did not have the skills and the habits needed for anticipating the likely *long-term* costs of their initiatives. The long-term significance of these activities, on both sides, lay in ingraining a sense of communal opposition, so that it would absorb numerous conflicts originating in varied domains: agrarian, political rivalries over elective bodies, competition for jobs. Yet, even as this opposition deepened, anthropologists working in the 1960s and later continued to find Muslims sharing religious and other cultural beliefs and practices with their non-Muslim neighbours (see various contributions to Ahmad 1973a; Fruzzetti-Ostor 1970).

Between the Arya Samaj, which we considered earlier, and Deoband, there was one crucial difference. Deoband sought to strengthen Sunni practice, an accepted orthodoxy, and therefore the Maulvis trained there could take over many of the numerous extant mosques. Led by Dayananda, the Arya Samaj, in contrast, was harsh on established Hindu institutions and practices; and therefore the vast stock of temples was closed to its functionaries and ideology. Further, in the Arya scheme of things, its spread hinged on its followers forming their own congregations; religious specialists were secondary to its vision. For their congregational worship, the Aryas had to build new premises from scratch. In the process, they generated energetic networks which worked also on diverse other activities that we considered earlier.

Reconfigurations

Separative impulses were appropriating the realms both of imagination and of ongoing experience; altogether these served to give the bar of separation greater cultural and emotional depth and density. What ideologues like Dayananda in the Arya Samaj and Rashid Ahmad at Deoband managed to do was to standardize, stereotype, such categories as "Muslim" and "Hindu". Overriding their shared humanity, the groups were being reified – being represented as if their differences were intrinsic, "natural", rather than being the results of historical, and ongoing, social processes.

Why were ordinary people willing to bear the costs of reorganizing their lives on this exclusive basis? The question will concern the next chapter, but a partial answer may be attempted here. In some cases, clearly, large categories saw substantial advantages in taking on the proferred identities. We have seen that Muslim peasants in Bengal or in Kerala saw advantage in building large, maulvi-led solidarities in order to be able to stand up to overweening Hindu *zamindars*. Hindu Jats in Haryana found in the Arya Samaj – in its texts, ideology, institutional forms, and ritual – resources that they hoped would help them challenge the lowly Shudra caste status accorded them by local Brahmins and other upper castes (p. 44). As the Jats absorbed the Arya ideology, it had a side effect: that of souring of their relationships with their Jat Muslim neighbours. Hindu Jats pressed the latter on *shuddhi*, trying to persuade them to become Hindu; and there was violence between the two groups, especially after Khilafat (N. Datta 1999: 184–86, 146–51). The relations continued to deteriorate, and the Arya Jats used the disorders of Partition for a major assault on the Muslim Jats.

Where did the ideologues get their authority for being able to persuade large numbers to follow them along this path? At one level, as in the Jat case, they were persuasive because their ideologies offered forms for social reorganization that promised to meet felt current needs. At another level, the authority of their appeals came from invoking ancient traditions. Coming down from the precolonial period were durable, exclusive networks of religious specialists, carrying their distinctive traditions and worldviews – which would have shaped their personalities too. An axiomatic, self-evident quality marked the truths of their particular traditions. To the later era of anxiety and uncertainty, such men brought matchless confidence, and offered transcendental certainty, grounded in the truths of ancient, holy scriptures.

The respective protagonists on the two sides would bring into play logics which they drew out of what they saw as their own traditions, wholly unrelated to what was happening on the other side. In Bengal, in Punjab and in western UP, they summoned their respective believers to autarkic identities: as Muslims, as Aryas, and so forth. More potently than any other social actors at the time, they were poised to appropriate the new communications – where the choice of script could already define a potential audience in some measure. In shaping their ideologies, they dug back into the depths of historical memories and scriptural resources.

The nineteenth century rediscovered also the possibility of large scale mobilization around religious and cultural symbols: symbols *decontextualized* in the sense that these could be charged up independently of any particular locality, time, or small social groups. In

Maharashtra, Tilak made much of the symbols of Ganapati and Shivaji to initiate activities, in 1894 and 1895, which added to his own political weight (Cashman 1975: Chaps 4 and 5). These protagonists had discovered that using such decontextualized symbols gave them a way to get around the segmentation which was long believed to impede wider coordination among Hindus. Likewise, on the Muslim side, we have seen the numerous strands leading back to Prophet Mohammad himself. As these several consolidatory campaigns ran their courses, the Hindu: Muslim interface began to harden – from a distinction into an opposition.

There have been new forms of relatedness furthermore: religious associations, *anjumans*, among Bengali Muslims, congregational worship in the Arya Samaj, and, later, the walking parties, *gasht*, of Tablighi Jamaat,[5] and the daily multipurpose gathering of youth in the *shakha* in the Rashtriya Swayamsevak Sangh. These have offered emotional satisfactions, ranging from the sense of ideologically inspired togetherness to the excitements of combat and violence in moments of mob action, when that became more common (Hansen 1999: 61–63). These are diverse considerations; and the next chapter will pursue other dimensions of this complex question.

Stated more generally, choices within the two spaces, within the two traditions, were responding to diverse considerations. Internally, these reflected the anxieties, historical memories, the textual traditions accepted as authentic within a space; the subgroups and their interrelationships; and, arising out of all this, the sense of possibilities for the future. The choices responded to the external context too: the other

---

[5] In the mid-1920s, to combat the Arya Samaji campaign for *shuddhi*, reconversion from other faiths to Hinduism, Tablighi Jamaat devised a new form of activity. It consisted in persuading lay Muslims everywhere to accept responsibility for their religious community. They were urged to form small, self-financing groups that would spend a day, three days, or 40 days in a year walking around, or otherwise travelling, to visit other Muslims. During its travel, the group's members would observe personal Islamic routines like the *namaz*, introspect on how Islamic their own lives were, urge their hosts to live proper Islamic lives – and urge them also to go on their own *gasht*, walking trips.This last gave the Jamaat a snowballing momentum, so its reach is global today (Sikand 2002; Mayaram 2006). The whole movement is an extraordinary display of the leadership of laymen, a possibility that Islamic theology has spurned historically (Mujeeb 1965: 528).

traditions in the vicinity and their historic configuration, the challenges from various external quarters, and the possibilities, say, of employment or of leverage in relation to one or another of groups seen as adversaries.

Choices within a tradition have to include some over how to relate to other traditions in the vicinity. The caste order had enabled the Brahminical tradition, rather uniquely, to establish, and maintain social barriers defensively – enabling it also, thereby, to withstand the political pressure that accompanied the Islamic impulse in north India. An option that the Brahminical tradition had devised historically remained available during the nineteenth century: to provide caste-like niches of graded distance, both physical and social, for followers of other religious traditions. This option provided for separate neighbourhoods for Muslims as a separate *jati*, as for other *jati*s, too.

The caste order did serve to integrate social diversity at the local level but, given resurgent religious traditions, its calculus of purity and pollution served to give the Muslims only a sense of outrage.[6] The choice made by the Muslim *ulama* in northern India and their associated elites, as we saw, was more categorical: to stand apart from other religious traditions, socially. It was the Brahminical option, in combination with the Muslim elite choice, that was leading, by the early twentieth century, to a hardening of a *bar of separation* between Muslims and Hindus in the subcontinent. To paraphrase Pradeep Jeganathan, the Sri Lankan anthropologist, "a space for recurrent violence" was emerging. More on this later.

౸౸

The more clearly the several social spaces were demarcated in exclusive, communal terms, the more these served to intensify the relationships within such a space, and to promote common practices, and a sense of being the "same" people – distinguishable by their names, their

---

[6] The provision in the caste order for niches for followers of other religious traditions is sometimes seen as a mark of Hindus' tolerance for religious diversity, an aspect of a valorized "pluralism". T. N. Madan has argued, however, that "this pluralism is both realized through and maimed by the all-pervasive reign of hierarchy in social thought and social practice and by the spirit of inclusivism/ exclusivism" (1997: 200). The space this found for other traditions did not always appeal to them.

social practices, their lifestyles, and their appearances. Within such spaces, there were of course internal hierarchies and differences. The ideological projects sought to promote a sense of commonality within the space, overriding the differences and the hierarchies; and to promote also a sense of timeless differences in relation to those outside the particular space. Recent thought has stressed the importance of "group names":

> ... The conspicuousness of group identity, regardless of intra-group diversity, cannot be separated from the use of group labels that enable people to recognize members of their own group and to stereotype outsiders ... (Schryer 2001: 710).

Group labels are part of the categories, and of systems of categories, in terms of which we comprehend the world we live in. These categories are the subject matter of "cognitive studies". The study of cognitions helps us see:

> how a group label enables people to recognize what they have in common despite variations in individual traits and social positions . ... At the same time, cognition accentuates inter-group differences.... These two aspects of categorization underlie social boundaries and group mobilization. ... The inner bond of [the group label] and [the referred group] including the mix of attributes associated with group labels [overrides the fact that group boundaries are in fact] arbitrary and conventional (Schryer 2001: 711).

As the nineteenth century wore on, these marks of commonality and difference were highlighted in the social maps that people were encouraged to learn, and to live out in their daily lives. Group labels – such as "Muslim" and "Hindu" – become parts of an ideology that:

> reshapes the perception of attributes.... . [A]s a form of essentialism, [it] gives the impression that group attributes are immutable; the group's place in a system of social stratification is portrayed as fixed, and internal inequalities are overlooked or more comprehensive categories imposed on what were once separate groups (*ibid.*: 712).

This situation of often massive hierarchies and internal differences (the caste order, *ashraf–ajlaf–ajral*), being wrapped under radically simplified group labels, and recourse to corresponding operative social maps: all this is clear enough – though it is not easily comprehended with our stock concepts. Baffled by this disjunction, scholars tend commonly to summon the apparently profound formula, "X were not monolithic", where X can stand for Muslim, Hindu, or whatever.

I wish to say two more things in closing this chapter. First, a striking aspect of our discussion so far has been the recurring references to a rather small number of men who had extraordinary influence on the shape of things. Why did so few lead the way? The answer, I think, lies in the colonial context. The West did present an enormous challenge: politically, economically, indeed also to the validity of received epistemologies; but there was more to it. It offered ideas for envisioning futures in keys very different from the past, but these could be blended variously with ideas from the past – and tinkered by ideologues following their own sense of the present and the future. For propagating these visions, there were new institutional forms and new technologies on the horizon. It was a complex juncture; and it took rare insight to recognize the possibilities, and to bring the several elements into concert.

Finally, in the last chapter we saw *why* elite groups tried to draw people with largely local, folk identities firmly into exclusive, scripturally oriented ones and, in this chapter, we have reviewed the kinds of resources that drove their campaigns. We have also seen some answers to the question: why did such vast numbers respond, even though they would have to suffer in the form of having their local communities cleaved, their familiar relationships disrupted? The next chapter will carry this question forward.

6
drifting apart

> Granted that a complex world precludes total comprehension and the absence of distortion; theory then must retain a sense of limits and an appreciation of ambiguity. But when that has been admitted, it remains that only general theoretical reflection, together with a sense of history, enables us to think through the meaning of our complex social world in a systematic way.
>
> Wilson 1975: 331

We have seen in earlier chapters something of the medieval ambiguities: alongside the many contexts of living and working together, the religious specialists had, by and large, stood apart and, in some cases, had worked on spreading their faith more or less competitively. The early nineteenth century in Haryana and western UP and in Bengal began rather disorderly moves to renegotiate the local hierarchies, challenging the regional land-controllers' social authority: that of Muslims in the first case, of Hindus in the second. By the third quarter of the nineteenth century, new kinds of religious institutions arose: a large *madrasa*, Deoband, in one case; an expansive congregational sect, Arya Samaj, in the other. Their projects of reform and renewal asked their followers not only to move to scripturally oriented beliefs and practices but also to rework their customary social arrangements separatively. Their impulses, arising in the anxieties of certain upper social strata, are clear enough, but we still have to resolve the puzzle: why did such vast numbers respond to these calls, letting these cleave into their local, familiar, social arrangements?

For working on this question, I have two points of departure. First, the growing access to new *technologies*, especially in communications; this had two major sets of implications:

132 *spirals of contention*

A. The new technologies gave the *religious (or at least communal) institutions* the means for multiplying their reach manifold. They could broadcast their messages – with virtually no holds barred. They offered their audiences fresh answers to the question, "who are we?", and urgent reasons for accepting the superiority of their particular answers. Both sides found, or devised, social forms, so their reach kept growing at low cost: the ubiquitous mosques; the new forms of belongingness, associated especially with the Arya Samaj (congregations), and later the Tablighi Jamaat (the travelling lay group), and the Rashtriya Swayamsevak Sangh (RSS) (the *shakha*, a group of young men meeting daily for a variety of activities); and the further amplification resulting from the two other processes noted below. The stress in the RSS is on ethnicity, not religion, but its exclusivity is no less for that (Saberwal and Hasan 2006 explores the origins and consequences of some of these low cost forms).

B. Independently of the above, similar new technologies brought growing numbers of people into unaccustomed, complex settings. Partly in response to the changing economic pulls and pressures, villagers travelled to a town or city nearby, or to an industrial centre, say the jute mills near Calcutta, or a metropolitan centre, say Bombay; or else, distant forces could disrupt their long familiar home areas – think of what 1857 did to Delhi. Entering unfamiliar social spaces, ordinary people could face complexities much greater than had been their experience hitherto. They had earlier lived with habits of mind that served to cope with their local exigencies of life; but some of these were not portable. A local shrine, the village caste matrix, a small town's pecking order – such "shared space" arrangements would stay behind.

In finding a niche in the new milieu, it sometimes helped to try new answers to the question, "who are we?" – and often the answers that worked were the ones coming from the active religious leaders and institutions. In the new locality, they would find institutions and personnel – a maulvi, a *gurudwara*, a temple – associated with the particular religious traditions which could give them access to important networks and resources. The corresponding identities would thereby be strengthened. To fall in with one of these clear-cut, well known identities would help "simplify" the complexity where one found oneself. Barbara Metcalf (2004: 184) cites the anthropologist Mattison Mines (1975) on "villagers [in Tamil Nadu], indistinguishable as Muslims at home, [who] dress, eat, and identify as Muslims when they go to the city, thus securing a basis for community in a context of physical dislocation."[1]

This turn to exclusive identities, amidst the new communications and related technologies, I shall argue, was boosted by another process whose force grew with passing decades. This is my second point of departure. Echoes from the medieval competitiveness of religious groups and traditions merged with the nascent contentions in early nineteenth century. In these skirmishes, aggression was in low key, principally of the *symbolic* sort. Over the next century and more, until 1947 and beyond, the protagonists of rival religious traditions grew more competitive, through campaigns at conversion and *shuddhi*. These efforts would be seen by the other side as aggressive, at the *societal* level. These sometimes loud campaigns were directed commonly at people whose religious beliefs and practices drew on more than one high religious tradition. Experiences of aggression at these levels, symbolic and societal, tended to shift the locus of the prevailing common sense; it predisposed minds to expect, if not to engage in, physical violence, as in riots: aggression, that is, at the *physical* level. The targets of aggression in these episodes, it will be remembered, were often the large categories, Muslim and Hindu.

To be at the receiving end of aggression generates anxieties which, in turn, may spur one to turn to others similarly placed. Organized groups' energies are a dual use resource, available for defence and offence alike. Their shared anxieties may find relief in aggression, which would generate anxiety on the other side, thereby setting up a self-aggravating cycle of anxiety, organization, aggression, and violence in its various forms – in which both sides can see themselves as victims, in equal measure.

Three very different kinds of processes, then, were converging:

- first, late nineteenth century *religious institutions* began energetically to advance renovated religious ideologies, purportedly of ancient lineages. Both sides had expansive impulses emulating, and surpassing, the Christian missionaries' style;
- second, *ordinary persons*' need for social and ideological anchors, as they coped with the unfamiliar complexities of life – and

---

[1] On Calcutta, Siddiqui (1973), Bose (1968); on Bombay, Kosambi (1980: 121–36). On Allahabad, a *much older* city, Bayly (1975: 39–46) suggests a considerable admixture of Hindus and Muslims during the late 1800s.

therefore their turn to the ideologies and associated identities reaching them in their neighbourhoods, old or new; and

- third, *contentious encounters* of a local sort, which began slowly to spiral up from the early nineteenth century in northern India, beginning to redraw the "us" – "them" boundaries, separatively. As the issues in contention grew in scale, and as the news of particular episodes spread through the media, the separative "us" "them" boundaries gathered further anxieties, and hardened, cementing the opposed identities, towards which other processes also were tending. The *micro* – "relatively short time-frames of face-to-face interaction"– and the *macro* – "the extended time-frames of long-standing institutional conditions that extend from the past into the present": both the micro and the macro were changing together, mediated by the news that travelled around (Sibeon 2004: 110, apropos Derek Layder's work). Put otherwise, local incidents and small-scale processes, expressed in local attitudes and activities, were influencing – and were being influenced by – processes of larger scales; the two levels were interconnected, *loosely*, by such devices as newspapers and fresh institutional initiatives.

At first glance it seems that these three sets of processes originated independently of each other. Yet, notably, "religion" was implicated in all three. It was towards one or the other *religious* complex, defined as a besieged identity in a threatening world, that the migrants and others gravitated; and religious ideologies and symbols entered the several levels of contention variously. The cumulative experience of aggression at multiple levels served to bind one into an exclusive religious category. The urgent calls of religious revivalists, the search for firm anchor in emerging settings of unprecedented complexity, and the rising spiral of social aggression – this triple dynamic was to reconfigure Indian society, separately, through the colonial period.

"Simplifying" Complexity

In trying to make sense of modern Indian history, we might remember that, already in the nineteenth century, society in India was stunningly complex – thanks partly to its fabled capacity for absorbing, and preserving, all manner of diversity. The secret of that capacity lay in the caste system: what was different could keep to its own niche, not much concerned about changes in other groups. The strong Indic tug towards cellular complexity did set it apart from other major civilizations – Chinese, Islamic, European. History has seen nothing like it anywhere else.

Precolonial complexities

It has been bad manners to see anything positive in the caste order publicly; the twentieth century gave it a bad press. An abundant anthropological literature, however, has urged a radically revisionist appraisal (for one review, see Saberwal 1996b). Here I wish only to indicate some aspects that have gone into shaping Indian history. Its agrarian division of labour underlay the society's agricultural productivity and wealth: an enduring magnet that long drew merchants, conquerors, and other seekers of opportunity from far and wide. Its ideologically strapped social grid gave the society defensive capabilities – so that it could survive adversity with its core social templates intact: this was a significant resource for resistance and resilience. The multi-stranded bonds *within* a *jati* would serve both to hold members to its internal codes, and also to facilitate cooperative, sometimes expansive, effort. Chapter 2 saw a *jati* as a pouch of social capital which has repeatedly demonstrated its protean potential: in facilitating chain migration – physically or occupationally; in underwriting mutual trust in commercial credit and elsewhere; in mobilizing for political objectives – on scales small to medium; and so forth.

All this complexity was kept in order through the intricate ideology of the caste system that invoked the principles of separation, hierarchy, purity, pollution, and much else. The medieval period added to that complexity another, large order of social differences through the several distinctive groups immigrating from the north: Arabs, Persians, Afghans, Turks, and even some Mongols. Borne along with the expansive surge of Islam, these groups had little use for the ordering capacities of the caste system. Given the capacities for resistance and resilience inherent in the latter, however, Islam found itself stalled in south Asia as it had not been in north Africa or in west, central, and southeast Asia. In my reading, then, the caste system was a source of considerable frustration for those who saw it as their sacred duty to work for the spread of Islam. This frustration may have led them, in some measure, to castigate the caste system sharply, even though hierarchies and discrimination have been common enough in Islamic societies too.

In the event, the accidents of history brought two major religious traditions into neighbourly intimacy. This was "a process of interpenetration which in scale and ambiguity has scarcely a parallel in world history before Europe's expansion into Asia (Ray 2003: 109)".[2] Yet neither side carried the cognitive and emotional resources that might have enabled it to comprehend, and perhaps appreciate, the inner logic of the other. There were the Dara Shikohs, but they pulled against the formidable bearers of scriptural authority. This diversity the secularists have long celebrated as an enriching plurality; they are dismissive of Mohammad Mujeeb's kind of juxtaposing of the radically contrasting conceptions underlying, say, a temple and a mosque (1965: 184f). As Mujeeb goes on to note, however, "shared" space can be experienced as threatening for someone immersed in a particular lifestyle: "… while the Muslim proclaimed his mission and trumpeted his intentions, Hindu influences, moving silently and unobtrusively like the waters of a flood, surrounded him from all sides, leaving only small islands where the flag of Islam flew high – and defenceless (1967: 379)." These influences flowed from Rajput Mughal princesses introducing their ideas concerning family structure into the royal household, from the anxious warriors consulting Hindu astrologers, from the Sufis' sometimes transgressive behaviour, from music and dancing girls, from the practices of various service castes, and much else (*ibid.*: 379ff). There remain in any case two kinds of questions: how did it all hold together? – and – how did people make sense of the labyrinthine complexity enveloping them?

[2] Here is an illustration of elements from the two traditions becoming interlinked. In Maharashtra, where the number of Muslims has been relatively small, two kinds of *purana*-like texts sought to "normalize" the presence of the Islamic tradition: (*a*) in order to legitimize the Maratha regime emerging in the eighteenth century, "historical" accounts began to be rewritten. In one, it was the grace of Siva that brought Paigambar, the Prophet Muhammad, and Yavanas, Muslims, into being, and brought Yavanas to rule over Delhi (Wagle 1997: 135f); and (*b*) in several cases, compositions by Muslims, seen to be in the *bhakti* tradition, stressed the ultimate identity of, say Isvara and Allah, and of Muslims and Hindus; yet these spoke critically of Brahminical beliefs and practices concerning caste distinctions and idol worship. These compositions were written implicitly from within a monotheistic Islamic standpoint (*ibid.*: 141–45). On the other hand, we have already referred to an acrimonious debate composed by Eknath, expressing sixteenth century tensions (p. 108).

An unfixed complexity

Social and political order in this milieu came from the play of several, unconnected processes. Niches of the caste order more or less regulated themselves, internally. Politically, on one side, there was the current rulers' interest in keeping things going, and their willingness to use force to that end, when thought necessary; and on the other, there were countless armed political entrepreneurs, active simultaneously at multiple levels besides the imperial. Their rights of conquest, if this happened, would be acknowledged swiftly, so the area could return to orderly existence speedily. And at the level of everyday existence, there was the people's imperative need to cooperate with each other: as neighbours, in commerce, in the government, and in other ways. And there was much creative give and take – in shared languages.

With all that, there was still a void, however; and social analysis has difficulty with identifying what is absent. "In all societies, many of the most interesting things are the absences," notes Alan Macfarlane (2004: 97), "and it is extremely difficult to be aware of these." I wish to point to an absence in the context we have been considering: *the absence of an ideology*, one that would address *all* the social diversity in the prevailing profusion of groups, and the kinds of differences between them; an ideology that would present the extant arrangements as a natural order of things in a manner widely acceptable. For all that has been at stake, terms like *sulh-i kul*, "peace between all", which appealed to Akbar, and, later secularism, are much too slender, short on ideological fibre. Put otherwise, the society was left with a large order of what might be called *unfixed complexity*, devoid of robust ideological, and institutional, cover.[3]

Governed by horse-borne men, in relatively swift communication with the emperor, the late seventeenth century Mughal empire was large enough to cover much of the subcontinent; but nearly all its subjects lived in social universes of rather a small scale. For nearly everyone, their meanings for life lay within these social niches; the larger social complexity was a fact of existence, which they took for granted, like the sun and the wind. Even for the well-heeled Banarasi Das, of Jain

---

[3] "Complexity" has entered this treatment from LaPorte 1975, especially, in it, Winner, pp. 40–76. Their principal concern is with complexity in modern western societies, notably the conundrums that major technological changes pose for large organizations, and for the political domain. The notion of "unfixed complexity", arising in ideological (and institutional) deficits, is my own.

merchant background, who taught the then Mughal governor of Allahabad "Hindi versification and poetic usage", and moved around between several north Indian towns, wherever he went his life turned around the local Jain neighbourhood. In the social beehive surrounding him, Banarasi showed little interest. "All that was humanly meaningful or significant lay for him eminently in the life of his community" (Lath 1981: xxiii–xxiv, viii). The insulations of these small worlds began to erode in the nineteenth century.

Complexity, nineteenth century increments

Against this backdrop of an inadequate ideological cover for the prevailing social complexity, the nineteenth century was a time of uncertainties and anxieties, arising in multiple sources. The new possibilities of travel and printing cleared the way for social reconfigurations; and we have seen the impulses that embraced these new possibilities vigorously. A new dimension to the prevailing complexity came from the colonial conjunction, and the consequent encounter with Europe. This latter meant coping with another language, and with bodies of knowledge organized in unfamiliar frameworks; these had to be faced at least in metropolitan institutions and in centres like Delhi College in the early 1800s. Christian missionaries advanced alternate religious schemes. Here and there, men sought to understand the nature of the European historical experience, contrasting it with India's (Raychaudhuri 1988).

This new complexity had another vital aspect. It enlarged, and made more complex, the possible scales of activities and of social relationships (Saberwal 1998: 63–71). As we saw above, the social milieu had indeed long been complex; but most people did not have to engage with that complexity in their everyday lives. The new possibilities of travel and printing began to translate what had earlier been a passive, objective complexity of the milieu into an unfamiliar, subjective complexity in personal encounters and experiences: the man from rural Bihar working in a jute mill near Calcutta, and losing his job – or getting caught in communal strife there.

Complexity: Diverse regional responses

Responses to these difficulties were to emerge informally within the prevailing, largely local and regional, social networks, and consequently there was much variation in the patterns from one region to another. In the Bombay of the early and mid-1800s, these networks stretched comfortably across the various caste and religious groups. Veena Naregal reports on the case of Fardunji Marzban (b. 1787), "a traditional *mullah* from Surat who was trained in Persian, Sanskrit, Hindustani and Gujarati and the Parsi scriptures, and evidently combined these with a keen entrepreneurial mind, became the first Gujarati publisher and the first native editor of a newspaper in western India" (2001: 177). She adds in a footnote that "He taught himself English in order to understand the new journalistic medium better" (*ibid.*: 178–87). His publications included the Gujarati translation of the Parsi scripture, *Khordeh Avesta*, which ultimately got him into trouble with Parsis, forcing him to leave Bombay for Goa. Marzban also became involved with the China trade, and even owned a ship. Similarly ramifying were the relationships of Ayesha, the butcher's widow (Siddiqi 2001). Out of such relatively relaxed networks emerged the shared responses reflected in the mid-century politics of Bombay city, then the writings of Dadabhai Naoroji, and ultimately the forming of the Indian National Congress (Dobbin 1972: Chaps 7 and 8). Later politics in Bombay too cleaved on communal lines.

The pattern in Punjab and UP was rather different. Several groups there acted, in contrast, as if they were under siege. At work were multiple spurs to insecurity: in Punjab, the experiences of extensive conflict in the eighteenth and early nineteenth centuries; in Delhi and western UP, the final passing of the old empire – and the brutal aftermath of 1857, especially for Muslims (though Hasan 2005 describes a remarkably relaxed milieu in late nineteenth century Delhi). The erstwhile intercommunal centres and networks of power, we have seen, became marginalized by the early nineteenth century. Alongside this, fresh claims were advanced – say by neo-rich merchants – and efforts made to protect old status. In this competition for status and influence, the rivals tended to rally around distinctive religious elements and the identities forming around them. Institutions like the Arya Samaj and Deoband offered their followers *moral* reasons for acting in concert with fellow believers – and apart from those of other faiths. To the stresses arising in the larger historical milieu were added those from growing contestation between neighbours.

The situation may be considered as a theme in historical social psychology. This is not a perspective in common use; but the classic synthesis, Lazarus 1966, offers a stimulating framework. Groups under stress are known to act in relatively rigid ways. Faced with a complex,

140 *spirals of contention*

somewhat threatening world, a common, if rigid practice is to simplify the categories in which we see that complex world. Stereotyping "outgroups" is one expression of this tendency. Another expression would be to reject large parts of the surrounding world as false knowledge, misguided practice, and so forth. Both the Arya Samaj and Deoband offered confident, starkly simplified ideologies for interpreting a social universe whose complexity was in fact growing. In the last chapter we noted the dismissive stance of Dayananda's principal text for Arya Samaj, *Satyarthaprakash*, towards the entrenched style of the Brahminical tradition as well as Christian and Islamic scriptures and beliefs, while exalting the ancient Vedic truths. On the other side, we noted earlier that Islam has carried several cultural styles historically: an open, outgoing one, as well as one that turned on the *shariat* (Chap. 1, p. 2f). In the circumstances of the mid-nineteenth century, we have seen that the architects of Deoband advanced the latter style. Their vision called on all true Muslims to purge their lives of all misguided beliefs and practices and to remake them on lines codified in the *shariat* a thousand years ago (Chap. 5).

As we saw earlier, roles, facilities, and institutions associated with the major religious traditions had spread out through the centuries – or could be replicated in new localities relatively easily. Men who migrated in the changing economic milieu of the late nineteenth century and later, often saw advantage in fitting into the frameworks of identities and differences in their host localities; and their choices would impress their kin and neighbours back home too. In their new settings, they needed to learn new kinds of social maps, and connect with adequate social networks, for coping with unaccustomed social situations; similar needs could arise as forces beyond their control affected the villages and towns they had long inhabited.

We have already seen something of this enlarging of scales in relation to UP towns in the nineteenth century. Such enlargement can also be seen among Muslim jute mill workers on the banks of the Hooghly and in their relationships with co-religionists in Calcutta. In their bid to cut labour costs, the jute mills had drawn low-paid workers from Bihar, Hindu as well as Muslim, and these men carried animosities from their home areas into their new inhabitations. These animosities were expressed in the Hindu objection to the killing of cows by Muslims at their festivals and, in retaliation, the Hindus killing a pig to provoke the Muslims. The 1890s were a time of oversupply of immigrant workers in the jute mills, and competition for work worsened the communal situation in mill areas. Several small-scale riots followed.

Muslims among the millworkers turned to the maulvis in their local mosques for help, and the maulvis' networks led them to the big Muslim merchants in Calcutta. The latter were predisposed to respond to the jutemen because they were themselves under some pressure from immigrant Marwari merchants; and they were imbibing distant pan-Islamic impulses too. Mediated by their maulvis, then, Bihari jute mill workers found support among the big Muslim merchants of Calcutta. The thin thread of common faith aided in a bit of social realignment (Chakrabarty 1990).

While jute mill workers, coming from eastern UP and Bihar to the vicinity of Calcutta, looked for support among local co-religionists in their moment of difficulty, Jats in Haryana, in about the same period, began to absorb and adapt the Arya Samaji framework to their own purposes. Thanks to the produce of their canal irrigated lands and preferred recruitment to the colonial army, Jats had done well – and felt unhappy with their low rank in the region's caste hierarchy. In Dayananda's *Satyarthaprakash*, however, they found justification for their particular social practices; and the Arya Samaj offered them a channel for giving some of their rituals a sanskritic touch, as well as an institutional framework through which to mobilize effort to build educational institutions. As they strengthened their identity as Aryas, they acquired too the Arya concern with cow protection, and Arya prejudices against neighbouring Jats who were Muslim – which was to lead to bloodshed in later years (N. Datta 1999).

Simplifying ideologies

The ideologies we have discussed, such as those from the Arya Samaj and Deoband, were radically simplifying; or so it seems to an outsider: for those who came to believe in them, these left nothing more to be desired. It is scarcely surprising that people should work with simple conceptions of the infinitely complex world around them: to be able to live in a complex society at all, we need countless simplifying notions so we may hold at bay the deluge of messages, events, and other phenomena that would otherwise engulf us (Berger and Luckmann 1966: 56–60, 135–40). What, then, was special about these late nineteenth century ideologies? These are striking because their stark simplifications were high on dogma and on opposition to their neighbours. Some of them were also low on the pragmatics of orderliness in a multi-religious society. These ideologies fostered collective practices that intensified the respective believers' mutual interactions within the fold, and their sense of mutual interrelatedness: it meant a "simplification of the social world" (Hansen 1999: 64). Later on, the Tablighi Jamaat was to promulgate a minimalist doctrine, stressing rather its practice of lay groups travelling for the faith. The attendant sense of togetherness could be an important resource for coping with uncertainties and anxieties – at least in the short run.

The coin had another side, of course: it served to attenuate one's bonds with one's neighbours whose own sense of interrelatedness was pulling away correspondingly. Moves towards social separativeness were getting justifications from "religious" authorities. Anxieties about one's prospects in the hereafter having been aroused by fantasies sanctioned by the respective religious tradition, the possibilities of appraising one's choices, and possibly changing course, were foreclosed. What would be the likely long-term consequences of such separativeness? As the decades passed, this question would be discouraged by the growing religious/communal sentiment; it became increasingly difficult to consider it in the light of ongoing experiences. Neighbours stacked themselves in religiously defined groups, in opposition, at times in incomprehending antagonism, to other groups also being defined around (different) religious nodes.

Parenthetically, we notice an asymmetry here which served to hide the separativeness of Hindus and to highlight that of Muslims. Hindu separativeness was integral to the caste order. In distantiating himself from a Muslim, a Hindu needed to refer only to the ancient principles of the caste order which, in his view, applied to everyone. A Muslim distantiating himself from a Hindu could be seen as doing something new – as being a separatist!

In the late nineteenth century, it was the protagonists of separative identities who moved more vigorously and gained the upper hand in the corresponding social spaces. This could be seen, for instance, in two moments in the life of Syed Ahmed Khan. On one side, he discovered that, in order to be able to proceed with building the college at Aligarh at all, he had to agree to let the *ulama* oversee religious thought and activity at Aligarh, superceding his own revisionist theology; on the other side, he threw his weight against Badruddin Tyabji in Bombay, who was trying to persuade Muslims to join the freshly launched Indian National Congress in large numbers (Metcalf 1982: 328f; Lelyveld 1978: 307ff; Seal 1968: 331–37).

The communal cleavage that climaxed in India, by the mid-twentieth century, was extraordinary in its depth and intensity. The implications of the technological changes we have considered hitherto, however, were relatively modest. To be able to account adequately for the kind of cleavage that emerged, we need to locate additional drivers of commensurate force. The next section will propose such a driver: the spirals of contention, to which our opening paragraphs referred, which contributed decisively to the adversarial hardening of religious identities.

Spirals of Contention

Addressing the Punjab Legislative Council in 1937, Muhammad Iqbal, the Punjabi litterateur and statesman, spoke of a "mutual lack of communication and trust between Hindu and Muslim". This, he said, was reflected in the preference for European to Indian police officers in both communities; and in the fact that Punjab University students had to write their final exams under "anonymous roll numbers to conceal their identity. The system was adopted, Iqbal claimed, because the Hindu examiners might fail Muslim candidates" and vice versa (Malik 1971: 87). In this last Iqbal was mistaken, for it is common to use numerical codes to track items in large sets; but his sense of the situation was shared by many.

Over the two decades, 1928 to 1947, numerous seemingly promising Constitutional formulae for India's future failed to find support from those who spoke for the Muslim League and the Indian National Congress – though agreement often seemed to be close (Hasan 1991: Chap. 9; Jalal 2001: 300–19; Prasad 2000: Chap. 5). In coming to Constitutional arrangements, each party has to take a certain risk about the unknown future, assuming that the other parties would act fairly and reasonably – abiding by not just the letter but also the spirit of the formal arrangements made. The prerequisite to such arrangements, then, is a level of mutual trust between the participants; and this mutual trust between Muslims and Hindus had been declining for several decades.[4] Why? The following pages will argue that this erosion

---

[4] The argument here builds on a decline in mutual trust, but there were other facets to the situation. For more than a decade after the Khilafat, Muslim political organizations were in grave disarray, and one could hold, with Mukul Kesavan (2007: 115f), that the Congress simply did not take anyone claiming to speak for Muslims seriously. But there may also have been a wariness about the efficacy of negotiating Constitutional formulae. The proponents of the 1916 Lucknow Pact between the Congress and the Muslim League had expected it to lead to lasting peace but politics ran at multiple levels; and almost immediately after the Pact came the "cow protection" attacks in 1917–18 and, following the Khilafat interlude, renewed conflict from the mid-1920s.

in mutual trust followed from the contentiousness which had been gathering force for several generations past.

The importance of social contention, or even of physical violence, has not entered our explanations and understanding of the widespread hardening of mindsets. At work has been a two way process: social insulation and social contention feed on, aggravate, each other. As the sense of mutuality between groups declines, the other side's actions and intentions become more suspect. The consolidation of exclusive identities was interactive: Ayesha Jalal calls it "dialogic" (2001: 57), even if the interaction and the "dialogue" became increasingly combative. Routine, innocuous events begin to seem ominous; indeed, one may inflect routine, innocuous acts in ways that would infuriate the other side. Conflict becomes more likely. Seen the other way, a feeling of being threatened helps cement one's commitment to those with whom one feels a sense of shared fate: that, then, is one's identity, an island of belonging and mutual support, against what are thought to be threatening others. In the making of identities, Rajat K. Ray has stressed the vital importance of "some real emotional bond" (2003: ix). The following pages will argue that a shared fear of the "other" side became the "real emotional bond" making religious identities firm; and conversely these firm, exclusive identities appeared to the other side to be increasingly threatening. Mohammad Mujeeb noted the crucial importance of "continuing conflict with others" for sustaining the Indian Muslims' sense of community (1967: 540); much the same could be said for the rise of Hindutva during the twentieth century.

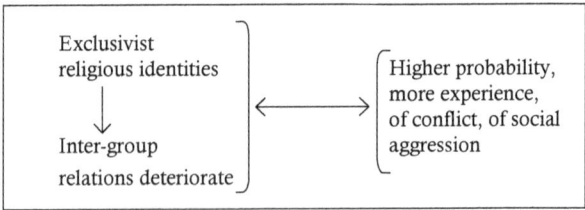

Varieties of social contention

At the heart of the drift in nineteenth and early twentieth century India were numerous moments of *social contention* which I analyze into three modes:

Symbolic. This kind of contention turned on deploying seemingly innocuous symbols publicly, in ways that offend. The utility of certain symbols in transcending a range of differences, and facilitating wider mobilization, was understood well by the end of the nineteenth century.

Societal. By the early twentieth century, an often aggressive endemic competitiveness was emerging, complete with doctrinal proclamations, and efforts at "conversions": efforts, that is, to bring into the respective folds those whose religious beliefs and practices fell short of the protagonists' doctrines.

Physical. The use of physical violence, of course, long antedates the emergence of mankind. In our context, however, the experiences of symbolic and societal contention were seen by the "other" side as assaults on their social and religious existence. Religious identities hardened in adversarial terms – making physical violence, and "communal riots", including struggles for control over, and violence to women, even more likely.

This sequencing of the symbolic, the societal, and the physical forms of aggression was not inevitable; in part, it is a device for orderly discussion. Already for the 1830s, Ranajit Guha (1983: 75n) cites an official report concerning the uprising led by Titu Mir (see below); the report made "allegations of cow killing, physical assaults on brahmans and forcible conversion to Islam". 70 years later, again, during an episode in Mymensingh in northeastern Bengal, in May 1907:

> Property, mainly of Hindu landholders, shopkeepers and mahajans, was this time the principal target, though there was also considerable destruction of images and some cases of rape and attempted forcible conversion (Sarkar 1973: 448).

These were still local happenings, however, though their spread and frequency were growing. Later generations saw dramatic increases in the scales of these forms of contention, and of their awareness and repercussions.

The campaigns of Gaurakshini Sabhas, Cow Protection Societies, were in full flow in the Bhojpur region straddling the UP–Bihar border in the 1890s; and the contestation on Baqr Id, 24 June 1893, went far beyond the symbolic: Hindus confiscated any cows intended for sacrifice in the town of Mau, in Azamgarh district, UP; there were massive Hindu assaults on a Muslim neighbourhood despite the posting of strong police pickets, and a stray party of Muslims was done to death. Many of the victims were Julahas, weavers:

> The repercussions of the Azamgarh events of 1893 were felt almost immediately in Bombay ... : [Muslim] Julaha migrants were to the fore in the Bombay riots which aimed at least in part to avenge the deaths of their brethren in north India . ... it appears that Hindus and Muslims of several classes scattered over a much wider geographical area than the site of any initial act of violence, were drawn into their respective religious community's concern for cow–protection or for *qurbani* [ritual sacrifice] (Pandey 1983: 124f).

The 1893–95 series of communal riotes in Maharashtra did begin over the protection of cows but reached into other issues between Muslims and Hindus in several districts (Cashman 1975: 68–73). Bimal Prasad places the "cow-protection movement" in a wider political and emotional context: the determination of a great many Hindus "that what was one of the objects of their depest veneration could not be slaughtered in a land where they constituted an overwhelming majority" (1999: 219). Two decades later, in 1917, Muslims in several villages in Shahabad, Bihar, were targeted too as diverse motivations came to fasten on cow protection. Through their parallel assaults on Muslims, who were alleged to sacrifice cows at Id, "true-blue" *zamindar* castes sought to assert their status and, at the same time, several middle-ranking castes – Goalas, Kurmis, and Koeris – sought to demonstrate their adherence to Brahminical values, and so claim higher status for themselves (Pandey 1990: 192–95).

Symbolic contention

> [By 1926 in Bengal] non-communal social phenomena were already being, on a sustained and day-to-day basis, harnessed into symbolic structures that were reproducing and intensifying communal identities (P. K. Datta 1999: 239–40).

The earliest studies of growing local skirmishes turn on such "classic irritant(s) [as] ... a Hindu procession accompanied by music passing before a mosque, or the Hindu's knowledge of a cow being slaughtered in the neighbourhood for its beef and hide" (Naidu 1980: 92). Sandra B. Freitag has given us accounts from Banaras, Bareilly, and Agra in what is now UP. As new groups came to wealth, or to strength of numbers, they sought to assert themselves through greater say in such matters as the routes taken by religious processions (Freitag 1989: Chaps 1, 3, and 4). In late nineteenth and early twentieth century UP, champions of "cow protection" mobilized material resources among the Hindus, employing caste-like measures of internal control to do so (*ibid.*: Chaps 2, 5, and 6). Apropos Bengal in the mid-1920s, Partha Chatterjee wrote that "the musical processions in question were usually immersion ceremonies following one or the other Hindu *puja*, patronized by landlords, traders, and other Hindu professionals and an important institution of demonstration of feudal wealth and power (1982: 19)."

The vocabulary for symbolic contention was used – or, if you prefer, abused – to perfection during the uprising led by Titu Mir in the Bengal of 1830–31:

> ... Krishnadeb Ray, a powerful Hindu landlord, ... raided a Muslim hamlet and burnt down some houses and a mosque. The insurgents returned the compliment by invading Ray's own residential village, Punrah. 'The Zemindars had put a slight on their religious feeling', reads the official report on this event, 'and they retaliated [by] seizing a cow which they killed in the public market place of the village, scattered the blood over the walls of a Hindu temple and hung up the four quarters of the animal in derision before it.' ... Desecration was used thus by both the parties to undermine each other's prestige ... (Guha 1983: 75).

The same vocabulary surfaced again a few years later during the Faraizi movement (p. 59).

As their reach grew, local issues gathered ideology. It availed of the sharp contrasts between scriptural Islam and Brahminical orthodoxy in their beliefs, practices, and underlying premises; and each had long defined those of the other side as misguided, or worse. The older contrasts were, by the 1870s, giving an edge to other themes like the struggle over Urdu and Hindi (Robinson 1975: 40–46); and were becoming institutionalized. To the fresh ideological thrusts of the Arya Samaj and Deoband, the bearers of older traditions – Sanatan Dharmis and Barelwis – responded competitively, making this a two-layered contestation. In one layer, Aryas and Sanatanis, for instance, tried to outdo each other in their assertiveness; in the other layer, both parties targeted Muslims (Freitag 1989: 139f; 142f); similarly at times on the Muslim side.

Long established practices began to grate mutually; new practices were introduced in order to defy or provoke the other side. Rafiuddin Ahmed (1981: 179) has examined the scene in rural Bengal as the schism widened. In Kushtia in 1897, things got to a point where Muslim peasants needed police protection in order to proceed with the customary cow sacrifice at the Id festival. Sumit Sarkar quotes a Mymensingh magistrate, writing on 1 June 1906: "the raiyats being well off do not mind paying cesses for most purposes, but object to pay for Kali pujas and other kinds of idolatry. The zamindars too object to their killing cows" (1973: 458). A generation later, in 1926, the "nature of popular Muslim feeling" in Kushtia was much sharper (see the speech quoted in Chatterjee 1982: 21f). Social and political equations may have changed by the twenty-first century; underlying attitudes have not.

Several generations of low-grade contentiousness served to push the prevailing common sense among several social clusters towards a belief in an abiding opposition between Hindu and Muslim. Recurrent local skirmishes heightened anxieties on both sides. The older bonds across differences of faith, and the fund of mutual trust and goodwill within local communities, declined. Adversarial attitudes tended to pervade the interpretation of otherwise neutral events, e.g., the publication of Census data. It was becoming easier for minor issues to slide into confrontations – each episode helping deepen a little the wider, ongoing process.

For the Bengal of the 1920s, Pradip Kumar Datta (1999) has documented the tendency for a variety of incidents to arouse anxious comments in newspapers, counterposing the interests of Hindus and Muslims. These included the 1911 Census, the death of a long silent, destitute man of unknown antecedents, and some women in rural areas deserting their husbands. In Punjab, numerous Arya propagandists would speak venomously about Muslims at Arya functions. Symbolic combat may break no bones, at least not immediately; but insults directed at core religious elements could arouse passions, sometimes lethally. The protracted pamphlet war between a leading Arya Samaji, Lekh Ram, and Mirza Ghulam Ahmad, founder of the Ahmediya sect, ended with Lekh Ram losing his life in 1897 (Jones 1976: 146–53).

While several drivers were at work to sharpen the Muslim–Hindu cleavage, there was little effort at fostering cross-cutting social networks, such as underpin mutual trust ordinarily, networks whose members may intervene to moderate and to defuse situations of conflict. Arya Samaji venom had been directed at Sanatana Dharma and

Sikhism too, but its divisive consequences were dissipated along the variety of cross-linkages – in shared beliefs, symbols, practices, textual traditions and, even more, in the persisting networks of family, kinship, intermarriage, and *jati*, which overrode these doctrinal differences. Late in his short life, Harishchandra, the late nineteenth century litterateur and lay religious leader in Banaras, counted the Brahmos and the Arya Samajis into the Hindu fold, along with the Vaishnava Sanatanis (Dalmia 1997: Chap. 6). Of cross-linkages between Muslims and Hindus, in governments, in religious amalgams, in literature, and much else, we have taken notice, but these had been giving way in recent generations. "Other things being equal", the weaker the cross-linkages between groups living in close proximity, the leaner their resources for resolving relatively minor issues before these escalate into active conflict. Ashutosh Varshney (2002) has recently advanced this dynamic to explain the incidence of urban communal conflict in India (for the underlying analytic tradition, see Gluckman 1965: 91–116).

Societal contention, demographic anxiety

Any concerted campaign seeking to persuade a target group to abandon its ancestral beliefs and practices, and religious identity, for those of the campaigners may be seen as a case of demographic aggression. We saw in Chapter 2, concerning Bengal and Punjab, that such efforts used to be relatively slow, localized, barely perceptible. Under the influence of Muslim religious men, large numbers grew into Islamic practices – without a decision to become Muslim ever being an issue. Later the scene changed a bit: as part of the late nineteenth century Islamic upsurge in Eastern Bengal, conversions from Hinduism were being staged at public meetings (Ahmed 1981: 103).

Demographic shifts between religious identities had by then become matters of periodic public attention, focussed by the decennial Census – and its worried interpretations. Pradip Kumar Datta has examined the 1909 text by U. N. Mukherji, *Hindus – a dying race*, and his later writings, interpreting census data alarmingly, to argue that Hindus are headed for extinction! Mukherji saw various pressures leading to that prospect: Hindus' caste exclusiveness; alleged Muslim wealth, so they could buy poor Hindu peasants' lands; and the superior Muslim physique, which drew Hindu widows to Muslim men (P. K. Datta 1999: 27–31). Propagandists continued to reiterate Mukherji's phrase, and theme, late into the twentieth century, seeking to freshen Hindu anxieties (*ibid.*: 22). We shall meet the Muslims' acute demographic anxieties in a moment.

Physical violence

We already have a sense of the frequency of physical violence in the relations between the two communities during the decades leading up to 1947, and the following pages will offer more. Here I wish to review some recent work on the social consequences of the experience of collective violence. Scholarly interest in this relationship in India was sparked by Veena Das's work on the aftermath of the 1984 Delhi pogrom against the Sikhs (1990). Two major bodies of work have come: one from Deepak Mehta and Roma Chatterji (2001), on Dharavi in Mumbai following the violence in 1992–93; the other from Rowena Robinson (2005), on Muslim survivors from Mumbai 1992–93 as well as Gujarat 2002. These studies show how major collective violence has gone into reconfiguring local social relations. It damages neighbourly trust in relationships across religious difference. It strengthens bonds with co-religionists. And it heightens a sense of vulnerability if one lives in an area where one's "own" community is in a minority, leading to efforts to shift where it is in majority; so that residential areas have tended to become more homogeneous with regard to religious identity. These recent findings accord both with earlier theoretical understandings[5] and with tendencies over the preceding century and more. Myriad expressions of collective violence will engage us below.

Aggression in its various forms had been in the air. We may separate its distinctive forms; but there are underlying attitudes and stereotypes running through them all. In a charged milieu, an aggressive act could set off a chain of reprisal and counter reprisal in the subcontinental theatre, shifting between localities, actors, victims, and modes of aggression opportunistically. This could work on different scales. For the late nineteenth and early twentieth centuries in eastern Bengal, Partha Chatterjee notes that Hindus were concentrated more in towns, Muslims in villages – though villages also had Marwari traders and moneylenders. Our author recounts the chains of events: Muslim assertiveness in an urban area, Hindu response with economic boycott

---

[5] In her work on Andhran inscriptions (the fourteenth to the seventeenth centuries), Cynthia Talbot sets her evidence on identity formation around the proposition: "prolonged confrontation between different groups intensifies self-identities" (1995: 70). N. Jayaram and Satish Saberwal reviewed the issues, amplifying the complex relationships between the variables (1996: 19, 514f, esp. fn. 11 there).

drifting apart 151

of Muslims in cities, and forceful Muslim retaliation against Marwari traders and moneylenders in villages. It simplified things, in a sense, to give the various underlying issues a communal label because the widespread social and economic opposition corresponded with a difference of religious identity: poorer but more numerous Muslim cultivators set against Hindu traders, moneylenders, *zamindars*, government servants, and professionals (1982: 20–30).

A somewhat analogous chain of events can be seen in the subcontinental arena in the 1920s. A galaxy of *ulama* and Gandhi had mounted that effort despite widespread reservations and expressions of mistrust. One part of the movement had sought to rally mass support around Islamic religious symbols and issues, especially around the "Khilafat", that is, the status of the Khalifa in Istanbul in Turkey, who claimed to be the protector of Islam's pilgrimage sites in Arabia. In order to broaden the movement, and increase the pressure on the British government to leave the Khalifa undisturbed, the Khilafat issue was run alongside a secular campaign, Non-cooperation.

In its initial phase, the movement witnessed communal bonhomie in unprecedented ways. As Khilafat–Non-cooperation gathered steam in 1921, however, the heightened religious passions found expression in conflict in northern Kerala. The Muslim Moplah peasants there had long chafed under their Hindu landlords. The Khilafat movement sought to arouse their identity as Muslims against the British; but their sentiments merged with their antagonism towards the landlords. The sense of being oppressed, alloyed with an anxious, heightened Islamic identity, led both to physical violence against a variety of targets, and also to demographic aggression, forcing some Hindu landlords to convert to Islam (Panikkar 1989: 49, 58, 121). However we designate the adversaries – agrarian classes or communal groups – the events were interpreted elsewhere as Muslim violence against Hindus; and this had consequences.

There were other violent incidents too, noted in the next chapter, and all this persuaded Gandhi that things were getting out of hand; he terminated the movement. There was a reaction because Muslim emotions had been roused to a high pitch. They felt let down. The communal situation became more fraught than ever before, and a long series of communal riots followed (Hasan 1991: 153ff). The riposte to the Moplah episode, meanwhile, came from Swami Shraddhananda, an Arya Samaj leader in north India, who arranged a coalition of Hindu groups – which worked then on the vast numbers whose ancestors had accepted Islam long ago but had kept their earlier bonds and cultural practices intact. Over a two year period starting in early 1923, in the region around Agra and Mathura, some 163,000 were persuaded to "return" to Hinduism (Sikand 2002: 32–36; Jordens 1981: 131–43). The campaign worked with the leaderships of caste groups which had taken their allegiance to Islam lightly. Tremors from the foregoing contributed to the souring of political relations in Bengal too (P. K. Datta 1999: Chap. 5).

The effectiveness of this effort led by Shraddhananda aroused old anxieties in the Muslim religious elite: that Muslims in India would be absorbed by Hindus wholesale, that the very existence of Islam in India was under threat. These fears energized the Tablighi Jamaat, whom we met in the last chapter (p. 127n), aiming to forestall future surprises of this kind. An earlier chapter considered the initial conversion of the Meo, who live southwest of Delhi (p. 24f); but their Islamic observances were perfunctory. They remained unresponsive to the Jamaat though it had been active among them for some years. Then in the early 1930s the Meo fell foul of the princely ruler of Alwar. The ruler had made heavy revenue demands, which appeared to be designed so as to fall on their small agricultural holdings. He construed their resistance to these demands as the opposition of Muslims because he was a *Hindu* ruler. For this self-serving interpretation, the Arya Samaj came to his support; and he unleashed state violence against his Meo subjects – earning thereby the colonial government's displeasure (Mayaram 1997: Chap. 3). The ruler had targeted them because they were Muslim; and this made the Meo somewhat responsive to the Islamizing labours of the Tablighi Jamaat for the first time. In the widespread violence of 1947, attending the Partition, the Meo came under comprehensive assault, triggered by the Princely states' rulers – because they were Muslim. The Meo responsiveness to the Tablighi Jamaat became stronger subsequently, even as they have hung on to their Mewati territorial identification (*ibid*: 1997: Chaps 5 and 6; Aggarwal 1971; Jamous 1996). Rather different anxieties have driven the Rashtriya Swayamsevak Sangh (RSS) and its affiliates with their patently aggressive agenda. The consequent social contestation, now silent now violent and raucous, continues down to our day (Mayaram 2006).

I wish to turn now to Sandra B. Freitag's work on public arenas in several cities in UP. Overlapping Muslim and Hindu festivals in Allahabad in 1919 had witnessed extraordinary public camaraderie. A similar conjunction following the Khilafat, five years later, was "devoted largely to the display of weapons and physical force by both Mohammedans and Hindus", noted an official report quoted by Freitag (1989: 230f). Between 1923 and 1927, incidents of violent communal conflict were widespread, sometimes reaching into rural areas, and occasionally were severe (Kohat in Balochistan, 1924; "several places from Rawalpindi to Calcutta" in 1925–26; Prasad 2000: 186, 237). In March 1925, Gandhi commented despairingly on the prevailing deficit of trust between Muslims and Hindus (*ibid*.: 235).

A few years later, following the execution of Bhagat Singh for terrorism, including the throwing of bombs in the Central Legislative Assembly, Congressmen in Kanpur gave a call for *hartal* in March 1931. Muslim merchants and others were not impressed, and the city exploded into large-scale rioting, looting, and arson (Freitag 1989: Chap. 7). The violence was serious enough to occasion two separate enquiries, one official and another by the Congress (Barrier 1976 has the Congress enquiry report). It also persuaded numerous Muslim families to move from neighbourhoods that were mixed to ones communally homogenous: a move for territorial separation within a city which, as Freitag notes, presaged later migrations on a far larger scale (*ibid*.: 246ff).

By the end of the nineteenth century, we saw earlier, rage at the sufferings of one's co-religionists in one place was beginning to find expression among migrants far away (p. 146). In the years following the Khilafat to 1947, as news of each dramatic incident spread, through word of mouth, rumours, and the print media, episodes of communal violence spread farther and became more frequent. An inflammatory vernacular press fanned the embers on both sides. Local incidents and arguments were grist for acerbic journalists – carrying tales of local skirmishes around, seeking larger circulations. As the wire services delivered dramatic news to partisan newspapers subcontinentally, local incidents influenced attitudes on a vast stage (Freitag 1989: 144f, on small-town journalism in UP; P. K. Datta 1999: Chap. 4, similarly in Bengal; Jalal 2001: 45, 68, 95. See the aftermath of Moplah events above.). These went to confirm for each side its own sense of being threatened, and its fears of the other side's intentions.

I have argued that communal violence reinforces and sharpens the consciousness of identities, among groups engaging in that violence, and among their victims; and it drains the reservoirs of mutual trust that have to underlie a sense of community. The effects of this erosion of trust can be seen directly in the political negotiations. The Lucknow Pact in 1916 between leaders of the Muslim League and the Congress, accepting weighted, separate representation nationally, had reflected a stock of mutual trust among the negotiators (Robinson 1975: 236–56). A decade later, following the turbulence of the Khilafat and its aftermath, such trust and confidence in each other was more elusive: the proposals by Jinnah (1927) and by the Motilal Nehru Committee (1928) foundered on such questions as separate electorates, weightage in legislatures for minorities at different levels, and the form of government, unitary or federal; and there were further infructuous proposals, counter proposals, and negotiations held under various auspices for the next two decades. The leadership of the Muslim League and the Indian National Congress could not agree on a Constitutional framework for the future (Hasan 1991: Chap. 9; Prasad 2000: Chap. 5; Wolpert 1984: Chaps 10, 17–21; Jalal 2001: 300–303). "Whatever the claims of inclusionary nationalism, there was a veritable absence of any inter-communitarian trust and scarcely any checks on nurturing hopes of dominating one another (Jalal 2001: 326)."

Summing Up

To conclude, then. By the late nineteenth century, in parts of north India – Haryana, western UP, Bengal – the Muslim–Hindu relations were already gathering tension. In some measure, the themes and the styles of skirmishes had long been rehearsed. When the respective religious festivals coincided, the associated processions' routes could be planned to provoke, the cow and the pig could be used strategically, the other side's religious symbols could be rubbished. In a setting of considerable political, economic, and social change, and anxiety, diverse religious ideologues emerged, and moved confidently to offer their respective audiences what looked like clear, scripturally sanctioned directions.[6] The ideologies on both sides happened to be disparaging of the other side: explicitly, in the foundational text of the Arya Samaj, *Satyarthaprakash*; indirectly, in the Deobandi call to Muslims to shed the un-Islamic falsehoods in which their everyday lives were said to be steeped. Both these institutions had to contend with rival sects active on their "own" side; and occasionally this added its own, competitively separative impulses.

---

[6] I owe some of my appreciation of the role of ideologies in this cycle of growing contention to Geertz's classic paper (1973).

drifting apart 155

Beyond such religious settings, adversarial attitudes found nourishment from litterateurs, such as Bankim Chandra Chatterji, and a variety of historians: amateurs like M. G. Ranade and V. D. Savarkar, alongside professionals like Jadunath Sarkar, R. C. Majumdar, G. S. Sardesai, all of them extolling "Shivaji as a great leader of Hindu resistance against Muslim tyranny" (Prasad 1999: 209–12). The spread of these ideologies served, then, to define the Hindu and Muslim identities clearly, exclusively, in more or less adversarial terms. These worked in mutually aggravative ways, raising the ideologies' credibility for their votaries – and a sense of their relevance – and stoking the other side's feeling of being threatened. In interpreting actions on "the other side", its hostile intentions would be taken for granted. Sociologists speak of the "institutionalization" of relationships; we can speak just as accurately of the institutionalization of animosities and conflict.

Separative impulses began to make sense to so many so speedily because these had arisen from several distinct directions: from the separativeness in the caste order, from the memories of earlier centuries, from the writings of historians and ideologues[7], from skirmishes in localities, and from those who spoke separatively for, and to, distinctive religious identities. These various interventions merged into long term spirals of contentiousness – symbolic, societal, and physical. In north India, a limited *adversarial* element had come down from the medieval period. Spurred by ideological triggers in the nineteenth century, and the spirals of contention, this adversarial element became more pervasive. Even as political leaders worked out the Lucknow Pact in 1916, there followed a series of communal riots in 1917–18: Shahabad, Allahabad, Calcutta, and elsewhere (Minault 1982: 58–60). In the gradually rising heat of public contention, through the decades, these diverse impulses fused together into powerful drivers. Ayesha Jalal notes the bitter aftermath in Punjab:

> It was a dismal manifestation of inverted pride on both sides of the religious divide. Conducted in the name of Hindus and Muslims, the bigotry was no less individual for being cast in communitarian idioms (2001: 249).

---

[7] Pradip Kumar Datta (2006) has scrutinized the writings of V. D. Savarkar and M. S. Golwalkar. The latter's corpus is examined by Jyotirmaya Sharma (2007) too, following his consideration of an earlier set of "Hindutva" ideologues (see Sharma 2003). For a wide-angled view of the rise of Hindutva in Indian society and politics, see Hansen 1999.

7

Concluding review

> The cellular formation of Indian society ever since its inception, and the new Islamic model of the unitary state and community, were two ideas that were profoundly at odds with each other. Each was of world significance, all-embracing in its sweep, and apparently capable of swallowing up the other. The Indian idea provided for the hierarchical existence of every group of human beings in its autonomous cell; the Islamic idea urged a fusion of all humanity with the true faith of Islam, and of the state with the egalitarian community of the faithful. ... The strong potential of each to penetrate the other posed internal dangers to both. However, the process of mutual inter-penetration kept open the possibility of hitherto untried modes of conflict resolution amongst mankind. These were ambiguous encounters at close quarters.
>
> Ray 2003: 125–26

> ... perhaps it is the unacknowledged "truth" of Partition that we need to confront as a nation so that we may find a moral consensus beyond the local "truths" of communalism. ...
>
> Rai[1]

The Society

Why, then, did we have the Partition?

As the prospect of the transfer of power from British to Indian hands had approached, accumulated tensions sparked into heightened violence. Going by the testimony, for early 1947, of the then Home Secretary, H. M. Patel, and other observers, the prevailing level of violence in Punjab was such as to signal a threat of civil war looming

---
[1] In *The Book Review*, June 2005, p. 33.

ahead (Patel 2005: 150f and elsewhere). To partition into two countries, and to move on, was about the only available option, however devastating its immediate implications. This state of virtual civil war had come in the wake of an inability of the two principal political parties to come to Constitutional agreements over two decades past which, I argued in the last chapter, reflected falls in levels of mutual trust – in the leadership and, even more, among substantial sections of people in large parts of eastern and northern India [4.2. Numbers in square brackets refer to "levels" in Fig. 1 on the next page].

How had things come to this pass? This erosion of mutual trust, this study has argued, was a consequence of more than a century of rising contestation [4.1, 4.11]. It began in low key skirmishes in the mid-nineteenth century, involving ascendent merchants and other new occupational groups, challenging the established patterns of dominance in urban centres. For security in the changing circumstances, one needed to bond with others who would be available, even though the cement of power had dissolved. To rally a following, religious themes like festive processions could be pressed even within localities; later, religious symbols like the cow helped to draw much larger numbers. In Maharashtra, Ganapati and Shivaji proved to be potent symbols for Tilak to mobilize Hindus in the 1890s; in Bengal in the next decade, the legacy of Bankim's writings helped fire up the (almost exclusively Hindu) Swadeshi movement. In several regions, furthermore, class differences, as between peasants and landowners, converged with religious differences, so that the rival parties could summon religious leaderships and symbols to their respective banners (Chap. 4). Even as religious identities were projected in these latter cases, the core issue often was a claim to higher status in the locality [2.1, 2.2].

Violence in some measure could often be expected; but subsequent generations saw its scales grow, as religious identities became more salient, and the rivals got better organized. Antagonisms flared up further by recurrent attempts to secure "conversions" from one faith to the other. There were campaigns to this effect from both sides: Arya Samaj called it *shuddhi*, and between 1923–25, Shraddhananda, an Arya leader, coordinated a vast effort in the Agra–Mathura region; and we noted efforts in the reverse direction in Bengal in the late nineteenth century, northern Kerala in 1921, and Kohat in Balochistan in 1924. I have interpreted these campaigns for conversion as societal violence, directed at the target community's social body. While the contestation had been principally symbolic early in the century, recourse to physical

158 *spirals of contention*

Fig. 1: THE ROAD TO PARTITION

1. In this chart, key moves include:
   - judging the relative importance of the several forces;
   - clustering similarly acting forces into nodes; and
   - identifying the more consequential nodes and their causal relationships.

2. In different regions, the several elements were oriented variously.
   Social and political processes varied accordingly.
   The chart seeks to reflect the central tendencies in the north and the east.

3. Levels 1 to 4 indicate growing proximity to the moment of choice in the 1940s.
   Nodes at Level 1 were part of the ambience, with extensive, diffuse, causal links.

Level 1

1.1 Separativeness of men of religion.
Memories of medieval contests:
monuments/altered property relations

1.2 British *perceptions*,
working, e.g., through Census;
and their *policie*s, deepening
the cleavage.

Level 2

2.1 Through nineteenth century,
locally ascendent Hindu groups –
building on caste, sect, commercial
wealth and, later, institutions – generated
pressures with which Muslim elites
had to cope: processions, electoral
and other contests, cow protection
movement, presence in government
jobs, large commerce, new professions.

2.3 Amidst nineteenth century
uncertainties +1857, the liveliest
initiatives arose in religious
traditions, fostering firm
identities. Polarization grew.
Arya Samaj, Deoband. Census.
District Board, other elections.
Urdu | Hindi

2.2 Regional *class* differences –
Bengal, Moplahs, Punjab.
Religious differences trumped
those of class.

Level 3
Early 1900s: *Separate Electorates*.
Consequently, numerous political
conversations on the two sides
held apart from those on the other
side.

Level 4
**4.1 Persistent tensions +
incidence of violence grew**

⟶ **4.2 Falling levels of mutual trust**

4.11 Post-Khilafat *shuddhi*:
societal aggression

TOWARDS PARTITION

---

violence was growing towards its end; and determined campaigns at "conversions", from both sides, gave the contestation yet another dimension. There was a virtually self-aggravating quality to all this social aggression (Chap. 6).

At another level, both Muslim and Hindu ideologues – religious authors, litterateurs, historians both amateur and professional[2] – delved into the past for ground on which to imagine for themselves, and for their fellows, futures more worthy than their present. Of the several sorts of ideologues, it is men who came to be associated with institutions, especially religious institutions, that came to exercise the greater influence (Chap. 5).

The invocations of the past sought to arouse and gather emotions. From Dayananda to Golwalkar, and their ideological progeny, all have sought to harness Hindus' emotions by invoking what they saw as past and present humiliations, in ways that, these men hoped, would override the historic segmentation by caste, sect, and language. In their visions, equating the Hindu with the Indian was implicit – and often explicit; in this image of the future, the place of the Muslims was at best blurred. Muslim ideologues were nostalgic about the effulgent polities in southern Europe, North Africa, west Asia, and India, where their co-religionists had held sway; and their visions for the future too sought to override a social segmentation that was different from that in the case of the Hindus, but not much less acute, despite the egalitarian bent in the Islamic vision. In the medieval period, numerous Muslims had crossed frontiers easily, finding welcome wherever co-religionists ruled. Some Muslim ideologues drew on this tradition to proclaim a universal Islam – one that would unite politically all Muslims everywhere, disregarding all territorial boundaries; but others saw India as home, one that their ancestors had made their own. Whereas on the Hindu side the ideologues were principally laymen, the key figures among Muslims, well into the twentieth century, were largely religious leaders (Chaps 2 and 3). The separative implications of the ideologues' visions converged with those from the local rivalries for status and dominance.

Alongside the slowly rising frequency of social contention, and partly in response to the Christian missionaries' challenge to the principal religious traditions, several movements for "reform" and "revival" arose among both Muslims and Hindus from the mid-nineteenth century. We considered at some length the two remarkable cases: the congregationalist Arya Samaj among the Hindus and the influential

---

[2] For literature in languages ranging from Gujarati to Assamese and even to Tamil: see Chandra 1992, Pandian 2007: 57f. For history, in Bengal and Maharashtra, Prasad 1999: 49–61.

Deoband *madrasa* on the Muslim side. These initiatives built on scriptural bases, and harnessed to their respective cause the printing press and other new means of communication. The ideologies that spread were exclusivist, summoning the respective believers to what were claimed to be ancient, revelatory creeds, bearers of sovereign truths. Yet they were open to new institutional forms: educational institutions to western designs, including in some measure Deoband itself; and other formal organizations, with elected office bearers, regular meetings, and the like. These elements were together making something of a public space. They were also orienting their audiences away from the familiar, away from some of their neighbours; and towards the remote, the unfamiliar, and the ancient, sometimes towards a language whose value in dealing with the world remained uncertain (Chap. 5).

In the conditions of the nineteenth century, the several more or less open religious traditions from medieval times – Ismailis, Sufis, Kabir, Dadu – which had allowed their followers alternate spaces of belief and practice, came in for sharp scrutiny as being steeped in error. Short on their own apparatus of scriptures, religious specialists, elaborate rituals, pilgrimages and the like, the alternate religious traditions were unable to offer much effective resistance to the exclusivists (Chap. 4). As the revivalists' campaigns gathered pace, polarization, communal competitiveness, and conflict grew [2.3].

Curzon's Partition of Bengal in 1905 was a milestone. The government claimed for it the rationale of administrative convenience, but clearly it was intended also to clip the wings of a troublesome (predominantly Hindu) political class in Calcutta; the Partition would raise a barrier between the predominantly Muslim eastern parts and Calcutta's articulate politicians. The intensity of nationalist (Hindu) protests, which later took to terrorist violence, persuaded the British to reverse this Partition; but Muslim leaders interpreted the whole episode as yet another illustration of Hindu reluctance to cede any opportunities to Muslims. The response to the 1905 Partition illustrated a frequently observable pattern. In a setting of limited opportunities, by the late nineteenth century, the situation was being seen widely as basically zero sum: if any advantage accrued to one side, the other saw itself as being the loser, at least in equal measure.

The separative social reconfiguration and the growing din of contestation together began to harden the communal lines – enough to generate a demand from Muslim elites for separate electorates: these were instituted by the government in 1909 and became part of an agreement between the Congress and the Muslim League in 1916. Creating two separate compartments for electoral competition, one for Muslims, the second for others including Hindus, it compartmentalized, too, many of the political conversations on the two sides (Chap. 4); and we have noted its own contribution to the declining levels of mutual trust [3].

Seeing the foregoing another way, the impulses for separativeness, which culminated in the Partition, can be tracked back to two major elements continuing from the medieval period, active already in the nineteenth century, and constituting a palpable tension in the public space from the late nineteenth century on. On one side was the feeling among some groups of Hindus, like the merchants and the other upper castes in areas of northern India, that their ancestors had suffered under Muslim dynasties, and they themselves were held down by dominant landowning Muslim groups in the region; these feelings were dismissive of the value of what had been vibrant shared spaces. This stance found institutional form, for instance, in the Arya Samaj and its subsequent activities.

The other impulse came from the pride in parts of the Muslim elite that their ancestors had been rulers and empire builders, in three continents, over many centuries past. Behind this belief lay diverse conquests that had originated in west and central Asia – conquests that had shared only the rubric of Islam, their leaders' religious identity. The nineteenth century saw nearly all Indians disempowered, and subjected to diverse pressures: political, economic, social; but this sense of loss of power was the acutest for some Muslim elites, heirs to the erstwhile rulers. From about the middle of the nineteenth century, and especially after 1857, many Muslims in northern India began to feel apprehensive about what they saw as Hindu ascendency. We shall consider shortly the texture of these Muslim anxieties.

Behind all this was still another level, part of the ambience, whose influences were widespread and diffuse. This included, of course, the medieval legacy. During that period the relations between Muslims and Hindus, over the subcontinental spread, had shown a great deal of variation. On one side were the numerous linkages, the sharing of power and status, trading activity especially along the coasts, and various shared languages and forms of literature, of the creative arts, and of devotion and veneration: a cluster sometimes called "India's composite culture". On the other side lay a sense of opposition, here active there passive, between at least some religious specialists. Between the two major religious traditions and their specialists, there had long been rivalry, neither side able to prevail decisively [1.1]. There had also been recurrent conflict on communal lines off and on; and a vocabulary for mutual insult and provocation (temple, mosque, cow, pig) evolved during the medieval period and was bequeathed to later centuries. As Chapter 1 reviewed, however, the medieval period also had remarkably open religious stances, including the history of Ismaili sects in Rajasthan, and that of Sufis in at least some of their phases (Eaton 1978; Ray 2003: 108–24, *passim*).

Alongside much cooperative activity, in government and in everyday life, then, there were also impulses to pull apart, but these were held back by shared interests and established habits. Societies host to such doctrinal multiplicity, we should remember, commonly have such ambiguity, such mixtures of conflict, disagreements, and mutual accommodation. Ambiguous interfaces are normal, letting complex societies tilt one way and then the other, responding to changing circumstances. In the circumstances of the nineteenth century, leading groups on the two sides felt impelled in somewhat divergent directions. To the vocabulary for mutual provocation inherited from the medieval period, the Arya Samaj and Deoband added potent institutional triggers by the late nineteenth century. Over the next several generations, all this would often have unintended consequences, reshaping the social ground in ways that provided social reasons for the fraught politics of later decades – which will engage us shortly.

There was besides an alien presence, that of the colonialists, that stirred the pot off and on. The nineteenth century British ideas about the proper constitution of society, around a scriptural religious tradition, took these religious categories as the natural framework for Indian society. Such moves as the Census enumerations, consequently, exaggerated the scripturally backed identities at the expense of the various folk syntheses; and once the national sentiment found a voice, as through the Indian National Congress, colonial functionaries were ever watchful for its rivals, patronizing and encouraging whoever would speak in loyalist tones – and hold promise of undercutting the regime's adversaries [1.2]. Chapter 4 sought to assess the weights of these several actors in the developments of the nineteenth century. While the British presence defined the context in some measure, in the themes that have absorbed my attention the most in this study, Indian actors were centre-stage; the British were marginal.

The process at work may be seen in another way. The nineteenth century contention between Muslims and Hindus had varied sources. There was, first, a core of adversarial sentiment in limited groups and settings, received from preceding centuries. At least a modicum of shared emotion, Rajat K. Ray has argued, is a vital core for larger solidarities to arise:

> You may 'invent' a tradition, 'construct' an identity, 'imagine' a nation, but however much you print or propagate, the 'project' will not be successful until you hit upon some real emotional bond (2003: ix).

This emotional base helped channel the contestation that arose during the nineteenth century on the diverse grounds noted earlier. The received, somewhat adversarial religious identities tended to absorb parts of the small-time animosity that all this contestation generated. The combination of an older emotional base and contemporary contestation enhanced the appeal of exclusivist ideologies, being offered with the aid of new technologies and institutional forms.

What helped these exclusivist ideologies to prevail, we saw in the previous chapter, was that they offered access to resources that turned out to be important for the times. These resources were, first, *radically simplying worldviews* for grasping a stunningly complex social milieu; second, *new institutional settings* which sometimes facilitated contacts with people, often strangers, and through them secured scarce, but vital, resources for emerging situations; and third, the *security of solidarities* and identities, which were useful for responding to the growing contestatory spiral of the late nineteenth and early twentieth centuries. From the perspective of particular persons and groups, each of these resources helped in coping with unfamiliar, often threatening, circumstances.

With passing years, routine issues between a Muslim and a Hindu, say competing for a job or contesting an election, would often be *interpreted* as a contest not between individuals or small groups but between comprehensive categories. By the late nineteenth century, we have seen, communal consolidations were in progress on both sides. Rajat K. Ray has offered an interesting interpretation of what happened early in the second millennium: that Islam had become Indian in the course of contestation and interaction with the congeries of indigenous traditions,

164 *spirals of contention*

an encounter during which the latter too redefined themselves – as Hindu (2003: 104). The hundred odd years beginning with the mid-nineteenth century saw another round of contestation and interaction through which the two traditions reshaped themselves in yet other directions.

The foregoing calls for a comment of a conceptual sort. In this review, summarized in Fig. 1, the reader would notice continuities from the medieval period through the nineteenth century on to the decision to Partition; some version of the separative impulses we noticed for the nineteenth century may be traced back to the medieval period and forward to 1947. To recognize such links, however, does not make the analysis *teleological*: by no means did the separate pockets of the medieval period ordain the skirmishes of the nineteenth century, or the growth of communalism, let alone Partition itself. The Partition was an aggregate, very large-scale phenomenon, embodying millions of discrete events, choices, and initiatives.

We have identified the logic underlying what actually happened, the variety of actors propelling that logic, and the course that society in India took. The metaphor of the "spiral of contention" summarizes a cumulative, self-aggravating, directional process whose "causes", we have argued, were continually renewed within the process itself, in the antagonisms getting lodged in widely shared attitudes, in the separative reconfigurations of social relationships. The process was cumulative; its course was not entirely predictable, and it was amenable to human intervention one way or the other. The process was somewhat *directional*, but not teleological. In the setting of the direction we may see such hands as those of the Arya leader Dayananda, the Deoband *alim* Rashid Ahmad, the Hindu ideologue V. D. Savarkar, or the founder of the Tablighi Jamaat, Muhammad Ilyas; but none of these men visualized separate sovereign states. The ideologies and institutions that they fostered contributed to a certain kind of separative social consolidation. In relation to these numerous, diverse projects, which their proponents surely thought were benign, the Partition turned out to be an unintended, unforeseeable consequence.

That humans by and large make their own society, and their own history – this is an elementary sociological dictum. It is the processes that accentuated separativeness that have loomed large in this analysis – because it seeks to account for the fact of Partition. This sequence has to be set against a flux of diverse agendas pursued, and choices made, during the nineteenth century and later. Agendas that helped harden separative identities and related social arrangements came to prevail, at a particular juncture, over those to the contrary. At other junctures, around different issues, the feelings of togetherness gained the upper hand. This happened, for instance, during the 1857 uprising; in the city of Lahore during the Rowlatt Satyagraha in 1919; and then again in 1920–22 during the Khilafat–Non-cooperation movement (on 1857, Ray 2003: Chap. 4; on Lahore in 1919, Kumar 1971b; on 1920–22, Hasan 1991: Chaps 5–6). In all these episodes, many Muslims and many Hindus rose to act together against the colonial regime but, whatever their intrinsic significance, these experiences did not emerge from, and did not generate, commensurate institutional arrangements of a durable sort, such as might have shaped the course of later developments. It was the direction that was set, and continually renewed, by recurrent contention – symbolic, societal, physical – that became determinative as the end of the colonial order drew close.

Before closing this section, I have one more reflection to offer on the overall process before us, a reflection that is admittedly speculative and tentative. An observer of the early nineteenth century society in India could well have concluded that the Hindus seemed to be highly "involuted" around the caste order – their kinship and marriage, the division of labour, effective modes of social control, indeed the quasi-political arrangements, all this and more was conducted with the caste order. In the colonial milieu however, we saw in Chapter 2, the *jati* bases, and the numerous sects generating fresh charisma, provided some leverage for movement. Some of this movement went into building new kinds of institutions – which provided additional leverage for beginning to reach out. Through some four or five generations, all these elements led at least small numbers towards a gradual spreading out, towards a "disinvolution" in this space, if a neologism be permitted.

The internal dynamic among Muslims has been remarkably contrasting. The growing focus on the Quran, the *hadis*, and the *shariat* contributed, alongside a stronger sense of solidarity, to an inward-turn, to what I have called Islam's stern, inward looking cultural style (p. 3). This inward *pull* is doubly noteworthy: at one level it tended to counter the kinds of outgoing vision that a Syed Ahmed Khan or an Iqbal might have advanced; at another level it reinforced the *push* into a hardening identity being generated through the experience of spiralling contention. Over the generations, one might ask, have the pull and the push together served to make large numbers of Muslims in south Asia somewhat more involuted, rather more turned in upon their faith, than their ancestors had been, say in the early nineteenth century?

The Politics

We have just been reviewing the core thrust of this study: the *social* processes which reconfigured Indian societies in ways that made probable an outcome like the Partition of 1947; but of course there were political processes too tending towards that outcome. In this concluding chapter, I wish to bring these latter on board, though I can do this only summarily.

Elite groups could form subcontinental associations like the Indian National Congress, the Muslim Educational Conference, and later the Muslim League; and European companies had already spread a web of railways speedily. Yet the late nineteenth century society in India was segmented heavily: by linguistic regions, by the colonial administrative arrangements, by the caste order (which placed Muslims at the margins in many local social contexts); by the history of assertion and aggression since the early nineteenth century, and by the urge in certain groups to consolidate in terms of Muslim and Hindu. Correspondingly, the pre-political sentiments and social networks found their initial points of coherence within the regions, and the nineteenth century politics in India was predominantly regional, its leaders being men like Surendranath Banerjea, Amir Ali, and Bipin Chandra Pal in Bengal; Pherozeshah Mehta, Gokhle, Badruddin Tyabji, and Tilak in Bombay; Syed Ahmad Khan and Madan Mohan Malaviya in UP; and Lajpat Rai in Punjab. In the framework of the Indian National Congress furthermore, Mukul Kesavan argues, there emerged a *nationalist* perspective built around the *economic critique* of the colonial regime in India, authored by Dadabhai Naoroji and R. C. Dutt, both leading lights in the Congress. Beyond that, on the question of the nature of the Indian nation, and on how to advance its cause, the Congess had split into the "Extremists" and the "Moderates" (2007: 108–10).

Into this multi-regional scene, Gandhi entered at a time when the regional stirrings were reaching out for wider linkages – and when the relations between Muslims and Hindus already carried a tense undertow, given the course of the past several generations. Gandhi had won his spurs in South Africa, working closely with both Muslim and Hindu Gujarati merchants and others, challenging the country's racist regime on civil rights. Immediately following his return to India in 1914, he travelled incessantly and, later, intervened in public issues in Bihar (on indigo in Champaran), Gujarat (textile workers in Ahmedabad, peasants in Kheda), and Punjab (Rowlatt Act, Jallianwala Bagh) in quick succession; and he reached out to the Ali Brothers, who had been in detention for their war time political activities, establishing a relationship that would underlie their later cooperation on the Khilafat.

We noted earlier the imperative in what has been India's heavily segmented society to stress the commonality of interests, to try to hold things together. This imperative clearly influenced many among those who led the national movement, among them Gandhi and indeed the young Jinnah. Gandhi's political vision was inclusive, respectful of the variety of faiths around him. Yet his bid to enlarge public politics, bringing the masses into that arena as actors, overrode, and disrupted somewhat, the earlier pattern of elite cooperation within the Congress. By 1920, Gandhi was stirring a countrywide following, despite his impatience when crowds were undisciplined. His public stature was virtually unrivalled, as leading (Hindu) merchants, part of a rising capitalist class, underwrote his spartan ventures.

Gandhi's style of leadership was too complex to get summary review here. Following Ravinder Kumar, we need take note of only a couple of elements. One was his operative conception of the nature of Indian society: Gandhi "looked upon the peoples of India as a loose constellation of classes, communities, and religious groups, and because he had no illusions about the nature of political society in the country, he was able to unite it in a way it had never been united before (Kumar 1971a: 12)." He was continuing with what had been Congress practice for a generation. For his style and his struggles, vast numbers made him an iconic figure, a Mahatma; yet the struggles' effectiveness depended on a range of key men from diverse backgrounds – men like Vallabhbhai Patel, Mohamed Ali, Rajendra Prasad, Abdul Gaffar Khan, and Rajagopalachari – men firmly embedded within their respective religious, caste, and territorial social categories, who could reach out to others too. Some of them were discovering the possibility of harnessing *jati* networks and identities to political effect, a discovery that became an axis for politics in India for generations to come.

The other striking element was Gandhi's sense of the efficacy of symbols in transcending cleavages. The protagonists for the cow in UP, Tilak in Maharashtra, and *Swadeshi* leaders in Bengal had all invoked symbols effectively for decades earlier; Gandhi went farther. Already in Transvaal in South Africa by 1908, he had organized several symbolic acts in collective protest against the civil disabilities imposed on Indians living there (Brown 1989: 56). In the symbols that he made into public issues later in India – Rowlatt Act, *khadi*, salt, foreign cloth – Kumar stresses his "attempt to relate political aspirations to moral ... objectives; to the flowering of the character and personality of his countrymen ..." (1971: 15). It is in the nature of symbols, however, that it takes time, and diverse engagement, for a generality of associations to gather to them: a generality that gives them their evocative power. Furthermore, even the secular symbols that Gandhi advanced came with his recognizably Hindu lifestyle, ideas, and vocabulary – from which, we have seen, key groups of Muslims had been drawing away. His political *motive* may have been secular; but he could not control others' responses to what he did. The responses were mediated by the widely understood social logics that had been spreading in society. With important exceptions like Abul Kalam Azad and Abdul Gaffar Khan, Muslims in the main held aloof – apart, of course, from the Khilafat episode. Khilafat, as Kesavan notes, was the only occasion when Gandhi worked with a *religious* symbol – and he soon came to grief (2007: 113).

Sensing his own weakening position, the ruler of the Ottoman empire had been promoting himself, since the 1870s, as the Khalifa, the religious Head, of Muslims everywhere, since his empire included the sacred sites for the Hajj in Arabia. As European powers, including Britain, pressed against the Ottomans, Muslims in India began to rally behind the Khalifa, part of the pan-Islamic impulse. After 1912, a rising generation of young Muslim leaders steered the nascent Muslim League into cooperating with the Congress, even if it would pit them against the colonial regime; and they drafted the hitherto apolitical Muslim *religious* leaders also onto their platforms. Their anxiety over the terms that would be offered to the Ottomans began to climb as the War approached its end. While the young Turks among Muslims were angry, their political leverage with the colonial regime, and through it with the British, was limited.

concluding review 169

At the end of World War I, however, Gandhi happened to be ascending to leadership in India's nationalist politics. The issue of the Ottoman empire and Khilafat, linked with Islam's sacred sites, was driving a wedge between the British and significant Muslim leadership in India; and Gandhi saw here a possible nationalist alliance – which might even dampen the Hindu–Muslim quarrels. Given his sensitivity to the potential of symbols, Gandhi responded to the Khilafat issue with alacrity. After the Rowlatt Act and Jallianwala Bagh, nationalist tempers were high. The national movement might be made comprehensive by adding the religious issue of the Khilafat to a general call for Non-cooperation with the colonial regime. This twinning of impulses launched what became by far the most powerful political movement hitherto in India. The course it took, and its aftermath, illustrate the simultaneous tug of two sets of cross-currents: one principally social, the other political. The first has engaged us at length; the second we need to take on board now.

In the chain of political links that Gandhi had been building, the weakest were those with Muslims. In South Africa he had worked closely with many Muslim Gujaratis. The leading Gujarati Muslim in politics in India in about 1920 was Muhammad Ali Jinnah; but their political styles were a study in contrast: challenging the colonial government through mass activity for Gandhi; concentrating on the legislative and other formal negotiatory arenas for Jinnah. The parting of ways came at the Nagpur session of the Congress in December 1920, as Gandhi's supporters, led by the Ali Brothers, secured the votes ratifying his call in support of the Khilafat and Non-cooperation.

The alliance Gandhi forged turned out to be difficult. Many Congressmen and others had questioned the wisdom of the Congress championing the Khilafat (Hasan 1991: 133). Even for Gandhi himself, while he proclaimed *non-violence* as a religious value, the Khilafat leadership maintained that their religious value was the preservation of the Khalifa, not non-violence; this stand was true to an established tradition (Hardy 1983). For Gandhi, non-violence was a canon with which to get a mass movement to learn to discipline itself. In this new style of politics, however, "all-India" politics became engaged with numerous local issues, so that the dynamic of the latter would affect the former (Brown 1989: 165). When Gandhi saw incidents of mass violence erupting in distant localities – North Kerala, August 1921 (against colonial officials and Hindu landlords), Bombay city, November 1921 (against Parsis and others thought to be allies of the colonial regime), and Chauri Chaura, Gorakhpur in UP, February 1922 (against local policemen) – Gandhi saw discipline going, and indiscipline growing. Unable to control these bouts of violence, he withdrew the Non-cooperation, for he attached great importance to the means employed, regardless of the ends in view (Nanda 1989: Chaps 16–18; Brown 1989: 84 and elsewhere; Amin 1995).

In all these episodes of violence, the attackers saw the principal target group as part of the colonial framework of oppression. In north Kerala, however, the perpetrators of violence happened to be Muslim and their target included their Hindu landlords – who were subjected to forced conversions to Islam too. The local communal divide lay open; and as the news travelled, it raised Hindu ire elsewhere. The kind of intellectual, emotional, organizational, and political resources – and historical precedents – that would have been needed to bridge the cleavage were not at hand. The larger communal divide surfaced with fresh vigour, and several aggravative initiatives took off soon thereafter. Shraddhanand's *shuddhi*, a campaign to convert vast numbers of Muslims to Hinduism at one go, we have noted earlier to be an act of societal aggression (Chap. 6). The mid-1920s saw too the activation, in the vicinity of Delhi, of the Tablighi Jamaat, the beginning of an enormous drive to re-Islamize, as it were, the millions who had long lived the faith minimally; and in Nagpur in central India began at the same time Rashtriya Swayamsevak Sangh (RSS), seeking to provide collective muscle for what its founders misconstrued as the feeble and beleaguered Hindus.

The Khilafat wave had carried the *ulama* up to political leadership; but when Ataturk in Turkey abolished the Khilafat, its votaries in India lost their prime cause. The Congress support for Khilafat had persuaded Muslims to join the party in strength during 1920–23 (Hasan 2002: 170–71 has figures, citing Gopal Krishna); but their participation fell off. The Congress sought to be an umbrella organization, admitting many who belonged, simultaneously, also to sectional parties like the Muslim League and the Hindu Mahasabha. Yet, given the logic of numbers, Muslims realized that their Hindu counterparts would always have the upper hand in the Congress. The large bulk of Muslims was oriented to regional parties, like the Unionist Party in Punjab and the Krishak Praja Party in Bengal (Wolpert 1984: Chap. 11; Gilmartin 1988: 109–52; Chatterji 1995). Separate electorates having been promulgated, however, they would be reminded continually that the centre of gravity of the Congress was not among Muslims. In the late 1930s and the 1940s, right up to 1947, the religious orthodoxy in the Jamiat-ul-ulama-i-Hind (JUH), led by some *ulama* from Deoband, tended to argue for a free "united" India that would be composed of "largely self-governing communities", in which the *ulama* would guide Muslims, through [Islamic] education and the *shariat* (Hardy 1971: 41; Metcalf 2005 on one key figure, Husain Ahmad Madani).

The possibility of mobilizing around the Muslim identity had been demonstrated to spectacular effect during the Khilafat. That issue had dissolved before its protagonists' eyes; but could that kind of mobilization not be repeated for Muslims? Returning to active leadership of the Muslim League in 1934, Jinnah applied himself to the task. At the 1937 elections, the provinces with Muslim majorities all got non-League ministries; and the next few years were thick with events. A key element in the picture was this: all Muslim political leaders with significant followings had their bases in their own provinces only; Jinnah, on the other hand, had been a significant figure in national politics for three decades, and he was President of the Muslim League, which had existed even longer as the only all-India Muslim party. The Congress had won at the 1937 elections dramatically – but not in Muslim constituencies. Shortly after the elections, Jinnah suceeded in persuading Sikandar Hayat Khan and Fazlul Haq – Premiers of Punjab and Bengal, leaders of independent, non-League coalitions in the two provinces – to enter the League, and enable him to speak for all Muslims at the Centre (Jalal 1985: 39f). Thereafter he would be able to sideline both the "Nationalist Muslims" in the Congress, and the JUH opposition to his vision.

The Muslim political consensus was forming around political separativeness, not around any of the alternatives we just noted; why? To this question the answer emerging in this study turns around the rising spiral of contention. We have argued that the communal animosities helped strengthen the *umma*, the sense of Islamic community, and to generate a lay consensus in the political realm.[3] The Muslim dossiers of Hindu (and Congress) misdeeds kept growing. Jalal mentions a

---

[3] Farzana Shaikh (1989) has tracked the idea of consensus, *ijma*, to its beginnings in the days of the Prophet. In the long-term ideology, however, this general idea has been something of a constant; the active, lay consensus has varied over time, congealing around one or another alternative available at the moment. This study has sought to account for the consensus in favour of a homeland for Muslims that emerged in the 1930s and 1940s.

pamphlet, "[p]ublished for the third time in 1921", pointing to the Hindu practice of untouchability, directed at Muslims (2001: 239; see also Bir Bahadur Singh's testimony in Butalia 1998: 167–70). For the period of the Congress government in UP, 1937 to 1939, Mukul Kesavan has examined the communal scene closely. The Congress government was almost wholly Hindu; nearly all Muslim legislators sat on opposition benches. In the sharp rise in incidents of communal conflict, Mukul Kesavan sees a belief among Hindu zealots that they had achieved Hindu Raj, entitling them to push hard on old tracks: play music before mosques, prevent kine-killing by Muslims. In these activities, local Congressmen too were often involved, and occasionally the government seemed to be favouring Hindus. In any case, whatever it did or did not do, the Congress was held responsible for everything that went wrong, for it led the government. The Muslim League seized on every incident to attack the Congress government in the legislature, to attack the party through publicity, and to arouse Muslim opinion in localities, cementing its claim to be the only true champion of the Muslims' cause (Kesavan 1990; Wolpert 1984: Chap. 12).

We have noted earlier that the level of mutual trust on the two sides was low. On one side, it limited the margins of manoeuvre available to the leadership. Whatever the leaders' own inclination, they all operated in competitive political arenas; and they had to be wary of what would cut ice with their constituents on the ground: the Congress leaders, for instance, had to watch lest it lose much of its base to the Hindu Mahasabha. The other side of the same coin was that the leaders of the Muslim League had good reasons to believe that a call in religious terms would bring in the votes: an estimate that would stiffen the resolve of those who took a hard line for Muslims to hold fast.

The Muslim League began to secure a mass base rapidly though its political organization remained minuscule; still, it was a bit odd for Jinnah, a flourishing barrister, to say that, in 1936–37, he "worked alone unassisted by ... a personal staff ... [for] the numerous letters that I had to dispose of" (Malik 1971: 384). Between 1937 and 1946, the Muslim League was able to generate a political wave in favour of a homeland for Muslims (Sayeed 1983: 276–78). It was a move of quite extraordinary daring; it was also a leap in the dark. There was nothing in its proponents', or in their adversaries', experience that would have enabled them to guess, even remotely, the likely, long trails of consequences. As the British prepared to leave, an Islamic mystique swept the country. The wave was strong enough to persuade, for instance, the numerous Chishti Pirs of Punjab to switch their support to the Muslim League in the mid-1940s (Gilmartin 1988: 213-22). This reversed both the historical Sufi inter-religious influence on Punjabi society and culture and, over the previous generation, the Chishti Pirs' support for the inter-communal Unionist Party in Punjab politics. The elections in 1945-46 were a watershed in south Asia's history. Concerning the demand for Pakistan, the verdict of the elections was unambiguous. In the negotiations for the transfer of power from British to Indian hands, the elections cemented Jinnah's claim to speak for India's Muslims. The wave so formed, however, proved to be so strong that it was to limit Jinnah's own room for manoeuvre during the last rounds of negotiation (on Punjab, Gilmartin 1988: 191-222; on 1946 negotiations, Jalal 1985: 186-89).

The single most vivid image associated with the Partition of 1947 is the savagery at work in both parts of Punjab; such savagery is not a necessary part of Partitions. Partitions *can* be cool. Think of the then United Arab Republic splitting in 1961 between Syria and the residual UAR (Egypt); or Czechoslovakia splitting in 1992 into the Czech and Slovak republics. One difference in India was the animosity that had ballooned over the decades; yet Punjab and Bengal both carried stocks of antipathy in equal measure. If Punjab bled so much more furiously in 1947, we have to go beyond the stores of antagonism. What set Punjab apart was the ubiquitous, demobilized armymen in the land of the "martial races", veterans of World War II and others: Hindus, Muslims, Sikhs. It was the possibility of arousing them to kill civilians with impunity that made the difference in Punjab (Wolpert 1984: 261f).

Was Partition Inevitable?

It is important to remember that the political separation was largely an unintended consequence of what had initially been only social separativeness. The underlying attitudes had formed here and there over the decades. If the mid-nineteenth century initiatives appear, in hindsight, to have led to the formation of the social base, ultimately, for the Partition, that outcome had not been intended by the *ulama*, the Arya Samaj, or any of the others. A social cleavage had, however, been deepened and made more general, becoming part of the prevailing common sense.

The spiral of contention that arose kept on generating waves of fresh emotion – emotions of fear and anxiety and all that goes with them. All this went into forging the (separative) social bondings; and this started its own dynamic, independent of its sponsors' preferences, providing the framework in relation to which later actors would craft their own political agendas. Lawrence Ziring wrote three decades after the event:

> As Jinnah noted in a 1948 speech: "Pakistan was made possible because of the danger of complete annihilation of [the] human soul in a society based on caste." The cry, 'Islam in Danger' exemplified this fear, it also galvanized an ethnically diverse and otherwise disparate people into a massive demand for national self-determination ... (1979: 145).

Arsenals both of attitudes and of weapons were ready to fire.

The foregoing fits into a general conception of society, as if it were a "system": one where information about its ongoing experiences serves to modify that "system"; the information is the *feedback* through which the society gets regulated or modified. These "feedbacks", however, may be "positive" or "negative". Positive feedback nudges a system to continue further along tracks already taken; negative feedback nudges it, instead, to *dampen*, to hold back on, continuing the movement in the current direction. The "systems perspective" is fruitful in situations of conflict too. The process of long-term social contention we have considered may be seen as a "system", in which the ongoing feedbacks were "positive". That is to say: each incident, and each report, of such conflict would (*a*) increase some individuals' sense of insecurity somewhat, and (*b*) push them a little more towards one of the exclusive identities being advanced. (*c*) This spread, and hardening, of exclusive identities would tend to reduce communication and understanding across them, make future incidents of conflict likelier, and – completing the loop – increase individual insecurities further. A "learning" process was at work here, a learning of fear – learning of a pathological sort. Systems subject to such escalating spirals – or, if you prefer, long-term "positive" feedbacks – have an inherent tendency to run out of control.[4] ("Negative feedback", in contrast, would have consisted of interventions that would serve to *dampen* the conflict, preventing the

---

[4] For more on the "systems" perspective on conflicts, see Jayaram and Saberwal 1996: 510–12.

spiral from escalating or even reversing it.) It has been the brunt of my argument that the moment of Partition should be seen as the climax of slow, multi-generational, virtually self-aggravating processes of this kind. Sustained positive feedbacks may of course be made benign by restructuring the whole system appropriately. In this latter perspective it could be argued that the restructuring called Partition, however ghastly its immediate costs, was in this sense a "benign" move.

Armed with hindsight, we can see the errors in leading twentieth century actors' judgments. The 1937 programme for mass contact among Muslims, instigated by Nehru, for instance, overlooked both the paucity of workers in the Congress suitable for the task (Prasad 2000: 378–81) and the strength of animosities on the ground. And there is Iqbal's 28 May 1937 letter to Jinnah, confident that Nehru's socialism is likely to cause "much bloodshed among the Hindus themselves"; that the Muslim masses' poverty can be removed by promulgating the *shariat*, "and its further development in the light of modern ideas"; and that, to do the latter, Muslims needed independence (Malik 1971: 386). Such projects and hunches had little backing in experience – and the misjudgements could at times be egregious.

A major difficulty, of course, was the enormous complexities – of the society, and of its historical circumstances – confronting these men. A great deal was unprecedented in the twentieth century: the 1930s and 1940s were the first occasion in Indian history when fresh Constitutional arrangements for sovereignty were being considered, not through conquest but through consultation with, and between, persons who saw themselves as acting on behalf of certain categories of people. The game was being played under rules whose long-term implications were unfamiliar in the Indian actors' experience.

For playing that game, there was first the question: what general principles should govern the Constitutional arrangements being negotiated? In *conquest states*, including the Chinese imperial regimes, the Saltanat and Mughals, and all the rest, the principle of hierarchy, from the sovereign down, used to settle the core of the question. In the colonial regime, another conquest state, power rested, first, in the hands of British rulers; and subordinate to them, it was subject to a kind of legal order derived from Britain. What would be the general principles for governing the subcontinent's late colonial, and post-Independence, polity? They could scarcely opt for a conquest state, such as a Babur or a Shivaji might have launched. On the mid-twentieth century horizon, an electoral democracy was the principal available option. Working that on a plain one-man-one-vote basis could be dismissed quickly as being "western", unsuited to India's situation – which would, Muslims feared, only ensure Hindu domination over them. Variations in the democratic option could include the extent of the franchise, and how the legislatures would be structured through devices like separate electorates and weightages for different categories. Securing consensus on such choices, however, needed mutual trust at a level that, for reasons we have seen, was unattainable. In the decision-making councils in 1946–47, that "minimal degree of political consensus" was lacking without which Constitution-making cannot proceed (Preuss 1991: 119, apropos Constitution-making in East and Central Europe in the wake of the 1989 revolutions; Ambedkar 1945: Part III for the Indian scene in the mid-1940s).

Seen another way, within the structure of Indian society, what were the limits of political mobilization? Here we have the general problem of the implications of turning India's cellular society over to elections, democratic procedures, civil society, and the like. Social diversity in unparalleled measure had been bound into thousands of *jati*s, and it had carried an extraordinary range of religious traditions too. Political competition needed mobilizing; and to attain any substantial scale, it was necessary to transcend the cellular barriers. Attempts at such transcendence had relied on general symbols, but symbols that would appeal effectively across the Muslim: Hindu interface were hard to find. The pools of symbols received from the medieval period were distributed, as it were, into two baskets. Those in one appealed to Muslims, those in the other to Hindus. Of course there were others, like Akbar or the Sufis or the ballads of love in Punjab; and although these are often invoked to assert "the composite culture" or India's "secular traditions", in the period and the public arenas we have considered, they emerged from the shadows but rarely.

When Gandhi seized on the Khilafat as a symbol, his non-Muslim followers were responding not to Khilafat but to Gandhi himself, for he had himself become by then a potent symbol (Amin 1995). After the post-Khilafat–Non-cooperation violence, Gandhi took care to frame his public issues around secular symbols but, by then, his appeal to Muslims at large had to refract through the plasma of antagonism that had been rising for two generations. With limited exceptions such as the Khilafat and the North Western Frontier Province, the strategy of transcendence failed to appeal to Muslims at large and, after 1909, there was also the structural barrier of separate electorates. The decision to Partition, then, may be seen as a move, deliberate or not, to simplify the political field somewhat (Ambedkar 1945: 212 had envisaged that a Partition would indeed simplify matters somewhat). Even in that simplified milieu, Pakistan split again in 1971, and India has, more than once, come close to the edge.

Suppose there had been no Partition; could that alternative have been worse? In terms of the ideology prevailing in Pakistan now, that alternative would have been unspeakably worse. How does it look from the viewpoint of post-Partition India? It may be argued that coping with the social heterogeneity, and turbulence, did stretch the political skills available in post-Partition India to their limits. Amidst a somewhat simplified political field, we may see the marks of a measure of social, political, and economic creativity: the integration of princely states, the vast churning of society including a modest assault on the caste order, the fairly orderly management of a democratic polity with all its regional pulls, some strength of civil society, and the recent rise in literacy, Panchayati Raj, industry, communications, and science and technology. Even the tension between Hindus and Muslims has been controlled over the past half century, after counting in all the riots and the fearful pogroms. In large part this tension has been deflected on to the international relations between Pakistan and India – turbulent as these have been. Suppose, however, that some agreement, other than the Partition, had been worked out in 1947. Counterfactual speculation is always tricky; still, there is the simple question: what would have happened to all the animosity that had accumulated over the generations in the northern and eastern parts? Perhaps the social geography of attitudes is more malleable than the rivers and mountains of physical geography; yet attitudes have their own intractabilities. An unpartitioned subcontinent, with numerous princely states going their own ways: could it have taken a Yugoslav, or a Sri Lankan, kind of road to breakdown?

We need to face up to the past in full measure, reckoning the costs, historically, of choices made – paths taken and those not taken – and think of the options for the future. Twentieth century politics and conflicts, especially after the Khilafat and Non-Cooperation movements had subsided, have carried several potent strains promoting a hard separativeness between the categories Hindu and Muslim. We have explored the social psychology underlying the link between separativeness and conflict. Hard lines of social separation foreshadow serious, continuing, and inescapable conflicts in a large, complex, society. For such societies, especially, it is imperative that we monitor our milieu, and review ongoing experience, continually, considering alternatives, and making choices for the future – with as much awareness of their likely consequences as we can muster. It seems to me that the social sciences, including history, have the resources now to enable us to grasp, in non-partisan ways, what has gone into the animosities of long-standing, and to comprehend accurately what really happened in the past. These offer us the resources, too, for trying to steer into the future with a sense of responsibility, and with close attention to the likely consequences of what we do, individually and collectively, trying as best we can to control the unwanted consequences. These clarify something of the nuggets that have come to us from sages, ancient and modern, through the millennia. Whether we shall have the patience and the judgment to listen to them is, of course, another matter.

bibliography

Aggarwal, Partap. 1971. *Caste, religion and power.* New Delhi: Shri Ram Centre for Industrial Relations.
Ahmad, Aziz. 1964. *Studies in Islamic culture in the Indian environment.* Oxford: Clarendon Press.
Ahmad, Imtiaz. 1969. Secularism and communalism, *Economic and Political Weekly*, vol. 4: 1137–58.
——— (ed.). 1973a. *Caste and social stratification among the Muslims.* New Delhi: Manohar.
———. 1973b. "Endogamy and status mobility among the Siddique Sheikhs of Allahabad, Uttar Pradesh", in idem, *Caste and social stratification among the Muslims*, pp. 157–94. New Delhi: Manohar.
——— (ed.). 1976. *Family, kinship and marriage among Muslims in India.* New Delhi: Manohar.
——— (ed.). 1981. *Ritual and religion among Muslims in India.* New Delhi: Manohar.
——— (ed.). 1983. *Modernization and social change among Muslims in India.* New Delhi: Manohar.
Ahmed, Rafiuddin. 1981. *The Bengal Muslims 1871–1906.* New Delhi: Oxford University Press.
Alam, Muzaffar. 1986. "Aspects of agrarian uprisings in north India in the early eighteenth century", in S. Bhattacharya and Romila Thapar (eds), *Situating Indian history: for Sarvepalli Gopal*, pp. 146–70. Delhi: Oxford University Press.
———. 1989. "Competition and co-existence: Indo-Islamic interaction in medieval north India", *Itinerario*, vol. 13: 37–59.
———. 2004. *The languages of political Islam in India, c. 1200–1800.* New Delhi: Permanent Black.
Ambedkar, B. R. 1945. *Pakistan, or Partition of India.* 2nd edn. Bombay: Thacker & Co.
Amin, Shahid. 1995. *Event, metaphor, memory: Chauri Chaura 1922–1992.* New Delhi: Oxford University Press.
———. 2002. "On retelling the Muslim conquest of north India", in Partha Chatterjee and Anjan Ghosh (eds), *History and the present*, pp. 24–43. New Delhi: Permanent Black.
Aquil, Raziuddin. 2006. "From Dar-ul-Harb to Dar-ul-Islam?: Chishti Sufi accounts and the emergence of Islam in the Delhi sultanate", in Satish Saberwal and

Mushirul Hasan (eds), *Assertive religious identities: India and Europe*, pp. 59–84. New Delhi: Manohar.
Bairy, Ramesh T. S. 2003. "Caste, community and association: a study of the dynamics of Brahmin identity in contemporary Karnataka". Unpublished Ph. D. dissertation. University of Hyderabad.
Baker, D. E. U. 1979. *Changing political leadership in an Indian province: the Central Provinces and Berar 1919–1939*. New Delhi: Oxford University Press.
Bandopadhyay, Sekhar. 1990. *Caste, politics and the Raj: Bengal 1872–1937*. Calcutta: K. P. Bagchi.
Banerjee, Himadri. 2006. "The other Sikhs: Sikhs and Sikhism in eastern India", Presidential Address, Modern Section. 66th Session, Indian History Congress. Santiniketan.
Barrier, N. Gerald (ed.). 1976. *Roots of communal politics*. New Delhi: Arnold-Heinemann.
Basu, Aparna. 1980. "Growth of education and Muslim separatism, 1919–1939", in B. R. Nanda (ed.), *Essays in modern Indian history*, pp. 223–43. New Delhi: Oxford University Press.
Bayly, C. A. 1975. *Local roots of Indian politics*. London: Oxford University Press.
———. 1983. *Rulers, townsmen and bazaars: north Indian society in the age of British expansion, 1770–1870*. Cambridge: Cambridge University Press.
———. 1985. "The pre-history of 'communalism'? religious conflict in India, 1700–1860", *Modern Asian studies*, vol. 19: 177–203.
Bayly, Susan. 1989. *Saints, goddesses and kings: Muslims and Christians in south Indian society 1700–1900*. Cambridge: Cambridge University Press.
Beckerlegge, Gwilym. 2006. *Swami Vivekananda's legacy of service: a study of the Ramakrishna math and mission*. New Delhi: Oxford University Press.
Berger, Peter and Thomas Luckmann. 1966. *Social construction of reality*. Harmondsworth: Penguin.
Bertocci, Peter. 1976. "Community structure and social rank in two villages in Bangladesh", in T. N. Madan (ed.), *Muslim communities of south Asia: culture and society*, pp. 28–52. New Delhi: Vikas.
Bhalla, Alok (ed.). 1994. *Stories about the Partition of India*. New Delhi: Harper Collins.
Bhargava, Rajeev. 2000. "History, nation and community: reflections on nationalist historiography of India and Pakistan", *Economic and Political Weekly*, vol. 35: 193–200.
Bharucha, Rustom. 2003. *Rajasthan: an oral history. Conversations with Komal Kothari*. New Delhi: Penguin.
Bhattacharya, Sabyasachi. 2003. *Vande mataram: the biography of a song*. New Delhi: Penguin.
Bose, Nirmal Kumar. 1941. "The Hindu method of tribal absorption", *Science and culture*, vol. 7: 188–94.
———. 1967. *Culture and society in India*. Bombay: Asia.
———. 1968. *Calcutta: A Social Survey*. Bombay: Lalvani Publishers.

Brass, Paul R. 1975. "Muslim separatism in the United Provinces: the social context and political strategy of the Muslim minority before Partition", in *idem*, *Language, religion and politics in north India*, pp. 119–81. Cambridge: Cambridge University Press.
Brown, Judith. 1989. *Gandhi: prisoner of hope*. New Haven: Yale University Press.
Butalia, Urvashi. 1998. *The other side of silence: voices from the Partition of India*. New Delhi: Viking.
———. 2001. "Partition and memory", *Seminar*, no. 497: 92–95.
Cashman, Richard I. 1975. *The myth of the Lokamanya: Tilak and mass politics in Maharashtra*. Berkeley: University of California Press.
Chakrabarti, Kunal. 2001. *Religious process: the puranas and the making of a religious tradition*. New Delhi: Oxford University Press.
Chakrabarty, Dipesh. 1990. "Communal riots and labour: Bengal's jute mill-hands in the 1890s", in Veena Das (ed.), *Mirrors of violence: communities, riots and survivors in south Asia*, pp. 146–84. New Delhi: Oxford University Press.
Chakravarti, Anand. 1975. *Contradiction and change: emerging patterns of authority in a Rajasthan village*. New Delhi: Oxford University Press.
Chandra, Bipan. 1984. *Communalism in modern India*. New Delhi: Vikas.
Chandra, Sudhir. 1992. *The oppressive present: literature and social consciousness in colonial India*. New Delhi: Oxford University Press.
———. 1998. *Enslaved daughters: colonialism, law and women's rights*. New Delhi: Oxford University Press.
Chatterjee, Partha. 1982. "Agrarian relations and communalism in Bengal, 1926–1935", in Ranajit Guha (ed.), *Subaltern studies I: writings on south Asian history and society*, pp. 9–38. New Delhi: Oxford University Press.
———. 1994. *The nation and its fragments: colonial and postcolonial histories*. New Delhi: Oxford University Press.
———. 1999. "On religious and linguistic nationalisms: the second partition of Bengal", in Peter van der Veer and Harmut Lehmann (eds), *Nation and religion: perspectives on Europe and Asia*, pp. 112–28. Princeton: Princeton University Press.
Chatterji, Bankim Chandra. (1881–82) 2005. *Anandamath, or the sacred brotherhood*. Trans. and ed. Julius J. Lipner. New Delhi: Oxford University Press.
Chatterji, Joya. 1995. *Bengal divided: Hindu communalism and partition, 1932–1947*. New Delhi: Foundation Books.
Chattopadhyaya, Brajadulal. 1998. *Representing the other? Sanskrit sources and the Muslims (Eighth to Fourteenth Century)*. New Delhi: Manohar.
Chaudhuri, Binay Bhushan. 2002. "Society and culture of the tribal world in colonial eastern India: reconsidering the notion of 'Hinduization' of tribes", in Hetukar Jha (ed.), *Perspectives on Indian society and history*, pp. 23–79. New Delhi: Manohar.
Chaudhuri, Maitrayee. 2004. "Introduction", in *idem* (ed.), *Feminism in India*, pp. xi–xlvi. New Delhi: Kali for Women.

Chowdhury, Indira. 2006. Institutional history, collective memory and the institutional archives, Occasional Papers (New Series). Delhi: Department of Sociology, University of Delhi.

Cohen, Abner. 1974. *Two dimensional man: an essay on the anthropology of power and symbolism in complex society*. London: Routledge & Kegan Paul.

Cohn, Bernard S. 1996. *Colonialism and its forms of knowledge: the British in India*. Princeton: Princeton University Press.

Conlon, Frank. 1977. *A caste in a changing world: the Chitrapur Saraswat Brahmans 1700–1935*. Berkeley: University of California Press.

Dalmia, Vasudha. 1995. "The only real religion of the Hindus: Vaisnava self-representation in the late nineteenth century", in Vasudha Dalmia and Heinrich von Stietencron (eds), *Representing Hinduism: the construction of religious traditions and national identity*, pp. 176–210. New Delhi: Sage Publications.

———. 1997. *The nationalization of Hindu traditions: Bharatendu Harischandra and nineteenth-century Banaras*. New Delhi: Oxford University Press.

Das, Veena. 1990. "Our work to cry: your work to listen", in *idem* (ed.), *Mirrors of violence: communities, riots and survivors in south Asia*, pp. 345–98. New Delhi: Oxford University Press.

Das Gupta, Ashin. 1979. *Indian merchants and the decline of Surat c. 1700–1750*. Wiesbaden: Steiner.

Datta, Nonica. 1999. *Forming an identity: a social history of the Jats*. New Delhi: Oxford University Press.

Datta, Pradip Kumar. 1999. *Carving blocs: communal ideology in early twentieth-century Bengal*. New Delhi: Oxford University Press.

———. 2006. "Hindutva ideas of the past", in Satish Saberwal and Mushirul Hasan (eds), *Assertive religious identities: India and Europe*, pp. 199–232. New Delhi: Manohar.

Denzin, Norman K. 1983. "Interpretive interactionism", in G. Morgan (ed.), *Beyond method: strategies for social research*, pp. 126–49. Beverly Hills: Sage Publications.

Devalle, Susana B. C. 1992. *Discourses of ethnicity: culture and protest in Jharkhand*. New Delhi: Sage Publications.

Dobbin, Christine. 1972. *Urban leadership in western India: politics and communities in Bombay city, 1840–85*. Oxford: Oxford University Press.

Dube, Saurabh. 1998. *Untouchable pasts: religion, identity, and power among a central Indian community, 1780–1950*. Albany, NY: State University of New York Press.

Eaton, Richard M. 1978. *Sufis of Bijapur 1300–1700. Social roles of Sufis in medieval India*. Princeton: Princeton University Press.

———. 1994. *The rise of Islam and the Bengal frontier, 1204–1760*. New Delhi: Oxford University Press.

———. 2000. *Essays on Islam and Indian history*. New Delhi: Oxford University Press.

bibliography 183

Elliot, H. M. and John Dowson (eds). 1867–77. *The history of India as told by its own historians: the Muhammadan period*, 8 vols. London: Trubner.
Eschmann, Anncharlot. 1997. "Religion, reaction and change: the role of sects in Hinduism", in Gunther-Dietz Sontheimer and Hermann Kulke (eds), *Hinduism reconsidered*, pp. 108–20. New Delhi: Manohar.
Faruqi, Ziyaul-Hasan. 1981. "Orthodoxy and heterodoxy in India", in Mushirul Hasan (ed.), *Communal and pan-Islamic trends in colonial India*, pp. 326–43. New Delhi: Manohar.
Fox, R. G. 1967. "Family, caste, and commerce in a north Indian market town", *Economic development and cultural change*, vol. 15: 297–314.
———. 1969. *From zamindar to ballot box: community change in a north Indian market town*. Ithaca, NY: Cornell University Press.
———. 1971. *Kin, clan, raja, and rule: state–hinterland relations in pre-industrial India*. Berkeley: University of California Press.
Freitag, Sandra B. 1989. *Collective action and community: public arenas and the emergence of communalism in north India*. Berkeley: University of California Press.
Fruzzetti-Ostor, Lina. 1972. "The idea of community among West Bengal Muslims", in P. Bertocci (ed.), *Prelude to crisis*, Occasional paper no. 80, pp. 79–88. Michigan State University: Centre for South and East Asian Studies.
Geertz, Clifford. 1973. "Ideology as a cultural system", in *idem*, *The interpretation of cultures: selected essays*, pp. 193–233. New York: Basic Books.
Gernet, Jacques. 1982. *A history of Chinese civilization*. Cambridge: Cambridge University Press.
Ghosh, Papiya. 1997. "Partition's Biharis", *Comparative studies of South Asia, Africa and the Middle East*, vol. 17: 21–33.
Ghosh, Suresh C. 2000. *The history of education in modern India 1757–1989*. Rev. edn. New Delhi: Orient Longman.
Giddens, Anthony 1979. *Central problems in social theory: action, structure and contradiction in social analysis*. London: Macmillan.
Gillion, Kenneth. 1968. *Ahmedabad: a study in Indian urban history*. Berkeley: University of California Press.
Gilmartin, David. 1988. *Empire and Islam: Punjab and the making of Pakistan*. Berkeley: University of California Press.
Gluckman, Max. 1965. *Politics, law and tribal society*. Chicago: Aldine.
Gordon-Polonskaya, L. R. 1971. "Ideology of Muslim nationalism", in Hafeez Malik (ed.), *Iqbal: poet-philosopher of Pakistan*, pp. 108–35. New York: Columbia University Press.
Gottschalk, Peter. 2001. *Beyond Hindu and Muslim: multiple identity in narratives from village India*. New Delhi: Oxford University Press.
Guha, Ranajit. 1983. *Elementary aspects of peasant insurgency in colonial India*. New Delhi: Oxford University Press.
Gupta, Narayani. 1981. *Delhi between two empires 1803–1931. Society, government and urban growth*. New Delhi: Oxford University Press.

Habib, Mohammad. 1958. "Life and thought of Ziauddin Barani", *Medieval India quarterly*, vol. 3: 197–252.
———. 1974. *Politics and society during the early medieval period: collected works*, vol. 1. New Delhi: People's Publishing House.
Haidar, Najaf. 2005. "A 'Holi riot' of 1714: versions from Ahmedabad and Delhi", in Mushirul Hasan and Asim Roy (eds), *Living together separately: cultural India in history and politics*, pp. 127–44. New Delhi: Oxford University Press.
Hangloo, R. L. 2000. *The state in medieval Kashmir*. New Delhi: Manohar.
Hansen, Thomas B. 1999. *The saffron wave: democracy and Hindu nationalism in modern India*. New Delhi: Oxford University Press.
Hardgrave, Robert L. Jr. 1969. *The Nadars of Tamilnad: the political culture of a community in change*. Berkeley: University of California Press.
Hardy, Peter. 1971. *Partners in freedom—and true Muslims: the political thought of some Muslim scholars in British India. 1912–1947*. Lund: Scandinavian Institute of Asian Studies.
———. (1972) 1998. *The Muslims of British India*. New Delhi: Foundation Books.
———. 1983. 'Force and violence in Indo-Persian writing on history and government in medieval south Asia', in Milton Israel and N. K. Wagle (eds), *Islamic society and culture: essays in honour of Professor Aziz Ahmad*, pp. 165–208. New Delhi: Manohar.
Harris, F. R. 1958. *Jamsetji Nusserwanji Tata: a chronicle of his life*. 2nd edn. Bombay: Blackie.
Hartung, Jan-Peter. 2006. "Standardising Muslim scholarship: The *Nadwat al-Ulama*", in Satish Saberwal and Mushirul Hasan (eds), *Assertive religious identities: India and Europe*, pp. 121–44. New Delhi: Manohar.
Hasan, Mushirul. 1991. *Nationalism and communal politics in India 1885–1930*. New Delhi: Manohar.
——— (ed.). 1995. *India partitioned: the other face of freedom*, 2 vols. New Delhi: Roli.
———. 1997. *Legacy of a divided nation: India's Muslims since Independence*. New Delhi: Oxford University Press.
———. 2002. *Islam in the subcontinent: Muslims in a plural society*. New Delhi: Manohar.
———. 2004a. *From pluralism to separatism: Qasbas in colonial Awadh*. New Delhi: Oxford University Press.
———. 2004b. "Muslims in secular India: problems and prospects in education", in *idem* (ed.), *Will secular India survive?*, pp. 277–319. Gurgaon: ImprintOne.
———. 2005. *A moral reckoning: Muslim intellectuals in nineteenth-century Delhi*. New Delhi: Oxford University Press.
Hazlehurst, Leighton W. 1966. *Entrepreneurship and the merchant castes in a Punjabi city*. Duke University Program in Comparative Studies on Southern Asia, Monograph No. 1.
Hodgson, Marshall G. S. (1974) 2004. *The venture of Islam: conscience and history in a world civilization*, 3 vols. Lahore: Vanguard Books.

Ikram, S. M. 1964. *Muslim civilization in India*. New York: Columbia University Press.
Iqbal, Muhammad. 2003 rpt. *The reconstruction of religious thought in Islam*. Lahore: Ilm-o-Irfan Publishers.
Irschick, Eugene F. 1969. *Politics and social conflict in south India: the non-Brahman movement and Tamil separatism, 1916–1929*. Bombay: Oxford University Press.
Jalal, Ayesha. 1985. *The sole spokesman: Jinnah, the Muslim League, and the demand for Pakistan*. Cambridge: Cambridge University Press.
———. 2001. *Self and sovereignty: individual and community in south Asian Islam since 1850*. New Delhi: Oxford University Press.
Jamous, Raymond. 1996. "The Meo as a Rajput caste and a Muslim community", in C. J. Fuller (ed.), *Caste today*, pp. 180–201. Delhi: Oxford University Press.
Jayaram, N. and Satish Saberwal (eds). 1996. *Social conflict*. Delhi: Oxford University Press.
Jeganathan, Pradeep. 2000. "A space for violence: anthropology, politics and the location of a Sinhala practice of masculinity", in Partha Chatterjee and Pradeep Jeganathan (eds), *Community, gender, and violence* (Subaltern Studies XI), pp. 37–65. New Delhi: Permanent Black.
Jones, Kenneth W. 1976. *Arya dharm*. New Delhi: Manohar.
Jordens, J. T. F. 1981. *Swami Shraddhanand: his life and causes*. Delhi: Oxford University Press.
Juergensmeyer, Mark. 1982. *Religion as social vision: the movement against untouchability in 20th-century Punjab*. Berkeley: University of California Press.
Kaviraj, Sudipta. 1995. *The unhappy consciousness: Bankimchandra Chattopadhyay and the formation of nationalist discourse in India*. Delhi: Oxford University Press.
Kesavan, Mukul. 1990. "Communal violence and its impact on the politics of India, 1937 to 1939", occasional papers on history and society, 2nd series, no. 23. Nehru Memorial Museum and Library.
———. 2007. "A new history of Indian nationalism", *Contemporary perspectives: history and sociology of south Asia*, vol. 1: 107–29.
Kessinger, Tom G. 1974. *Vilyatpur 1846–1968: social and economic change in a north Indian village*. Berkeley: University of California Press.
Khan, Abdul Rashid. 2001. *The All India Muslim Educational Conference: its contribution to the cultural development of Indian Muslims 1886–1947*. Karachi: Oxford University Press.
Khan, Dominique-Sila. 1997. *Conversions and shifting identities: Ramdev Pir and the Ismailis in Rajasthan*. New Delhi: Manohar.
Khan, I. A. 1978. "A note on the conception of Akbar's religious policy", in Debiprasad Chattopadhyaya (ed.), *History and society: essays in honour of Professor Niharranjan Ray*, pp. 455–65. Calcutta: K. P. Bagchi.
Khan, M. Ishaq. 1994. *Kashmir's transition to Islam: the role of Muslim rishis (Fifteenth to eighteenth century)*. New Delhi: Manohar.
Kling, Blair. 1976. *Partner in empire: Dwarkanath Tagore and the age of enterprise in eastern India*. Berkeley: University of California Press.

Kopf, David. 1969. *British orientalism and the Bengal renaissance*. Berkeley: University of California Press.
——. 1979. *The Brahmo Samaj and the shaping of the modern Indian mind*. Princeton: Princeton University Press.
Kosambi, Meera. 1980. "Bombay and Poona: A socio-ecological study of two Indian cities 1650–1900". Unpublished Ph. D. dissertation. University of Stockholm.
Kothari, Rajni (ed.). 1970. *Caste in Indian politics*. New Delhi: Orient Longman.
Kudaisya, Medha M. 2003. *The life and times of G. D. Birla*. New Delhi: Oxford University Press.
Kumar, Ravinder (ed.). 1971a. *Essays on Gandhian politics: the Rowlett Satyagraha of 1919*. Oxford: Clarendon Press.
——. 1971b. "The Rowlatt satyagraha in Lahore", in *idem* (ed.), *Essays on Gandhian politics: the Rowlett Satyagraha of 1919*, pp. 236–97. Oxford: Clarendon Press.
Kumar, Sunil. Forthcoming. "Politics, the Muslim community and Hindu–Muslim relations reconsidered: north India in the early thirteenth century", in Rajat Datta (ed.), *Rethinking a millennium: India from the eighth to the eighteenth centuries, festschrift Harbans Mukhia*.
LaPorte, Todd R. (ed.). 1975. *Organized social complexity: challenge to politics and policy*. Princeton: Princeton University Press.
Lath, Mukund (ed.). 1981. *Ardhakathanaka: half a tale. A study in the interrelationship between autobiography and history*. Jaipur: Rajasthan Prakrit Bharati Sansthan.
Lazarus, Richard. 1966. *Psychological stress and the coping process*. New York: McGraw-Hill.
Lelyveld, David. 1978. *Aligarh's first generation: Muslim solidarity in British India*. Princeton: Princeton University Press.
Lipner, Julius J. 2005. "Introduction", in his translation of Bankimchandra Chatterji, *Anandamath, or The Sacred Brotherhood*, pp. 1–124. New Delhi: Oxford University Press.
Longohr, Vickie. 2001. "Educational 'subcontracting' and the spread of religious nationalism: Hindu and Muslim nationalist schools in colonial India", *Comparative studies of south Asia, Africa, and the middle East*, vol. 21: 42–49.
Lutt, Jurgen. 1976. "The movement for the foundation of the Benares Hindu University", *German scholars on India: contributions to Indian studies*, vol. 2, pp. 160–95. New Delhi: Cultural Department, Embassy of the Federal Republic of Germany.
Macfarlane, Alan. 2004. "To contrast and compare", in Vinay K. Srivastava (ed.), *Methodology and fieldwork*, pp. 94–111. New Delhi: Oxford University Press.
Madan, T. N. 1997. *Modern myths, locked minds: secularism and fundamentalism in India*. New Delhi: Oxford University Press.
Madan, T. N. and B. G. Halbar. 1972. "Caste and community in the private and public education of Mysore state", in Susanne H. Rudolph and Lloyd I. Rudolph (eds), *Education and politics in India: studies in organization, society, and policy*, pp. 121–47. New Delhi: Oxford University Press.

bibliography 187

Mahadevan, Raman. 1976. "The origin and growth of entrepreneurship in the Nattukottai Chettiar community of Taminadu 1880–1930". Unpublished M. Phil. dissertation. New Delhi: Centre for Historical Studies, Jawaharlal Nehru University.
Majumdar, R. C. 1960. *Glimpses of Bengal in the nineteenth century*. Calcutta: Firma K. L. Mukhopadhyay.
Malik, Hafeez. 1963. *Moslem nationalism in India and Pakistan*. Washington, D. C.: Public Affairs Press.
——— (ed.). 1971. *Iqbal: poet–philosopher of Pakistan*. New York: Columbia University Press.
Mallison, Francoise. 1997. "Hinduism as seen by the *Nizari Ismaili* missionaries of western India: the evidence of the *ginan*", in Gunther-Dietz Sontheimer and Hermann Kulke (eds), *Hinduism reconsidered*, pp. 189–201. New Delhi: Manohar.
Mandelbaum, David G. 1970. *Society in India*. Berkeley: University of California Press.
Mann, Michael. 1986. *The sources of social power. I: a history of power from the beginning to A. D. 1760*. Cambridge: Cambridge University Press.
Markovits, Claude. 1991. "Businessman and the partition of India", in Dwijendra Tripathi (ed.), *Business and politics in India: a historical perspective*, pp. 284–307. New Delhi: Manohar.
Masselos, J. C. 1973. "The Khojas of Bombay: the defining of formal membership criteria during the nineteenth century", in Imtiaz Ahmad (ed.), *Caste and social stratification among the Muslims*, pp. 1–20. New Delhi: Manohar.
Mayaram, Shail. 1997. *Resisting regimes: myth, memory and the shaping of a Muslim identity*. New Delhi: Oxford University Press.
———. 2006. "Do Hindu and Islamic transnational religious movements represent cosmopolitanism and difference?", in Satish Saberwal and Mushirul Hasan (eds), *Assertive religious identities: India and Europe*, pp. 323–55. New Delhi: Manohar.
Mehta, Deepak and Roma Chatterji. 2001. "Boundaries, names, alterities: a case study of a 'communal riot' in Dharavi, Bombay", in V. Das, A. Kleinman, M. Lock, M. Ramphele and P. Reynolds (eds), *Remaking the world*, pp. 201–49. Berkeley: University of California Press.
Merton, Robert. 1936. "The unanticipated consequences of purposive social action", *American sociological review*, vol. 1: 894–904.
———. (1948) 1968. "The self-fulfilling prophecy", in *idem*, *Social theory and social structure*, pp. 475–90. New Delhi: Amerind.
Metcalf, Barbara. 1982. *Islamic revival in British India: Deoband, 1860–1900*. Princeton: Princeton University Press.
———. 2004. *Islamic contestations: essays on Muslims in India and Pakistan*. New Delhi: Oxford University Press.
———. 2005. "Reinventing Islamic politics in inter-war India: the clergy commitment to 'composite nationalism'", in Mushirul Hasan and Asim Roy (eds), *Living*

together separately: cultural India in history and politics, pp. 389–403. New Delhi: Oxford University Press.
Miller, Roland E. 1976. *Mappila Muslims of Kerala: a study of Islamic trends*. Hyderabad: Orient Longman.
Minault, Gail. 1982. *The Khilafat movement: religious symbolism and political mobilization in India*. Delhi: Oxford University Press.
———. 1998. *Secluded scholars: women's education and Muslim social reform in colonial India*. New Delhi: Oxford University Press.
———. 2000. "Qiran Al-Sa'adain: the dialogue between eastern and western learning at Delhi College", in Jamal Malik (ed.), *Perspectives of mutual encounters in South Asian history 1760–1860*, pp. 260–77. Leiden: Brill.
Mines, Mattison. 1972. *Muslim merchants: the economic behaviour of an Indian Muslim community*. New Delhi: Sri Ram Centre for Industrial Relations.
———. 1975. "Islamization and Muslim ethnicity in South India", in Dietmar Rothermund (ed.), *Islam in southern Asia: a survey of current research*, pp. 55–57. Wiesbaden: Steiner.
———. 1984. *The warrior merchants: textiles, trade, and territory in south India*. Cambridge: Cambridge University Press.
Misra, S. C. 1964. *Muslim communities in Gujarat: preliminary studies in their history and social organization*. Bombay: Asia.
More, J. B. P. 1997. *The political evolution of Muslims in Tamilnadu and Madras 1930–1947*. Hyderabad: Orient Longman.
Morgan, Gereth. 1983. "Research as engagement: a personal view", in *idem* (ed.), *Beyond method: strategies for social research*, pp. 11–18. Beverly Hills: Sage Publications.
Mujeeb, Mohammad. 1967, 1995 rpt. *The Indian Muslims*. New Delhi: Munshiram Manoharlal.
Mukerji, Dhurjati Prasad. 1948, 1979 rpt. *Sociology of Indian culture*. Jaipur: Rawat.
Murad, Mehr Afroz. 1976, 1996 Indian rpt. *Intellectual modernism of Shibli Numani: an exposition of his religious and political ideas*. New Delhi: Kitab Bhavan.
Naidu, Ratna. 1980. *The communal edge to plural societies: India and Malaysia*. New Delhi: Vikas.
Naim, C. M. 2004a. "Ghalib's Delhi: a shamelessly revisionist look at two popular metaphors", in *idem*, *Urdu texts and contexts: selected essays*, pp. 250–73. New Delhi: Permanent Black.
———. 2004b. "How Bibi Ashraf learned to read and write", in *idem*, *Urdu texts and contexts: selected essays*. New Delhi: Permanent Black.
Nanda, B. R. 1989. *Gandhi, pan-Islamism, imperialism, and nationalism in India*. Bombay: Oxford University Press.
Nandy, Ashis. 2005. "Telling the story of communal conflicts in south Asia: Interim report on a personal search for defining myths", in Jamal Malik and Helmut Reifeld (eds), *Religious pluralism in south Asia and Europe*, pp. 298–317. New Delhi: Oxford University Press.

Narayanan, Vasudha. 2002. "Religious vocabulary and religious identity: a study of the Tamil *Cirappuranam*", in David Gilmartin and Bruce B. Lawrence (eds), *Beyond Turk and Hindu: rethinking religious identities in Islamicate south Asia*, pp. 74–97. New Delhi: India Research Press.

Naregal, Veena. 2001. *Language politics, elites, and the public sphere: western India under colonialism*. New Delhi: Permanent Black.

Nicholas, Ralph. 1981. "Understanding a Hindu temple in Bengal", in Adrian Mayer (ed.), *Culture and morality*, pp. 174–90. New Delhi: Oxford University Press.

Oberoi, Harjot. 1994. *The construction of religious boundaries: culture, identity and diversity in the Sikh tradition*. New Delhi: Oxford University Press.

Omvedt, Gail. 1976. *Cultural revolt in a colonial society: the non-Brahman movement in western India, 1873–1930*. Bombay: Scientific Socialist Education Trust.

Owens, Raymond L. and Ashis Nandy. 1978. *The new Vaisyas: entrepreneurial opportunity and response in an Indian city*. New Delhi: Allied Publishers.

Pandey, Gyan. 1983. "Rallying around the cow: sectarian strife in the Bhojpuri region, c. 1888–1917", in Ranajit Guha (ed.), *Subaltern Studies II: writings on south Asian history and society*, pp. 60–129. Delhi: Oxford University Press.

Pandey, Gyanendra. 1990. *The construction of communalism in colonial north India*. New Delhi: Oxford University Press.

Pandian, M. S. S. 2007. *Brahmin and non-Brahmin: genealogies of the Tamil political present*. Delhi: Permanent Black.

Panikkar, K. N. 1975. "Social and intellectual history of modern India", Presidential Address, Sec. III, Indian History Congress.

———. 1989. *Against lord and state: religion and peasant uprisings in Malabar, 1836–1921*. Delhi: Oxford University Press.

Parekh, Bhikhu. 1989. *Colonialism, tradition and reform: an analysis of Gandhi's political discourse*. New Delhi: Sage Publications.

Parmu, R. K. 1969. *A history of Muslim rule in Kashmir 1320–1819*. New Delhi: People's Publishing House.

Patel, H. M. 2005. *Rites of passage: a civil servant remembers*. New Delhi: Rupa and Co.

Phukan, Shantanu. 2001. "'Through throats where many rivers meet': the ecology of Hindi in the world of Persian", *Indian Economic and social history review*, vol. 38: 33–58.

Pollock, Sheldon. 1993. "Ramayana and political imagination in India", *Journal of Asian studies*, vol. 52: 261–97.

Prasad, Bimal. 1999, 2000. *The foundations of Muslim nationalism. A nation within a nation*, 2 vols. in *idem, Pathway to India's Partition*. New Delhi: Manohar.

Preuss, Ulrich K. 1991. "The politics of constitution making: transforming politics into constitutions", *Law and policy*, vol. 13: 106–23.

Qureshi, Ishtiaq Husain. 1962. *The Muslim community of the Indo-Pakistani subcontinent 610–1947*. Gravenhage: Mouton.

Radhakrishnan, P. 1993. "Communal representation in Tamil Nadu, 1850–1916: the pre-non-Brahmin phase", *Economic and Political Weekly*, vol. 28: 1585–97.

Ramanujan, A. K. 1989. "Is there an Indian way of thinking? An informal essay", *Contributions to Indian sociology*, vol. 23: 41–58.
Rao, M. S. A. 1979. *Social movements and social transformation: a study of two backward caste movements in India*. Delhi: Macmillan.
Rao, U. Bhaskar. 1967. *The story of rehabilitation*. Delhi: Ministry of Labour, Employment and Rehabilitation, Government of India.
Rao, V. Nagendra and Rekha Chowdhary. 2006. "Evolution of political Islam in Jammu and Kashmir", in Satish Saberwal and Mushirul Hasan (eds), *Assertive religious identities: India and Europe*, pp. 295–319. New Delhi: Manohar.
Ray, Rajat K. 2003. *The felt community: commonalty and mentality before the emergence of Indian nationalism*. New Delhi: Oxford University Press.
Raychaudhari, Tapan. 1988. *Europe reconsidered: perceptions of the West in nineteenth century Bengal*. Delhi: Oxford University Press.
Rizvi, S. A. A. 1977. "Islamic proselytisation (seventh to sixteenth centuries)", in G. A. Oddie (ed.), *Religion in south Asia*, pp. 13–33. New Delhi: Manohar.
Robinson, Francis. 1975. *Separatism among Indian Muslims: the politics of the United Provinces' Muslims, 1860–1923*. New Delhi: Vikas.
———. 1983. "Islam and Muslim society in south Asia", *Contributions to Indian sociology*, vol. 1: 185–203.
———. 2001. *The 'Ulama' of Farangi Mahall and Islamic culture in South Asia*. New Delhi: Permanent Black.
Robinson, Rowena. 2005. *Tremors of violence: Muslim survivors of ethnic strife in western India*. New Delhi: Sage Publications.
Rodinson, Maxime. 1971. *Mohammed*. London: Penguin Books.
Rowe, William L. 1973. "Caste, kinship, and association in urban India", in A. Southall (ed.), *Urban anthropology*, pp. 211–49. New York: Oxford University Press.
Roy, Asim. 1983. *The Islamic syncretistic tradition in Bengal*. Princeton: Princeton University Press.
Rudner, David. 1989. "Banker's trust and the culture of banking among the Nattukottai Chettiars of colonial south India", *Modern Asian studies*, vol. 23: 417–58.
Saberwal, Satish. 1976. *Mobile men: limits to social change in urban Punjab*. New Delhi: Vikas.
———. 1995. *Wages of segmentation: comparative historical studies on Europe and India*. New Delhi: Orient Longman.
———. 1996a. *Roots of crisis: interpreting contemporary Indian society*. New Delhi: Sage Publications.
———. 1996b. "Tradition and resilience: mobilizational energy in the Brahminical order", in S. Gopal and R. Champakalakshmi (eds), *Tradition, dissent, and ideology*. New Delhi: Oxford University Press.
———. 1998. "Enlargement of scales, plural traditions, and rule of law: comparative reflections on European and Indian history", in Satish Saberwal and Heiko Sievers (eds), *Rules, laws, constitutions*, pp. 62–82. New Delhi: Sage Publications.

Saberwal, Satish. 2001. "Framework in change: Colonial Indian society", in Susan Visvanathan (ed.), *Structure and transformation: theory and society in India*, pp. 33–57. New Delhi: Oxford University Press.
———. 2003. "Review of Ajit K. Dalal and Girishwar Misra" (eds), *New directions in Indian psychology: Volume 1—Social psychology*, in *Sociological Bulletin*, vol. 51: 269–72.
———. 2004a. "Anxieties, identities, complexity, reality", in Mushirul Hasan (ed.), *Will secular India survive?*, pp. 93–124. Gurgaon: ImprintOne.
———. 2004b. "Traditions and actors: 'communities' reconfigured in 19th century India", in Partha N. Mukherji and Chandan Sengupta (eds), *Indigeneity and universality: A South Asian response*, pp. 268–94. New Delhi: Sage Publications.
———. 2005a. "Integration and separation of traditions: Muslims and Hindus in colonial India", in Satish Saberwal and Supriya Varma (eds), *Traditions in motion: religion and society in history*, pp. 272–95. New Delhi: Oxford University Press.
———. 2005b. "'Why did we have the Partition?' The making of a research interest", *Journal of research practice*, vol. 1 (1): Article M3. http://irp.icaap.org/content/v1.1/saberwal.html.
———. 2006. "Foreword", in *The Mushirul Hasan omnibus*, pp. v–xiv. New Delhi: Manohar.
Saberwal, Satish and Mushirul Hasan (eds). 2006. *Assertive religious identities: India and Europe*. New Delhi: Manohar.
Saiyed, A. R. and Mohammad Talib. 1985. "Institutions and ideas: a case study in Islamic learning", in Christian W. Troll (ed.), *Islam in India: studies and commentaries*, vol. 2, *Religion and religious education*, pp. 191–208. New Delhi: Vikas.
Samaddar, Ranabir. 2006. "Identity assertions as contentious acts", in Satish Saberwal and Mushirul Hasan (eds), *Assertive religious identities: India and Europe*, pp. 271–94. New Delhi: Manohar.
Sanyal, Usha. 1996. *Devotional Islam and politics in British India: Ahmad Riza Khan Barelwi and his movement, 1870–1920*. New Delhi: Oxford University Press.
Sarkar, Sumit. 1973. *The Swadeshi movement in Bengal 1903–1908*. New Delhi: People's Publishing House.
Sayeed, Khalid bin. 1967. *The political system of Pakistan*. Boston: Houghton Mifflin.
———. 1983. "The origins of Pakistan and the nature of its persistent crises", in Milton Israel and N. K. Wagle (eds), *Islamic society and culture: essays in honour of Professor Aziz Ahmad*, pp. 269–88. New Delhi: Manohar.
Scammell, G. V. 1981. *The world encompassed: the first European maritime empires c800–1650*. London: Methuen.
Schryer, Frans J. 2001. "Multiple hierarchies and the duplex nature of groups", *Journal of the royal anthropological Institute* (n. s.), vol. 7: 705–21.

Seal, Anil. 1968. *The emergence of Indian nationalism: competition and collaboration in the later nineteenth century*. London: Cambridge University Press.
Shackle, Christopher and Javed Majeed (eds). 1997. *Hali's Musaddas: the flow and ebb of Islam*. Delhi: Oxford University Press.
Shah, A. M. 2002. *Exploring India's rural past: a Gujarat village in the early nineteenth century*. New Delhi: Oxford University Press.
Shaikh, Farzana. 1989. *Community and consensus in Islam: Muslim representation in colonial India, 1860–1947*. Cambridge: Cambridge University Press.
Sharma, Jyotirmaya. 2003. *Hindutva: exploring the idea of Hindu nationalism*. New Delhi: Penguin.
———. 2007. *Terrifying vision: M. S. Golwalker, the RSS and India*. New Delhi: Penguin.
Sibeon, Roger. 2004. *Rethinking social theory*. London: Sage Publications.
Siddiqi, Asiya. 2001. "Ayesha's world: a butcher's family in nineteenth-century Bombay", *Comparative studies in society and history*, vol. 43: 101–29.
Siddiqui, M. K. A. 1973. "Caste among Muslims of Calcutta", in Imtiaz Ahmad (ed.), *Caste and social stratification among the Muslims*. New Delhi: Manohar.
Sikand, Yoginder. 2002. *The origins and development of the Tablighi Jamaat (1920–2000)*. New Delhi: Orient Longman.
———. 2005. *Bastions of the believers: Madrasas and Islamic education in India*. New Delhi: Penguin.
Singh, Upinder. 2004. *The discovery of ancient India: early archeologists and the beginnings of archeology*. Delhi: Permanent Black.
Sinha, Surajit. 1962. "State formation and Rajput myth in tribal central India", *Man in India*, vol. 42: 35–80.
Southern R. W. 1962. *Western views of Islam in the middle ages*. Cambridge, Massachusetts: Harvard University Press.
Srinivas, M. N. 1966. *Social change in modern India*. Berkeley: University of California Press.
Stein, Burton. 1977. "Temples in Tamil country, 1300–1750 AD", *Indian economic and social history review*, vol. 14: 11–45.
Stephens, Ian. 1964. *Pakistan: old country new nation*. Harmondsworth: Penguin.
Stewart, Tony K. 2002. "Alternate structures of authority: Satya Pir on the frontiers of Bengal", in Davil Gilmartin and Bruce B. Lawrence (eds), *Beyond Turk and Hindu: rethinking religious identities in Islamicate south Asia*, pp. 21–54. New Delhi: India Research Press.
Stokes, Eric. 1978. *The peasant and the raj: studies in agrarian society and peasant rebellion in colonial India*. New Delhi: Vikas.
Subramanian, Lakshmi and Rajat K. Ray. 1991. "Merchants and politics: from the great Mughals to the East India Company", in Dwijendra Tripathi (ed.), *Business and politics in India: a historical perspective*, pp. 19–85. New Delhi: Manohar.
Taft, Frances H.1994. "Honor and alliance: reconsidering Mughal–Rajput marriages", in K. Schomer, J. L. Erdman and D. O. Lodrick (eds), *The idea of Rajasthan explorations in regional identity, vol. II: Institutions*, pp. 217–41. New Delhi: Manohar.

Talbot, Cynthia. 1995. "Inscribing the other, inscribing the self: Hindu–Muslim identities in pre-colonial India", *Comparative studies in society and history*, vol. 32: 692–722.
Talib, Mohammad. 1998. "Jamia Milia Islamia: career of Azad Talim", in Mushirul Hasan (ed.), *Knowledge, power and politics: educational institutions in India*, pp. 156–88. New Delhi: Roli Books.
Templeman, Dennis. 1996. *The northern Nadars of Tamil Nadu: an Indian caste in the process of change*. Delhi: Oxford University Press.
Timberg, Thomas A. 1978. *The Marwaris: from traders to industrialists*. New Delhi: Vikas.
Tiwari, Bajrang. 2001. *"Bhakti ke brihad aakhyan me 'satpurushon' ki peera* [The sufferings of 'worthy men' in *bhakti*'s grand narrative]", *Tadbhav* (Lucknow), no. 6 (October): 42–59.
———. 2003. *"Madhyakalin satta-vimarsh ka ek pahlu* [An aspect of the medieval political discourse]", *Tadbhav* (Lucknow), no. 9: 77–104.
Trivedi, Madhu. 2005. "Invoking sorrow: *marsiya* in north India", in Satish Saberwal and Supriya Varma (eds), *Traditions in motion: Religion and society in history*, pp. 127–46. New Delhi: Oxford University Press.
Unger, Roberto M. 1987. *Plasticity into power: comparative – historical studies on the institutional conditions of economic and military success*. Cambridge: Cambridge University Press.
van den Dungen, P. H. M. 1968. "Changes in status and occupation in nineteenth-century Panjab", in D. A. Low (ed.), *Soundings in modern south Asian history*, pp. 59–94. London: Weidenfeld and Nicolson.
van der Veer, Peter. 1996. *Religious nationalism: Hindus and Muslims in India*. Delhi: Oxford University Press.
Varshney, Ashutosh. 2002. *Ethnic conflict and civic life: Hindus and Muslims in India*. New Delhi: Oxford University Press.
von Gunebaum, G. E. 1955. "The problem: unity in diversity", in *idem* (ed.), *Unity and variety in Muslim civilization*, pp. 17–37. Chicago: University of Chicago Press.
Wagle, N. K. 1997. "Hindu–Muslim interactions in Medieval Maharashtra", in Gunther-Dietz Sontheimer and Hermann Kulke (eds), *Hinduism reconsidered*, pp. 134–52. New Delhi: Manohar.
Wallace, Anthony F. C. 1957. "Mazeway disintegration: the individual's perception of socio-cultural disorganization", *Human organization*, vol. 16, Summer 1957: 23–27.
Waltham, Clae. 1972. *Shu Ching: Book of history*. London: Allen & Unwin.
Wani, Muhammad Ashraf. 2005. *Islam in Kashmir (fourteenth to sixteenth century)*. Srinagar: Oriental Publishing House.
Webster, John C. B. 1976. *Christian community and change in 19th century north India*. Delhi: Macmillan.
Williams, Raymond B. 1984. *A new face of Hinduism: the Swaminarayan religion*. Cambridge: Cambridge University Press.

Wilson, Harlan. 1975. "Complexity as a theoretical problem: wider perspectives in political theory", in Todd R. LaPorte (ed.), *Organized social complexity: challenge to politics and policy*, pp. 281–331. Princeton: Princeton University Press.
Wink, Andre. 1990. *Al-Hind: the making of the Indo-Islamic world. I: Early medieval India and the expansion of Islam. Seventh to eleventh centuries*. Leiden: E. J. Brill.
———. 1997. *Al-Hind: the making of the Indo-Islamic world. II: The slave kings and the Islamic conquest, 11th–13th centuries*. Leiden: E. J. Brill.
Winner, Langdon. 1975. "Complexity and the limits of human understanding", in Todd R. LaPorte (ed.), *Organized social complexity: challenge to politics and policy*, pp. 40–76. Princeton: Princeton University Press.
Wolpert, Stanley. 1984. *Jinnah of Pakistan*. New York: Oxford University Press.
Wood, Anand. 1985. *Knowledge before printing and after: the Indian tradition in changing Kerala*. New Delhi: Oxford University Press.
Zelliot, Eleanor. 1992. *From untouchable to dalit: essays on Ambedkar movement*. New Delhi: Manohar.
Ziring, Lawrence. 1979. "The phases of Pakistan's political history", in C. M. Naim (ed.), *Iqbal, Jinnah, and Pakistan: the vision and the reality*, South Asian series No. 5, pp. 145–76. Syracuse: Maxwell School of Citizenship and Public Affairs.
Zutshi, Chitralekha. 2003. *Languages of belonging: Islam, regional identity, and the making of Kashmir*. New Delhi: Permanent Black.

about the author

Satish Saberwal (1933–2010) was Professor of Sociology, Centre for Historical Studies, Jawaharlal Nehru University, New Delhi. Prior to that, he worked at the University of Alberta and McGill University, Montreal, and was a Fellow at the Indian Institute of Advanced Study, Shimla. His fieldwork was among the Embu in central Kenya and the lower castes in a Punjabi industrial town. His publications include *Wages of Segmentation: Comparative Historical Studies on Europe and India* (1995); *Roots of Crisis: Interpreting Contemporary Indian Society* (1996); *Social Conflict* (1996, co-edited); and *Rules, Laws, Constitutions* (1998).

index

1857 64f, 87, 88, 96, 118, 132, 139, 161, 165
1947 xvi, 126, 152, 166, 173, 177
actors and structures xxvi, 86, 109, 110f
Ad Dharm 38, 42
Aggarwal, P. 25, 152
aggression xv, 4, 23, 27f, 29, 80, 85, 86, 93, 94, 96, 110, 126, 127, 128, 134, 143n, 144, 145, 151, 156, 157, 166, 169f, 176
and exclusive identities xxiii, 27, 69, 97, 133, 150, 153
Ahmad, A. 13, 28
Ahmad, I. xx, 26, 70, 72, 125
Ahmad, Rashid 125, 164
Ahmed, Rafiuddin 53, 59, 63, 64, 68, 71, 72, 78, 79, 85, 106, 118, 122f, 148, 149
Ahmediyas 68, 70, 85, 148
ajlaf 17, 64, 69–72, 78, 129,
Akbar xxiii, 6, 10, 12, 58, 99, 111, 137, 176
akhlaq 7, 29
Alam, M. 5, 6, 7, 8, 9, 25, 29, 98, 118f
Ali, Amir 166
Ali, Mohamed 167, 169
Aligarh Muslim University 51, 76
antecedent institutions 56, 65f, 73, 74, 75, 84, 90, 123, 142
Ambedkar, B. R. 176, 177
ambiguous relationships xvii, xxi, 32, 108f, 131, 136, 156
Amin, S. 4, 14f, 170, 176

animosities *see* attitudes
anjuman 68, 75, 127
Ansari, M. A. 77
anxieties *see* insecurity
Aquil, R. xxv, 6, 26, 42n
aristocracies in decline 56f, 118
Arya Samaj xxiii, 43, 44, 50, 52n, 53, 54, 68, 76, 77, 104, 112f, 125, 126, 127, 131, 132, 139, 140, 141, 147, 148, 149, 152, 154, 159, 161, 162, 173
see also Dayananda, Sraddhananda
arzal 70, 129,
ashraf 17, 62, 63f, 65, 66, 69–72, 78, 116, 124,129
ashraf–ajlaf–arzal 129
attitudes xvi, xxii, xxvi f, 11, 12, 21, 42f, 45, 49n, 50, 61, 63, 67, 69, 78, 83, 84, 100, 102f, 108, 112, 135, 140, 148, 150, 153, 164, 170, 173, 174, 177
Aurangzeb 25, 58, 99, 103
Aziz, Shah Abdul 88

Bairy, Ramesh T. S. 37
Baker, D. E. U. 61
Banarasi Das *see* Lath
Bande Mataram 66, 92f
Bandyopadhyay, S. 40
Banerjea, Surendranath 49f, 166
Banerjee, H. 40
Bansawi, Shah Abdul Razzak 9, 90
bar of separation xiv, 94, 125, 128
baraka 8, 67
Barelwi 67, 68, 79, 120, 121, 147

index 197

Barrier, N. G. 153
Basu, A. 78
Bayly, C. A. xx, 27n, 60n, 88, 91f, 93, 133n
Bayly, S. 18, 62, 97
Beckerlegge, G. 43, 46, 104
Benares Hindu University 51
Bengal 15, 42, 46, 58, 59, 64, 72, 75, 78, 85, 88f, 96, 97, 98, 102, 118, 122f, 126, 131, 147, 148, 149, 152, 154, 157, 170, 173
conversions 19–22
Berger, P. 141
Bertocci, P. 72
bhadralok 49, 107
bhakti 9f, 46, 108, 136n
Bhalla, A. ix
Bhargava, R. ix, xx
Bharucha, R. 19
Bhattacharya, S. 66, 92
Bohra 19n, 62, 76
Bombay city 76, 98, 139, 169
Bose, N. K. xix, 17, 133n
brahmins 21, 22, 24n, 25, 36, 42, 44, 45, 88, 112, 113, 114, 126, 128, 136n
 in early colonial governments 33, 36ff, 64
 revolts against 38, 53
 Chitrapur Saraswat 41, 43
Brahmo Samaj 42, 44, 46, 47f, 48ff, 53, 98, 106, 112, 113, 149
Brass, P. R. 57, 81
Brown, J. 46, 169, 170
Butalia, U. ix, xiii, 172
Cashman, R. I. 38n, 51, 127, 146
caste 4, 5, 17, 21, 28, 29, 38, 39, 52, 63, 87, 112, 113, 116, 117, 127, 128, 129, 135, 136n, 137, 142, 147, 152, 155, 159, 165, 166, 167, 174, 177
 lower castes 18, 38, 40, 42, 44, 70, 114, 126
 see also jati

Census 64, 72, 85f, 148, 149, 162
Central Asia 3f, 5, 23, 100,
 see also horses and horsemen
Chakrabarti, K. 43
Chakrabarty, D. 141
Chakravarti, A. 41
Chandra, B. xxi
Chandra, S. 39, 51, 103f, 159n
Chatterjee, P. ix, 85, 147, 148, 150f
Chatterji, Bankimchandra 53, 66, 92, 102f, 107f, 112, 155
Chatterji, J. 170
Chatterji, R. 69, 150
Chattopadhyaya, B. D. xxiv
Chaudhuri, B. B. 17
Chaudhuri, M. xix
China 1, 4, 29, 81, 100, 116, 135, 139, 175
Chowdhary, R. 59
civilizations and cultural styles 1–3, 98, 101, 104, 105, 116, 140, 165
Cohen, A. xxvi
Cohn, B. S. 84
colonial period 87, 119, 130
 early renegotiations 33, 79, 90f
colonial rule 49n, 83, 86, 87f, 93, 117, 165, 170, 175
 consequences 84, 162
commerce 11, 28, 54, 61, 62, 91, 94, 95, 100
 see also merchants
common sense, shifts in xxvii, 68, 115, 133, 148, 173
communal conflict 170, 172
 pre-colonial xx
communications xxiii, 39, 80, 82, 83, 94, 113, 122, 124, 126, 130, 131ff, 138, 160, 166
comparativism 78fff, 83, 116
complexity 110f, 116, 134–43, 141, 162, 175, 178
 in caste system 135
 medieval inputs 135f

colonial increments. 138
  see also unfixed complexity
conflict 67ff, 108, 111, 144, 150, 160, 162, 177, 178
  cross-cutting ties in 148f
  institutionalization of 155
  media and scale 134, 148, 153, 170
  see also aggression
Conlon, F. 41, 114
consequences, intended and unintended xxvii f, 21, 87, 98, 101, 108, 125, 162, 164, 172, 173, 178
contention 91, 93, 104, 106, 113, 134, 139, 148, 157, 166, 171, 174
  symbolic, societal, physical 133, 143–55, 157f, 165
  and learning 53, 67, 174
conversions 145
  to Islam 8, 16–26, 31, 149, 151, 170
  to Hinduism (*shuddhi*) xxxiii, 43, 69, 126, 127n, 133, 157, 170
cow protection 145f, 147, 168

Dalmia, V. 35, 43, 104, 114, 149
darvesh 8
Das Gupta, A. 11f
Das, V. xx, 150
Datta, N. 43, 126, 141, 148
Datta, P. K. 4, 59, 108, 146, 149, 152, 153, 155n
Dayananda, Swami xxi n, 85, 96, 105, 112, 113f, 125, 159, 164
  see also Arya Samaj
definition of situation xxvii f, 21
Delhi College 64, 99, 118, 138
Denzin, N. K. 30
Deoband xxiii, xxxi, 56f, 64, 65, 66, 67, 68, 70, 71f, 79, 80, 90, 101, 105, 117, 131, 139, 140, 141, 147, 154, 160, 162
  impetus, vision, strengths 118–25
  focus on the Prophet 119f
  see also *fatwa*, Rashid Ahmad

desecration of symbols 23
Devalle, S. B. C. xxii
disempowerment 87ff, 96, 108
Dobbin, C. 53, 62, 76, 98, 139
Douglas, M. 110
Dube, S. 42, 47

Eaton, R. M. 8, 12, 19–22, 59, 162
education, modern 37, 39, 45, 57, 60, 75, 76, 78, 82, 87, 88, 89, 109, 113, 114, 121, 141
  see also institutions, Aligarh, Jamia Millia Islamia
Eknath 108
elections 1937 171
elections 1945–46. 81, 94, 96, 173
elective bodies 106f, 109, 125
  see also separate electorates
elite bifurcation 32, 55, 81, 82, 86, 95
Elliot, H. M. and J. Dowson 85
epistemologies, power of western 53
Eschmann, A. 41
Europe 1, 29, 52, 84, 98ff, 104, 116, 135, 138, 159, 176
exclusivism 48, 83, 87, 93, 95, 96, 102, 104, 108, 109, 117, 121, 124, 125, 128, 132, 133, 134, 141, 144, 155, 160, 174

Farangi Mahall 58, 66, 90, 124
Faruqi, Z. H. 105
fatwa (pl. *fatawa*) 115, 121f, 115, 121f
Fort William, College of 84, 99
Fox, R. G. 27, 39
Freitag, S. B. xx, 61n, 68, 92, 93, 146f, 152f
Fruzzetti-Ostor, L. 125

Ganapati 45, 93, 127, 157
Gandhi, Mohandas Karamchand 46, 77, 151, 153, 166–70, 176
gasht 127
Geertz, C. 55, 154n

Gernet, J. 1
Ghosh, P. 57, 71
Ghosh, S. 50
Giddens, A. xxviii
Gillion, K. 52
Gilmartin, D. 58f, 67, 77, 113, 170, 173
Gluckman, M. 149
Gordon-Polonskaya, L. R. 76
Gottschalk, P. 30
Great Tradition xxiv, 96, 109
Guha, R. 35, 59, 64, 68, 145, 147
Gupta, N. 60
guru 42, 43, 113

Habib, M. 6, 28
hadis xxxi, 3, 79, 120, 116, 119f, 165
Haider, N. xx, 28
hajj, haji 68, 79, 96, 120, 168
Halbar, B. G. 50, 51, 76, 77
Hali, A. H. 66, 104
Hangloo, R. L. 22
Hansen, T. B. 115, 127, 142, 155n
Hardgrave, R. L. 38n
Hardy, P. 17, 55, 169, 171
Harishchandra of Benaras 44, 103f, 114, 149
Harris, F. R. 76
Hartung, J.P. 67, 124
Hasan, M. ix, xvi, 56f, 64, 68, 70, 71, 73, 75, 77, 84f, 132, 139, 143, 151, 154, 165, 169, 170
Hazlehurst, L. W. 61
Hierarchy 128n, 129, 131, 135f, 141, 156, 175
Hindu and Muslim xv, 28, 83, 86,103f, 112, 127, 141, 142, 148, 154, 156, 159, 166, 167, 172, 177
   cordial relations 9, 13ff, 30, 150, 152, 165
   conflict between xx f, 10f, 69, 108, 125, 146, 150f, 169, 176,
   validity of categories xxiv f, 125, 129
   see also shared spaces

index 199

Hindu College, Calcutta 48, 53
Hindu Mahasabha 172
Hindus 106, 112, 115
   multiple traditions and perceptions 36, 44ff, 46
   ascendent groups' challenge 91, 139, 157
   see also Arya Samaj
Hindutva 113, 115, 144, 155n
historiography xvii, xxi, 85, 155, 159n
Hodgson, M. G. S. 2, 3n, 4, 8, 57, 61, 100, 120
horses and horsemen 3f, 31, 81f, 100, 137
humiliations 4, 38, 88, 102, 108, 159, 161
Huq, Fazlul 78, 171
Husain, Fazl-i 78

ideas 44ff, 47, 48, 56, 83, 87, 98
   see also interests
identities xxii, xxv n, xxvii, 20, 30, 31, 59f, 68, 70, 72, 89, 93, 102, 108, 113, 114, 116, 118, 124, 126, 128, 130, 132, 133, 134, 140, 141, 144, 149, 150, 151, 155, 157, 162, 167
   see also names
ideologies xxiii, 29, 39, 42, 43, 55, 88, 89, 93, 101, 108, 110f, 114, 122, 125, 126, 127, 130, 134, 135, 137, 141, 147, 154f, 159, 164
   simplifying 129, 132, 140, 141ff
   see also Islamic ideology
ijma 171n
Ikram, S. M. 58
Ilyas, Muhammad 164
imam 72
immigrants' descendants 5, 15, 56, 62, 65, 82
Indian National Congress 50, 106, 139, 162, 166, 167,169
   and Muslims. 85, 142, 143, 153f, 161, 168, 170ff, 175
industry 52n, 62, 78, 82, 94, 132, 140

insecurity xvi, 12, 29, 35, 86, 93, 97, 110, 126, 127, 131, 133, 134, 138, 139, 142, 144, 148, 149, 154, 155, 174
  Muslims' xxv, 26, 56f, 65, 88ff, 94, 96,106f, 116, 136, 142, 146, 152, 153, 161
  Hindus' 31, 96,107f; 112, 114, 149
institutions xxx, 29, 43, 44, 48–54, 57, 76ff, 79, 80, 86, 89, 93, 99, 100, 101, 109, 110, 111, 112, 116, 118, 126, 130, 132, 134, 140, 141, 160, 164, 165
importance of resources 47ff, 51, 54, 66, 76
interests xxvi f, 43, 59, 62, 71, 111, 162
  see also ideas
involution and "disinvolution" 165f
Iqbal, M. 76, 98, 100, 104f, 143, 165, 175
Irschick, E. F. 53
Islamic expansion 63, 135
  see also conversions
Islamic ideology 59, 64, 69, 71, 105, 111, 127n, 136n, 156, 159
  learning 57, 73f, 101, 105, 115, 119, 122, 123 conforming to 62, 68, 75, 77, 79, 116, 117, 121, 127, 140, 154
  see also Deoband
Ismailis 8, 13, 18f, 76, 94, 160, 162

Jagir 27, 82
Jalal, A. ix, 66, 87, 124, 143, 144, 153, 154, 155, 171f, 173
Jamia Millia Islamia 77
Jamiatul-ulama-i-Hind 171
Jamous, R. 25, 152
jati xxx, 5, 24, 25, 27, 33–41, 46, 52, 53, 54, 61, 69f, 79, 82, 85, 102, 106, 114, 128, 135, 149, 165, 176
  in mobility 35
  see also Brahmins, Jats, Nadars

Jats 21, 34, 40, 44, 126, 141
Jayaram, N. 150n, 174n
Jeganathan, P. 128
Jinnah, M. A. 95, 154, 167, 169, 171, 173, 174, 175
Jones, K. W. 43, 50, 52, 53, 54, 76, 104, 112, 113, 148
Jordens, J. T. F. 152
Juergensmeyer, M. 38n

Kabir 9f, 108, 160
kalima 26
Kanpur 1931 violence 61n, 153
Kashmir 22ff, 31, 59
Kaviraj, S. xvii, 102f, 108
Kesavan, M. 143n, 166, 168, 172
Kessinger, T. G. 40
Khan, A. R. 75f
Khan, Ajmal 77
Khan, D. S. 8, 13, 18f
Khan, I. A. 7
Khan, M. I. 22ff
Khan, Sikandar Hayat 171
Khan, Syed Ahmad 56, 58, 75, 77, 84, 98, 100, 123n, 142, 165, 166
  see also Aligarh
Khilafat and Non-cooperation 62, 96, 126, 143, 151, 165, 167, 168–71, 176, 177
Khoja 19, 62, 70
Kidwais 57, 70
Kling, B. 98
Kopf, D. 42, 45, 46, 48, 49, 53, 84, 104
Kosambi, M. 133n
Kothari, R. 40
Kudaisya, M. M. 76
Kumar, R. 165, 167f
Kumar, S. xxv

LaPorte, T. R. 137n
Lath, M. 11, 14n, 35, 138
Lazarus, R. 139
Lelyveld, D. 66, 100, 142
Lipner, J. J. 93, 103, 112

index 201

literati 52, 58, 62, 73, 79, 97
literature 13ff, 102f, 104, 155, 159n
Little Tradition 95
  see also Great Tradition
Longohr, V. 50
Luckmann, T. 141
Lucknow Pact xxxiii, 143n, 153, 155
Lutt, J. 51

Macfarlane, A. 137
Madan, T. N. xix, xxi, xxiv, 22n, 50, 51, 76, 77, 101, 128n
madrasa xv, 58, 75, 121
  see also Delhi College, Deoband, Farangi Mahall
Mahadevan, R. 39
Majeed, J. 66, 104
Majumdar, R. C. 48
Malaviya, Madan Mohan 51, 166
Malik, H. 88f, 143, 172, 175
Mallison, F. 62
Mandelbaum, D. G. xix
Mann, M. iii
Manrique, Fray Sebastiao 12
mansabdari 82
Markovits, C. 60, 61
marsiya 14
Marzban, Fardunji 139
Masselos, J. C. 62
Mayaram, S. 72, 127n, 152
Mehta, D. 69, 150
Meos 20, 24, 72, 95, 152
merchants, medieval 12, 35, 60, 100, 135
  nineteenth–twentieth centuries 33, 39, 43, 44, 52, 55, 56, 58, 60ff, 66, 78, 80, 91, 96, 97, 101, 112, 139, 141, 150, 153, 161, 167
Merton, R. xxviii
Metcalf, B. 59, 64ff, 67, 72, 74, 92, 98, 104, 115, 117–24, 132, 142, 171
micro and macro 134, 159, 169
migrant men 39f, 63, 132f, 135, 140, 146, 153
Miller, R. E. 77

Minault, G. xx, 60, 64, 75, 117, 118, 155
Mines, M. 35, 71, 132
Misra, S. C. 19n
missionaries 40, 85, 96, 97, 112, 133, 138, 159
mlechha 10
mobility 25, 39ff, 71f, 96, 123
  see also jati, sects, institutions
Mobilization 53, 60, 83, 85, 129, 176
  kin and jati 27, 34, 92, 114, 135
  symbols and ideology 86, 92f, 94, 126, 139, 171, 176
  positive and negative axes 109
Moplah 62, 64, 68, 150, 169f
More, J. B. P. 71, 77
Morgan, G. xxxiv
Mughals xxiii, 3, 12, 19, 20, 24n, 29, 34, 56, 57, 60, 81f, 87, 88, 100, 101, 111, 116, 136, 137, 175
  literati's interest in the West 99
  see also akhlaq
Mujeeb, M. xviii, 6, 8, 22, 48, 58, 60n, 101, 125, 127n, 136, 144
Mukerji, D. P. xx, xxix, 98
Murad, M. A. 73f
Muslim Educational Conference, All India 75f, 166
Muslim League 71, 75, 81, 143, 153f, 161, 166, 168, 171, 172f
Muslims and Hindus see Hindu and Muslim
Muslims 140, 168f
  neglect by sociologists xix f
  elite sense of seige. 88, 97, 161
  jatis 69–73, 117
  forging the community 63–67, 79, 144
  orthodoxy 58, 71, 75, 89, 105, 125, 171
  liberals 73ff see also Syed Ahmed Khan
  see also Deoband, Shibli Numani, social composition, Tablighi Jamaat

Mutazilis 7

Nadar 38, 39, 76
Nadwatul Ulama 67, 74, 123
Naidu, R. xvi, 146
Naim, C. M. 64, 75
names, importance of xxvi, 128f
Nanak 108f
Nanda, B. R. 170
Nandy, A. xxvii, 40
Naoroji, Dadabhai 166
Narayanan, V. 13
Naregal, V. 37, 40, 45f, 64, 82, 114, 139
Nicholas, R. 46
non-Brahmin movements 38
Non-cooperation *see* Khilafat
non-violence 169
Numani, Shibli 73f, 75, 98, 123f

Oberoi, H. 95
Omvedt, G. 38n, 51, 53
Owens, R. L. 40

Pandey, G. xvii, 72, 84, 90f, 92, 94, 146
Pandian, M. S. S. 37f, 47, 88, 104, 113, 159n
Panikkar, K. N. 62, 75, 151
pan-Islamism 68, 141, 168
Parekh, B. 45
Parmu, R. K. 23
Partition of Bengal 1905, 49n, 78, 85, 107, 160
past: remembering or forgetting xiii, xvii f, xxii f, 27f, 30, 33, 53, 56, 83, 87, 90, 92, 102–5, 112–18, 126, 127, 130, 136n, 155, 159, 177f
Patel, H. M. 156f
Phukan, S. 14
Phule, Jotiba 38, 40, 53
pir 8, 120, 173, 173
poetry 23, 66, 73, 76, 105
politics 25, 78, 87ff, 106f, 139, 143n, 155n, 161, 162, 166–73

Pollock, S. 3, 5, 15, 31
Prasad, B. ix, xvii, xviii, xxxiii, 49, 60n, 62, 73, 82, 86, 89, 143, 146, 153, 154, 155, 159n, 175
Preuss, U. K. 176
professions 47, 54, 57, 60, 109, 112, 114
Punjab 21, 50, 58, 67, 78, 95, 96, 126, 139, 143, 149, 156, 167, 173, 176
   see also Arya Samaj, Unionist Party
qasba 56, 82, 90, 96

Qureshi, I. H. xxi, 116f

Radhakrishnan, P. 38, 77
Rajputs 17, 24, 25, 41, 56, 74, 82, 101, 103, 136
Ramakrishna Mission 43, 46,113
Ramanujan, A. K. 47
Rao, M. S. A. 42, 43
Rao, U. B. xvi
Rao, V. N. 59
Rashtriya Swayamsevak Sangh (RSS) 108, 115, 127, 132, 152, 170
Ray, R. K. xxi, xxivf, 2, 10, 28, 35, 42, 56, 60, 61, 62, 82, 88, 118, 120, 121, 136, 144, 156, 162, 163f, 165
Raychaudhuri, T. 98, 103, 138
reconfiguration of Indian society xxii, xxvii, 83, 102, 118, 125ff, 130, 131, 134, 138, 150, 160, 164
Rizvi, S. A. A. 22, 25
Robinson, R. 69, 150
Robinson, F. xx, 57n, 58, 60n, 90, 92, 106, 107, 119, 124, 147, 154
Rodinson, M. 74
Rowe, W. L. 40
Roy, A. 15, 19n
Rudner, D. 39, 61

Saiyed, A. R. 119
Saltanat 5ff, 16, 19, 22, 24, 26, 28f, 57, 101, 175
Samaddar, R. 59, 75, 78
Sanatan Dharm 68, 97, 105, 147, 148

Sanyal, U. 67, 119, 121, 124
Sarkar, S. 49, 85, 89, 95, 103, 107, 145, 148
Satnamis 42, 47
Satyarthaprakash see Arya Samaj
Savarkar, V. D. xxi n, 108, 115, 155n, 164
Sayeed, Khalid bin xviii, 172
scales 150
  enlarging of 138, 140, 145, 146, 147, 153, 157, 166, 167, 169, 176
Scammell, G. V. 100
Schryer, F. J. xxvi, 129
Seal, A. 77f, 95, 106, 142
sects xxx, 33, 41–48, 54, 159, 165
  in mobility 106
  lay influence in 43f, 127n, 142
  Swaminarayan 43, 47
  see also Arya Samaj, Brahmo Samaj, Ramakrishna Mission, Sri Narayan Dharma Paripalana (SNDP), cow protection
Sen, Keshub Chandra 46
separate electorates 86, 154, 160f, 170, 176, 177
separativeness 142, 154, 155, 159f, 161, 164, 165, 171, 173, 174, 177
  responsibility for 83–87
Shackle, C. 66, 104
Shah, A. M. 24
Shaikh, F. 68, 89, 171n
shakha 127, 132
shared spaces 108, 132, 136, 139, 148, 152, 161
softness of 95ff, 149, 160, 161f
shariat xxxi, 3, 7, 8, 9, 26, 65, 67, 71, 74, 79, 80, 101, 115, 116, 119, 140, 165, 175
  see also Deoband
Shariatullah, Haji 59, 96, 122
Sharma, J. xxi, 113, 155n
Shias 7f, 63, 66, 68
  see also Ismailis, Khojas, Bohras
Shivaji 45, 93, 112, 127, 155, 157

Shraddhananda, Swami 151, 170
Sibeon, R. xxvi, 134
Siddiqi, A. 24, 71, 139
Siddiqui, M. K. A. 133n
Sikand, Y. 70, 72, 77, 89, 99, 127n, 152
silsila xxv, 7, 96
  see also Sufis
Singh, U. 53
Sinha, S. 17
skills 54, 56, 57, 100, 101, 106, 125, 177
social composition: "Indian Muslims" 55–63
social psychology xxii, 13, 178
  historical 139f
sociology, its history xix
South India xxiii f, 13, 55, 62, 77, 97, 104
Southern, R. W. 100
sovereign truths 10, 124, 126, 160
Sri Narayan Dharma Paripalana (SNDP) 41f, 43
Srinivas, M. N. xix
Stein, B. 46
Stephens, I. xviii
Stewart, T. K. 15
Stokes, E. 27n
structures *see* actors
Subramanian, L. 35, 56, 60, 62
Sufis xxv, 8f, 18, 20f, 22f, 26, 58, 62, 65, 67, 90, 94, 101, 120f, 136, 160, 162, 176
  see also silsila, Bansawi
Sulh-i-kul 6, 137
Surat 12, 62
Swadeshi 49n, 93, 112, 157, 168
symbols 45, 46, 84, 92, 102, 107, 115, 122, 126f, 134, 145, 146–49, 151, 154, 157, 168, 169
systems perspective 174f

Tablighi Jamaat xxxiv, 127n, 132, 142, 152, 170

Taft, F. H. 111,
Tagore, Dwarkanath 97f
Tagore, Rabindranath 85
Talbot, C. xxv, 28, 31, 150n
Talib, M. 77, 119
teleology vs. direction 164f
Templeman, D. 76
Timberg, T. A. 39
time horizons xx f, xxii, 30
Titu Mir 59, 68, 122, 145, 147
Tiwari, B. 10
tribal absorption, by Hindus and Muslims 17f
Trivedi, M. 13f
trust 135, 148, 150
  commercial 61
  between Hindus and Muslims 29, 143, 153f, 157, 161, 172, 176
Tyabji, Badruddin 95, 142, 166
ulama (pl. for alim) xxv, 3, 5, 10, 26, 29, 63, 65, 74, 75, 76, 78, 79, 101, 111, 115f, 128, 142, 151, 170, 171, 173
  see Deoband, Barelvi
umma 4, 8, 33, 63–69, 80, 171
  alternatives to 69–78
unfixed complexity 137f

Unger, R. M. 3, 4
Unionist Party, Punjab 59, 170, 173
UP 65, 77f, 84, 89f, 93, 94, 120, 126, 131, 139, 140, 146, 147, 152, 154, 172
Urdu–Hindi 84, 90, 94, 117, 122, 147

Vallabhacharya 10
Van den Dungen, P. H. M. 40
Van der Veer, P. 115
variations: over time, space, and social strata xxiii, 44, 161
Varshney, A. 149
violence *see* aggression
Vivekananda, Swami xxi n, 104
vocabulary for mutual provocation 11, 79, 93, 140, 146, 147, 154, 162, 172
von Grunebaum, G. E. 105, 119n
vulnerability, feelings of 88, 150

Wagle, N.K. 108, 136n
Wahdat al-shuhud 9
Wahdat al-wujud 8
Waliullah, Shah 65, 115, 116, 118
Wallace, A. F. C. 32
Waltham, C. 1
Wani, M. A. 22f, 31
Webster, J. C. B. 85, 97
West Asia 4, 23, 58, 61, 81, 100, 159
western learning 75, 76, 77, 80, 97–102, 123 and "reform" 98
Williams, R. B. 43, 47
Wilson, H. 131
Wink, A. 61, 95
Wolpert, S. 95, 154, 170, 172, 173
Wood, A. 51

Zelliot, E. 38n
Ziring, L. 174
Zutshi, C. 23

For Product Safety Concerns and Information please contact our EU
representative GPSR@taylorandfrancis.com
Taylor & Francis Verlag GmbH, Kaufingerstraße 24, 80331 München, Germany

www.ingramcontent.com/pod-product-compliance
Lightning Source LLC
Chambersburg PA
CBHW070308230426
43664CB00015B/2684